All the Words You Need

Englischer Grundwortschatz
zum Nachschlagen und Lernen

von Wolfgang Hamm

D1727330

Ernst Klett Schulbuchverlag
Stuttgart Düsseldorf Berlin Leipzig

All the Words You Need

Englischer Grundwortschatz zum Nachschlagen und Lernen

von Wolfgang Hamm, Marktredwitz

Inhalt

Gedruckt auf Papier aus chlorfrei gebleichtem Zellstoff, säurefrei.

1. Auflage

1 5 4 3 | 1999

Die letzte Zahl bezeichnet das Jahr dieses Druckes. Alle Drucke diese Auflage können im Unterricht nebeneinander benutzt werden.
© Ernst Klett Schulbuchverlag GmbH, Stuttgart 1995. Alle Rechte vorbehalten.

Redaktion: Inge Schäfer, Verlagsredakteurin

Umschlagbild und Illustrationen: Christian Gutendorf, Stuttgart
Druck: Röck,Weinsberg
ISBN 3-12-519710-4

I. Einführung

First things first

All the Words You Need ist kein Wörterbuch im üblichen Sinne. Wie schon der Titel sagt, wurden nur diejenigen Wörter, Ausdrücke und Redewendungen aufgenommen, die man nach rund 5-6 Jahren grundlegenden Englischunterrichts beherrschen sollte, um englischsprachige Partner verstehen und sich ihnen verständlich machen zu können. Kein reines Nachschlagewerk also, sondern ein Arbeitsbuch, das zum Lernen und Wiederholen des englischen Grundwortschatzes anregen und ermutigen möchte.

Eine Besonderheit von *All the Words You Need* liegt darin, daß das Einzelwort nicht alleine mit seiner deutschen Entsprechung in einer Liste steht. Vielmehr wird anhand alltagsbezogener Beispielsätze gezeigt, wie man das Wort tatsächlich anwenden kann:

agree [ə'griː]	zustimmen, einverstanden sein
I agree with you.	Ich stimme dir zu.
I don't agree to this plan.	Ich bin nicht mit diesem Plan einverstanden.

An mehreren Stellen wird die Liste durch Schilder – *signs* – unterbrochen, die einem Besucher des englischsprachigen Raums begegnen:

Kleine Witze – *jokes* – machen deutlich, daß beim Arbeiten mit *All the Words You Need* der Spaß und die Freude nicht zu kurz kommen:

Der Hauptteil des Buches besteht in einer alphabetisch geordneten englisch-deutschen Wortliste. Darauf folgt eine kurze deutsch-englische Liste zum Nachschlagen der Wörter. Bevor man mit dem englisch-deutschen Hauptteil beginnt, sollte man die folgende Hinweise zum Wörterlernen und zur Benutzung der Liste lesen.

How to learn words … and not forget them

Ein Schüler sagt stolz: „Ich muß mir die neuen Wörter nur ein-, zweimal durchlesen, schon kann ich sie."

Ein anderer deckt mit einem Papierstreifen die englischen Wörter ab und versucht, aus dem Gedächtnis zu sagen, wie das Wort auf Englisch heißt.

Ein Mädchen schreibt jedes englisches Wort dreimal ab und spricht laut dazu. Ihre Freundin nimmt alle Wörter auf einen Kassenrecorder auf. Dann hört sie sich die deutschen Wörter an, stoppt die Kassette und sagt das englische Wort oder schreibt es auf.

Und wieder ein anderer hat alle Wörter in seinen Computer eingegeben. Er ruft die einzelnen Wörter durch Tastendruck ab.

Und du – wie lernst du Wörter? Ist eine Methode dabei, die du selbst anwendest, oder hast du dir eine eigene Taktik zurechtgelegt?

Vielleicht probierst du die eine oder ander der oben beschriebenen Methoden einmal selber aus. Vielleicht sind aber auch die folgenden *tips* eine kleine Hilfe.

First tip: Die List mit der Liste – oder: „Geteiltes Leid ist halbes Leid"

„Ich verzweifle noch an diesen endlos langen Listen von englischen Vokabeln, Ausdrücken und Redewendungen," meint ein Schüler. Geht es dir auch so?

Vielleicht solltest du einmal versuchen, die Vokabellisten durch Querstriche zu teilen. Man hat nämlich herausgefunden, daß sich gerade die Anfangs- und Endpunkte besser in das Gedächtnis „eingraben" als die Vokabeln in der Mitte einer Tabelle. Schon nach fünf bis sieben Wörtern solltest du einen Trennungsstrich ziehen, damit die „Eckwörter" nur wenige „Kernwörter" umschließen.

cash [kæʃ]	Bargeld
How much cash have you got on you?	Wieviel Bargeld hast du dabei?
∞ pay in cash	bar bezahlen
cassette [kə'set] ✎ Entertainment electronics	Kassette
∞ cassette recorder	Kassettenrekorder
∞ video cassette	Videokassette
castle ['kɑːsl] ✎ In town	Schloß, Burg
cat [kæt] ✎ Animals	Katze
catalogue ['kætəlɒg]	Katalog
catch [kætʃ], **caught** [kɔːt], **caught**	fangen
The cat has caught a mouse.	
∞ catch a train/ bus/…	einen Zug/Bus/ … erreichen
∞ catch a cold	sich erkälten
cathedral [kə'θiːdrəl]	Kathedrale, Dom
cattle ['kætl] ✎ Animals	Vieh, Rinder
☛The cattle look very healthy.	Das Viel sieht sehr gesund aus.
cauliflower ['kɒliflaʊə] ✎ Vegetables	Blumenkohl
cause [kɔːz]	verursachen
The storm caused a lot of damage.	Der Sturm richtete großen Schaden an.
⇨ because [bɪ'kɒz]	weil

Second tip: Die Vokabelkartei –
oder: „Von der Intensivstation zur Heilung"

Tausendfach bewährt hat sich das System einer Vokabelkartei.

Besorge dir einen Karton (ca. 20 cm lang, 12 cm breit und 8 cm hoch), schneide dir entsprechend große Zettel, oder noch besser stabile Kärtchen, z. B. im DIN A 7-Format (ca. 10,5 cm x 7,5 cm; DIN A 4 3mal falten = 8 Zettel!). Jetzt teilst du dir deinen Zettelkasten in drei Fächer auf. In das erste Fach kommen immer alle gerade beschriebenen Zettel: Auf der Vorderseite steht das englische Wort, auf der Rückseite das deutsche. Statt der deutschen Entsprechung, oder als Ergänzung dazu, kannst du auf der Rückseite auch eine kleine

Zeichnung anbringen. Mehr über die Vorteile dieser Methode erfährst du, wenn du die *tips* 3 - 6 liest.

Nachdem du die neuen Vokabeln in Fach 1 eingeordnet hast, solltest du sie am nächsten Tag gleich einmal überprüfen oder, um es auf Englisch zu sagen, „den ersten Check machen". Wenn du ein Wort weißt, gibst du den Zettel in Fach 2. Die nicht gewußten Wörter bleiben in Fach 1 – der „Intensivstation". Am nächsten Tag überprüfst du die Vokabeln von Fach 1 erneut. Gewußte wandern ein Fach weiter, unsichere Kandidaten bleiben. Nach ein paar Tagen verfährst du genauso mit Fach 2. Sicher gewußte Wörter können in Fach 3 gebracht werden, problematische bleiben noch ein paar Tage auf Station 2. Wenn erst einmal die Intensivstation (Fach 1) geräumt ist, können neue Patienten (sprich: Wörter) aufgenommen werden. Wenn du nach ein paar Wochen sogar die Wörter von Station 3 sicher beherrschst, werden diese „als geheilt" in die Freiheit, das heißt aus der Kartei „entlassen".

Third tip: vocabulary poster

Schau dich einmal in deinem Zimmer um. Wie die meisten Schüler in deinem Alter hast du dir sicher auch einige Plakate, Poster oder Bilder von bekannten Stars aufgehängt. Während der eine lieber Pferdeposter mag, bevorzugt der andere Fußballspieler, Autos oder amerikanische Trucks. Das ist natürlich sehr unterschiedlich. Eines aber haben alle gemeinsam: Was man an der Wand hängen hat, merkt man sich besser als das, was irgendwo im Schrank oder in einer Kiste wie in einem Silo „abgelagert" und nicht selten der Verrottung preisgegeben ist. Das gilt auch für Wörter. Deshalb: Wörter raus aus welkenden Vokabelheftseiten und an ein Plakat geschrieben! Da ist auch ein bißchen Kreativität und Phantasie gefragt!

Du wirst in all den Jahren, in den du Englisch lernst, festgestellt haben, daß es Wörter gibt, die man sich einfach nicht merken kann. Meist sind es solche, die nicht im entferntesten eine Ähnlichkeit mit der deutschen Sprache haben. Oder weißt du sofort, was *to believe, to decide* usw. bedeutet? Nicht? Dann hilft dir vielleicht das *vocabulary poster*.

Dabei ist es wichtig, daß du nicht nur englisch-deutsche Wortpaare (möglichst groß, mit dickem Stift) auf das Plakat schreibst. Laß dir etwas einfallen: Woran denkst du, wenn du dieses oder jenes Wort hörst? Mache eine Zeichnung dazu. Oder klebe einen Ausschnitt aus

einem Warenhauskatalog auf. Dabei muß das Poster nicht besonders schön sein. Es ist nur wichtig, daß du die einzelnen Vokabeln immer wieder siehst. Erst dann kann man sich Wörter merken, die man sonst leicht vergißt oder mit anderen verwechselt. Vielleicht probierst du das *vocabulary poster* einmal selbst aus.

Fourth tip:
vocabulary wallpaper

Das beim *vocabulary poster* gesagt gilt auch für das *vocabulary wallpaper*. Die im Zimmer aufgehängte Tapentenbahn bietet jedoch noch mehr Platz für deine phantasievollen Aufschriften.
Manche Schüler schreiben die Wörter mit verschiedenen Farben oder in unterschiedlicher Größe, kreisen schwierige Wörter ein oder unterstreichen sie. Originale Bildausschnitte aus Illustrierten und Katalogen sind eine gute Möglichkeit, die Einzelwörter ohne Angabe der deutschen Bedeutung zu erklären.

6

Fifth tip:
vocabulary stickers

Besorge dir verschiedenfarbiges Kartonpapier. Schneide Kreise unterschiedlicher Größe aus. Hast du schwierige Vokabeln zu lernen, kannst du dir deine Stickers entsprechend beschriften und vielleicht mit erklärenden Symbolen versehen. Wenn du die einzelnen Stickers an verschiedenen Plätzen in eurer Wohnung aufhängst oder an Türen und Möbeln anklebst, wirst du den Wörtern mehrmals täglich begegnen, sie sehen, lesen und dadurch – unbewußt – leichter behalten.

Sixth tip: vocabulary folder

Bist du ein Sammlertyp? Dann werden dich die folgenden Tips zum Anlegen einer Wortschatzsammlung besonders interessieren. Aber selbst wenn das Sammeln von Dingen dich sonst überhaupt nicht interessiert, solltest du es einmal ausprobieren, denn die englisch-deutsche Wortliste in diesem Buch bietet dir besondere Hilfestellungen.

Wenn du die Wortliste durchblätterst, werden dir Kästchen wie dieses auffallen, das unter dem Stichwort *danger* steht:

✎ Danger and accidents

Es bedeutet, daß du dir ein Ordnerblatt mit der Überschrift *Danger and accidents* anlegen solltest. Darauf kannst du alle Wörter eintragen, die du zu diesem Thema findest. Die Zeichnungen im Kästchen geben dir nur ein paar Denkanstöße. Dein eigenes Blatt (vielleicht werden auch mehrere Blätter daraus) wird natürlich ganz anders aussehen.

Und welche Wörter gehören nun zum Thema *Danger and accidents*? Auch hierfür gibt dir die Wortliste Tips. Bei jedem Wort, das zu diesem Thema paßt, findest du den Eintrag „✎ Danger and accidents."

Beispiele:

aid [eɪd] ≈ help ∞ first aid ✎ Danger and accidents

fire ✎ Danger and accidents

ambulance [ˈæm-bjʊləns] ✎ Danger and accidents

Auch für eine ganze Reihe weiterer Wortfelder werden in der Vokabelliste entsprechende Vorschläge gemacht. Du kannst dir, wenn die den Anregungen folgen willst, einen *English folder* mit Blättern zu folgenden Themen anlegen:

- ✎ Animals
- ✎ In the <u>b</u>athroom
- ✎ The human <u>b</u>ody
- ✎ Clothes
- ✎ Colours
- ✎ Countries
- ✎ <u>D</u>anger and accidents
- ✎ <u>D</u>ays of the week
- ✎ Drinks
- ✎ <u>E</u>lectricity in the household
- ✎ <u>E</u>ntertainment electronics
- ✎ Food
- ✎ Fruit
- ✎ Furniture
- ✎ <u>H</u>ouse and flat
- ✎ Musical <u>i</u>nstruments

- ✎ Jobs
- ✎ <u>L</u>aying the table
- ✎ <u>M</u>onths and seasons
- ✎ People
- ✎ <u>P</u>lace and direction
- ✎ Relatives
- ✎ My <u>s</u>chool bag
- ✎ <u>S</u>ports and games
- ✎ School <u>s</u>ubjects
- ✎ Expressions of <u>t</u>ime
- ✎ Tools
- ✎ In <u>t</u>own
- ✎ Transport
- ✎ Vegetables
- ✎ The <u>w</u>eather

(Hinweis: Besteht eine Überschrift aus mehreren Wörtern, geben Dir die unterstrichenen Anfangsbuchstaben an, unter welchem Stichwort das Kästchen zu finden ist:
Beispiel: „Musical <u>i</u>nstruments" steht unter „instrument", also beim Buchstaben „I".
Bei „musical" steht nur der Hinweis „✎ *Musical instruments*".)
Wenn du bei einem Stichwort einen solchen Hinweis findest, trägst du es unter der entsprechenden Überschrift in deinem *folder* ein:

Auf diese Weise legst du dir eine eigene Wortschatzsammlung an, ähnlich wie ein Briefmarken- oder Münzensammler. Im Laufe der Zeit wächst diese Sammlung, wird ergänzt und vervollständigt. Die Einzelwörter werden auf diese Weise gelernt und wiederholt. Es bleibt selbstverständlich dir überlassen, ob du immer die deutsche Bedeutung der Begriffe hinzuschreibst; vielleicht wäre es besser, sie durch eine einfache Zeichnung oder Abbildung aus Illustrierten oder Katalogen zu erklären, oder auch durch einen Beispielsatz. So entsteht ein *personal dictionary,* geschrieben und gestaltet von dir selbst.
Selbstverständlich kannst du auch Ordnerblätter zu weiteren Themen hinzufügen, die dir einfallen. Oder du kannst die Blätter nach deinem eigenen Geschmack untergliedern, z. B. *Animals* in *Pets* und *Wild animals*.

Es wäre auch eine gute Idee, ein paar Seiten im *folder* für unregelmäßige Verben zu reservieren. Bewußt wurde darauf verzichtet, eine alphabetisch geordnete *List of irregular verbs* aufzunehmen. Sinnvoller und für dich gewinnbringender wäre es, beim Auftauchen eines unregelmäßigen Verbs die drei Formen nach Symbolen zu ordnen und erst dann einzutragen.

Beispiele:

◯	△	△	◯	◯	◯
catch	caught	caught	cut	cut	cut
make	made	made	put	put	put

◯	△	▢	◯	△	◯
sing	sang	sung	run	ran	run
go	went	gone	come	came	come

Beim Lesen der Wörter in der englisch-deutschen Liste werden dir sicher auch Einträge wie dieser auffallen:

button ['bʌtn]	Knopf; *Button*
press/push a	einen Knopf
button	drücken

Button gehört in die Gruppe von englischen Wörtern, deren Bedeutung jedem Deutschsprachigen bekannt sein dürfte. Sie haben Einzug in den Alltag gefunden und werden ohne Zögern benutzt.

Ein Vorschlag zur Arbeit mit diesen Wörtern, die aus dem Englischen ins Deutsche übernommen wurden: Immer wenn dir ein solches Wort auffällt, solltest du es ebenfalls in deinen *folder* eintragen, z. B. so:

English/American	German	Erklärung
button	Button	„Knopf" aus Plastik mit einer Inschrift; zum Anstecken

In der Spalte *Erklärung* kannst du durch einen kurzen Satz die Bedeutung des Begriffs angeben. Schon nach kurzer Zeit wirst du überrascht sein, wieviele Wörter dieser Art du kennst, und wie leicht du dir so deren Ableitungen merken kannst.

Seventh tip:
how words are formed

Viele Schülerinnen und Schüler haben verständlicherweise Schwierigkeiten mit dem umfangreichen englischen Wortschatz. Sie glauben nämlich, jedes einzelne Wort auswendig lernen zu müssen.

Lautet eine Überschrift im Englischbuch beispielsweise *The Visitor from York*, so brechen sie schnell in Verzweiflung aus: „Was heißt denn *visitor?"* Wenn du auch zu jenen gehörst, die vielleicht noch nichts oder wenig über Vor- und Nachsilben gehört haben, dann solltest du jetzt aufmerksam weiterlesen.

To visit – besuchen lernt man gewöhnlich schon im ersten Unterrichtsjahr. Wenn man weiß, daß mit der Endung *-or* und *-er* viele Haupt- oder Namenwörter *(nouns)* aus Tätigkeitswörtern *(verbs)* gebildet werden, ist schon viel erreicht!

Denke nur an ein einfaches Beispiel wie *to sail – a sailor* oder die Ableitung vom Hauptwort *garden* zum Beruf *gardener*.

Hier ist eine Liste mit weiterene wichtigen Nachsilben:

-ion	*to decide* (sich entschließen)	*decision* (Entschluß)
-ation	*to inform* (informieren)	*information* (Information)
-able	*to understand* (verstehen)	*understandable* (verständlich)
-y	*dirt* (Schmutz)	*dirty* (schmutzig)
-ful	*success* (Erfolg)	*successful* (erfolgreich)
-less	*hope* (Hoffnung)	*hopeless* (hoffnungslos)
-en	*short* (kurz)	*shorten* (kürzen)
-ize	*modern* (modern)	*modernize* (modernisieren)

Vielleicht ist dir auch schon aufgefallen, daß viele englische Tätigkeitswörter genauso lauten wie die entsprechenden Hauptwörter, z. B. *to cut* (schneiden) – *a cut* (ein Schnitt), oder wie die entsprechenden Eigenschaftswörter *(adjectives)*, z. B. *to clean* (reinigen) – *clean* (sauber). Wenn du z. B. das Eigenschaftswort *dirty* (schmutzig) kennst und einen Satz wie *Don't dirty your clothes* hörst, kannst du leicht erschließen, daß *to dirty* „schmutzig machen" heißen muß.

Sehr nützlich beim Erschließen von teilweise unbekannten Wörtern ist es auch, wenn man die Bedeutung einiger wichtiger Vorsilben kennt. Bestimmt weißt du schon was *un-* heißt. Du kennst Gegensatzpaare wie *happy* (glücklich) – *unhappy* (unglücklich), *fair* und *unfair*.

Weitere wichtige Vorsilben sind:

dis- (un-, nicht, Gegenteil von)	*disadvantage* (Nachteil)
	disappear (verschwinden)
in-/im-/ir- (in-, nicht, Gegenteil von)	*indirect* (indirekt)
	impossible (unmöglich)
	irregular (unregelmäßig)
co- (zusammen, mit)	*cooperation* (Zusammenarbeit)
super- (über-)	*supernatural* (übernatürlich)
sub- (unter-)	*subway* (Unterführung)
	subtitle (Untertitel)
re- (wieder)	*retell* (nacherzählen)
	reappear (wieder auftauchen)
trans- (jenseits, hinüber)	*transatlantic* (transatlantisch, überseeisch)

Eighth tip:
English numbers

Obwohl viele Schülerinnen und Schüler schon vor Beginn des Englischunterrichts die Zahlen von 1 bis 10 aufsagen können, fällt auf, daß die Zahlen später immer wieder Schwierigkeiten machen. Wiederhole zunächst die Grundzahlen (*cardinal numbers*):

1	one	[wʌn]	21	twenty-one	[twentɪ'wʌn]
2	two	[tu:]	22	twenty-two	[twentɪ'tu:]
3	three	[θri:]	23	twenty-three	[twentɪ'θri:]
4	four	[fɔ:]	30	thirty	['θɜ:tɪ]
5	five	[faɪv]	40	forty	['fɔ:tɪ]
6	six	[sɪks]	50	fifty	['fɪftɪ]
7	seven	['sevn]	60	sixty	['sɪkstɪ]
8	eight	[eɪt]	70	seventy	['sevntɪ]
9	nine	[naɪn]	80	eighty	['eɪtɪ]
10	ten	[ten]	90	ninety	['naɪntɪ]
11	eleven	[ɪ'levn]	100	a hundred	[ə'hʌndrəd]
12	twelve	[twelv]	101	a hundred and one	
13	thirteen	[θɜ:'ti:n]	203	two hundred and three	
14	fourteen	[fɔ:'ti:n]	364	three hundred and sixty-four	
15	fifteen	[fɪf'ti:n]	1000	a thousand	[ə'θaʊznd]
16	sixteen	[sɪks'ti:n]	2004	two thousand and four	
17	seventeen	[sevn'ti:n]	4889	four thousand eight hundred	
18	eighteen	[eɪ'ti:n]		and eighty-nine	
19	nineteen	[naɪn'ti:n]	1,000,000	a million	[ə'mɪljən]
20	twenty	['twentɪ]	12,000,000	twelve million	

Besonders beim Datum oder der Angabe einer bestimmten Reihenfolge ist es wichtig, die Ordnungszahlen (*ordinal numbers*) zu kennen:

1st	first	[fɜ:st]	21st	twenty-first	[twentɪ'fɜ:st]
2nd	second	['sekənd]	22nd	twenty-second	[twentɪ'seknd]
3rd	third	[θɜ:d]	23rd	twenty-third	[twentɪ'θɜ:d]
4th	fourth	[fɔ:θ]	30th	thirtieth	['θɜ:tɪəθ]
5th	fifth	[fɪfθ]	40th	fortieth	['fɔ:tɪəθ]
6th	sixth	[sɪksθ]	50th	fiftieth	['fɪftɪəθ]
7th	seventh	['sevθ]	60th	sixtieth	['sɪkstɪəθ]
8th	eighth	[eɪtθ]	70th	seventieth	['sevntɪəθ]
9th	ninth	[naɪnθ]	80th	eightieth	['eɪtɪəθ]
10th	tenth	[tenθ]	90th	ninetieth	['naɪntɪəθ]
11th	eleventh	[ɪ'levnθ]	100th	hundredth	['hʌndrədθ]
12th	twelfth	[twelfθ]	101st	hundred and first	
13th	thirteenth	[θɜ:'ti:nθ]	203rd	two hundred and third	
14th	fourteenth	[fɔ:'ti:nθ]	364th	three hundred and sixty-fourth	
15th	fifteenth	[fɪf'ti:nθ]	1000th	thousandth	['θaʊzndθ]
16th	sixteenth	[sɪks'ti:nθ]	2004th	two thousand and fourth	
17th	seventeenth	[sevn'ti:nθ]	4889th	four thousand eight hundred	
18th	eighteenth	[eɪ'ti:nθ]		and eighty-ninth	
19th	nineteenth	[naɪn'ti:nθ]	1,000,000th	millionth	
20th	twentieth	['twentɪəθ]	12,000,000th	twelve millionth	

Ninth tip: learning by games

Wie ein Jongleur – *a juggler* – Bälle, Ringe oder Keulen hochwirft und wieder aufzufangen versucht, solltest du versuchen, mit den Wörtern zu „spielen": *Let's have fun with "All the Words You Need!"* Denn nur wer Spaß und Freude hat, lernt leicht. Vielleicht sind die folgenden Anregungen zur Spielen mit *All the Words You Need* gerade das Richtige für dich oder deine Lerngruppe.

1. A spelling game

Jeder neue Buchstabe wird in der Wortliste so vorgestellt ➡
Hinter dem Buchstaben wird in eckigen Klammern seine Aussprache angegeben. (Eine solche Ausspracheschrift steht übrigens auch hinter jedem Stichwort.)

A [eɪ] is for

Wiederhole das englische Alphabet mit Hilfe der einzelnen Überschriften: *A* [eɪ], *B* [bi:], *C* [si:] usw. Dann kannst du zusammen mit einigen Mitspielern folgendes *spelling game* spielen: Suche dir ein Wort aus der Liste und buchstabiere es laut, z. B. *mother:* [em əʊ ti: eɪtʃ i: ɑː]. Wer das Wort als erster erkannt hat, macht weiter.

2. A is for ...

In einer kleinen Gruppe von 3-4 Teilnehmern sagst du: „A is for apple, but s is for ...". Innerhalb von 15, 20 oder 30 Sekunden müssen alle Teilnehmer möglichst viele Wörter mit *s* aufschreiben. Sieger ist, wer die meisten gefunden hat.

3. Which word comes before, which word comes after ...?

Suche dir ein Wort aus der Liste heraus. In einer kleinen Gruppe von 3-4 Teilnehmern schreibst du das Wort auf einen Zettel und zeigst ihn den anderen. Diese sollen nun so schnell wie möglich das Wort suchen und aufschreiben, das deinem Wort vorangeht und das Wort, das ihm folgt. Sieger ist, wer die beiden Wörter als erster richtig geschrieben vorlegen kann.

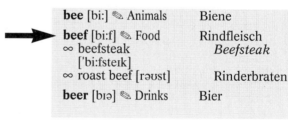

bee [bi:] ✎ Animals	Biene
beef [bi:f] ✎ Food	Rindfleisch
∞ beefsteak ['bi:fsteɪk]	*Beefsteak*
∞ roast beef [rəʊst]	Rinderbraten
beer [bɪə] ✎ Drinks	Bier

4. Opposites and words with similar meaning

Wo immer es sinnvoll ist, wird in der Wortliste das Gegenteil eines Stichwortes durch das Symbol „⇔" angegeben.

front ⇔ back

Ein Wort mit gleicher oder ähnlicher Bedeutung wird durch das Symbol „≈" angegeben.

gift [gɪft] ≈ present

Suche dir entsprechende Beispiel aus der Wortliste und frage deine Mitspieler: „What's the opposite of ...?" oder „Which word means alsmost the same as ..." Wer die richtige Antwort weiß, darf die nächste Frage stellen.

5. Find the right order

Such dir mehrere Wörter mit einem bestimmten Anfangsbuchstaben heraus und schreibe sie ungeordnet auf:

skirt   sky   skin   ski

Deine Partner müssen sie so rasch wie möglich in alphabetische Reihenfolge bringen:

ski   skin   skirt   sky

6. Letter mix

Du nimmst ein Wort und „schüttelst" alle Buchstaben durch. Deine Partner müssen das Wort erraten. Sie wissen nur den Anfangsbuchstaben. Als zusätzliche Hilfe kannst du die Seitenzahl im Buch angeben.

7. Coded words

Hier sehen wir den berühmten Detektiv Sherlock Holmes bei der Arbeit. Er versucht gerade, einen Brief in Geheimschrift zu entziffern. Natürlich knackt er den Code mit Leichtigkeit, denn er besteht aus dem einfachen Prinzip: A=1, B=2, C=3 usw.

Weise deine Spielpartner in den Code ein. Einer von euch sucht ein Wort aus der Liste und schreibt es verschlüsselt auf. Wer erkennt das Wort zuerst?

Eine anderer Geheimcode wäre z. B. A=B, B=C, C=D usw. Welches Wort ist das nach diesem Prinzip verschlüsselte Wort „TJTUFS"?

Erfindet euren eigenen Code und schreibt euch gegenseitig Wörter – oder ganze Botschaften (natürlich auf Englisch!) – zum Erraten auf.

Vielleicht fallen Euch selbst noch viele weitere spannende oder lustige Spiele zur Wortliste ein.

Tenth tip: Experimente erwünscht!

Grundsätzlich kann man feststellen, daß nicht jeder Mensch auf ein und dieselbe Weise lernt. Überlege dir selbst, wie du am besten Wörter lernen kannst. Vielleicht probierst du die einzelnen Vorschläge aus. Mit der Bereitschaft, die gewohnten, altbekannten Lerntechniken aufzugeben und einmal etwas Neues zu wagen, wirst du sicher den Erfolg haben, den du dir wünschst.

Denke daran, daß dein Gehirn all diejenigen Dinge besser speichern wird, die ihm ungewöhnlich, ja seltsam erscheinen. Das Normale wird leicht vergessen, nur das Merkwürdige ist „merk-würdig"!

Und: Oft ist es wirklich besser, ein Wort zu schreiben, als nur zu lesen!

II. Englisch-deutsche Wortliste

In der folgenden englisch-deutschen Wortschatzliste findest du einige Zeichen, die dir helfen sollen, dich besser zu orientieren:

≈   weist auf ein Wort hin, das die gleiche oder eine ähnliche Bedeutung hat, z. B. **ache** ≈ pain.

⟺   bezeichnet ein Wort mit der entgegengesetzten Bedeutung, z. B. **hot** ⟺ cold.

⇨   sagt dir, daß es vom Grundwort noch Ableitungen der selben Wortfamilie gibt, z. B. **act** ⇨ action.

→   verweist auf ein anderes Stichwort in der Wortschatzliste, unter dem du zusätzliche Erläuterungen und Anwendungsbeispiele findest, z. B. **aeroplane** → air, plane.

∞   Dieses Zeichen findest du bei manchen Untereinträgen zu einem Stichwort. Es bedeutet, daß es sich um eine Wortzusammensetzung oder eine feste Verbindung mit spezieller Bedeutung handelt, z. B **about** ∞ How about/What about ...?

☛   Besonders aufmerksam solltest du bei diesem Zeichen sein: ACHTUNG - FEHLERQUELLE! Es erinnert dich daran, daß bei diesem Stichwort gerne Fehler gemacht werden.

Zwei Beispiele aus dem Buchstaben A:

also ['ɔːlsəʊ] ≈ too, as well
> She plays the guitar. She also sings.
> ☛ *Too* und *as well* benutzt man in der Umgangssprache häufiger:
> She sings, too/as well.

any ['enɪ] → some
> ☛ *Any* steht in Fragen und verneinten Sätzen.
> Have you got any peaches?

 Ein sehr wichtiges Zeichen ist der Bleistift. Er weist dich darauf hin, daß du ein Wort auf ein bestimmtes Blatt deines *English folder* eintragen kannst, z. B. **cat** ✎ Animals.
Ausführliche Hinweise hierzu findest du auf Seite 7-8.

Außer diesen Symbolen werden folgende Abkürzungen verwendet:

s.o.	someone
s.th.	something
etw.	etwas
jdm.	jemandem
jdn.	jemanden

A [eɪ] is for

a [ə]/**an** [ən] ein/eine
  a pear
☛ Vor einem Selbst-
  laut steht *an:*
  an apple

be **able** to do s.th. fähig /in der Lage
['eɪbl] sein, etw. zu tun
  The police were Die Polizei
  able to catch the konnte den Dieb
  thief. fangen.

about [ə'baʊt] 1. ungefähr
  about 20 ungefähr 20
  2. über (ein Thema)
  a book about ein Buch über
  dinosaurs Dinosaurier
  They are talking Sie reden über
  about last das letzte
  weekend. Wochenende.
  She asked me Sie fragte mich
  about my nach meinen
  hobbies. Hobbys.

∞ How about/ Wie ist es mit
  What about you? dir?
  How/What Wie wär's mit
  about a glass of einem Glas
  lemonade? Limonade?

above [ə'bʌv] über, oberhalb
⇔ below (von)
✎ Place and direction
  The plane flew ... über den
  above the clouds. Wolken.
  Aber: He jumped ... <u>über</u> die
  <u>over</u> the wall. Mauer (hinweg).

abroad [ə'brɔːd] im/ins Ausland
  They are abroad
  at the moment.
  They went
  abroad last week.

accident ['æksɪdənt] Unfall
✎ Danger and accidents
  He was killed <u>in</u> ... <u>bei</u> einem
  an accident. Unfall ...
∞ It happened <u>by</u> Es geschah
  accident. <u>zufällig.</u>

account [ə'kaʊnt] Konto
∞ bank account Bankkonto
∞ savings account Sparkonto

ache [eɪk] ≈ pain Schmerz(en)
  I have <u>an ache</u> in Ich habe
  my left leg. <u>Schmerzen</u> im
  linken Bein.

∞ I have <u>a</u> Ich habe Kopf-
  headache. schmerzen.

across [ə'krɔs] (quer) über, (quer)
✎ Place and direction durch
  He walked Er ging über die
  across the road. Straße.
  We swam across Wir schwammen
  the river. durch den Fluß.
  They live across Sie wohnen
  the road. gegenüber.

act [ækt] ➪ react/ 1. handeln, etw.
action/active unternehmen
  We have to act
  before it is too
  late.

≈ behave 2. sich verhalten
  He acted strange-
  ly yesterday.

  3. (eine Theater-/
  Filmrolle) spielen

  She has acted in
  more than ten
  films.
➪ actor/actress Schauspieler(in)
✎ Jobs

action ['ækʃn] Handlung
  This film is full of Dieser Film ist
  action. sehr handlungs-
  reich/voller
  Action.

active ['æktɪv] aktiv
⇔ passive
  the active (voice) das Aktiv (in der
  Grammatik)

activity [æk'tɪvɪtɪ] Tätigkeit
  Her favourite
  activities are
  swimming and
  reading.

actually ['ækʃʊəlɪ] eigentlich
  What do you Was willst du
  actually want? eigentlich?

ad [æd] (short for Anzeige, Annonce,
→ advertisement) Inserat

address [ə'dres] Adresse, Anschrift

adult ['ædʌlt] Erwachse(r);
≈ grown-up erwachsen
✎ People
  a book for adults

advantage Vorteil
[əd'vɑːntɪdʒ]
⇔ disadvantage

adventure [əd'ventʃə]   Abenteuer

advertisement [əd'vɜ:tɪsmənt]/**ad-vert** ['ædvɜ:t]/**ad**   Anzeige, Annonce, Inserat
He put an ad in the newspaper

advice [əd'vaɪs]   Rat, Ratschlag
Your advice was good.   Dein Rat war gut.
☛ *advice* darf nicht mit *an* gebraucht werden.
I need <u>some</u> advice.   Ich brauche <u>einen</u> Rat.
That was a good <u>piece of</u> advice.   Das war <u>ein</u> guter Rat.

aeroplane ['eərəʊpleɪn] → air, plane ✎ Transport   Flugzeug

be **afraid** [ə'freɪd]   Angst haben, (sich) fürchten
Are you afraid <u>of</u> snakes?   Hast du Angst <u>vor</u> Schlangen?
She's afraid of flying.   Sie hat Angst vor dem Fliegen.
I'm afraid they have lost their way.   Ich (be)fürchte, sie haben sich verirrt.
☛ <u>I'm afraid</u> I must go now.   Ich muß jetzt <u>leider</u> gehen.

after ['ɑ:ftə] ✎ Expressions of time   nach
after lunch/school/the party
First I did my homework, and after that I went swimming.   … und danach …
The dog ran after the car.   … lief … nach.
∞ look after   sich kümmern um, versorgen
Can you look after my hamster while I am away?

afternoon [ɑ:ftə'nu:n] ✎ Expressions of time   Nachmittag
<u>this</u> afternoon   <u>heute</u> nachmittag
<u>in</u> the afternoon   <u>am</u> Nachmittag, nachmittags

again [ə'gen]   wieder, noch einmal
Come again soon.

Could you say that again, please?
He played that CD again and again.   … immer wieder.

against [ə'genst]   gegen
Are you for or against this idea?

age [eɪdʒ]   Alter
at the age of 15   im Alter von 15

agent ['eɪdʒənt]   Agent(in), Vertreter(in)
∞ travel agent ✎ Jobs   Reisefachfrau/-mann
at the travel agent's   im Reisebüro
⇨ agency   Agentur; Geschäftsstelle
∞ travel agency   Reisebüro

ago [ə'gəʊ]   vor
✎ Expressions of time
☛ *ago* wird nachgestellt:
two years <u>ago</u>   <u>vor</u> zwei Jahren
long ago/a long time ago   vor langer Zeit

agree [ə'gri:]   zustimmen, einverstanden sein
I agree with you.   Ich stimme dir zu.
I don't agree to this plan.   Ich bin nicht mit diesem Plan einverstanden.

aid [eɪd] ≈ help   Hilfe
∞ first aid ✎ Danger and accidents   Erste Hilfe

air [eə]   Luft
∞ by airmail   mit Luftpost
∞ airline   Fluggesellschaft
∞ airplane ≈ (aero-)plane ✎ Transport   Flugzeug
∞ airport   Flughafen

alarm [ə'lɑ:m]   Alarm
∞ alarm clock   Wecker

alive [ə'laɪv] ⇔ dead   lebendig, am Leben
Is he still <u>alive</u>?   <u>Lebt</u> er noch?
☛ *alive* steht nie vor einen Hauptwort:
a <u>living/live</u> [laɪv] animal   ein <u>lebendes</u> Tier
a <u>lively</u> discussion   eine <u>lebendige</u> Diskussion

all [ɔ:l]
  all children
  all my friends

  all day
  all the time
  all my life

  all over the
  country
∞ all right / alright
∞ not at all
∞ nothing at all

alle; ganz
  alle Kinder
  alle meine
  Freunde
  den ganzen Tag
  die ganze Zeit
  mein ganzes
  Leben lang
  überall im Land,
  im ganzen Land
  in Ordnung
  überhaupt nicht
  überhaupt nichts

allow [əˈlaʊ]
  My parents don't
  allow me to go to
  discos.

  Dogs are not
  allowed in the
  shop.
∞ be allowed to
  → may
  Nobody was
  allowed to leave
  the room.

erlauben, zulassen
  Meine Eltern
  erlauben mir
  nicht, in die
  Discos zu gehen.
  Hunde sind im
  Laden nicht
  zugelassen.
  dürfen

  Niemand durfte
  den Raum
  verlassen.

almost [ˈɔ:lməʊst]
≈ nearly
  I have almost
  finished work.

fast, beinahe

  Ich bin fast mit
  der Arbeit fertig.

alone [əˈləʊn]
  He lives alone in
  the house.
∞ leave s.o. alone.

allein
  Er lebt allein im
  Haus.
  jdn. in Ruhe
  lassen

along [əˈlɒŋ]
✎ Place and direction
  She is walking
  along the road.
∞ come along
∞ get along with
  s.o.

entlang

  ... die Straße
  entlang.
  mitkommen
  mit jdm. aus-
  kommen

aloud [əˈlaʊd]

  Could you read
  the letter aloud,
  please?
☛ Vor einem
  Hauptwort sagt
  man *loud:*
  a loud noise

laut, mit lauter
Stimme
  Könntest du den
  Brief bitte laut
  vorlesen?

  ein lautes
  Geräusch

already [ɔ:lˈredɪ]
  I've already
  packed my bag.

schon, bereits
  Ich habe ...
  schon gepackt.

☛ In Fragen sagt
  man *yet:*
  Have you packed
  your bag yet?

  Hast du ... schon
  gepackt?

alright /all right
[ɔ:lˈraɪt] ≈ okay, OK

in Ordnung

also [ˈɔ:lsəʊ] ≈ too,
as well
  She plays the
  guitar. She also
  sings.
☛ *Too* und *as well*
  benutzt man in
  der Umgangs-
  sprache häufiger:
  She sings, too/as
  well.

auch, ebenfalls

although [ɔ:lˈðəʊ]
≈ though
  He went out
  without a coat,
  although it was
  very cold.

obwohl

always [ˈɔ:lweɪz]
⇔ never ✎ Ex-
pressions of time
  He always sings
  in the bath.

immer

8 am [eɪˈem] → pm
✎ Expressions of time
  at 11 am

8 Uhr morgens

  um 11 Uhr
  vormittags

ambulance [ˈæm-
bjʊləns] ✎ Danger
and accidents
∞ ambulance man

Krankenwagen

Sanitäter

America [əˈmerɪkə]
✎ Countries
⇨ American

  She's an Ameri-
  can.
  the Americans
  an American city

Amerika

Amerikaner(in);
amerikanisch
Sie ist Amerika-
nerin.
die Amerikaner
eine amerikani-
sche Großstadt

among [əˈmʌŋ]
  The sugar bowl is
  among the cups.
  There is a special
  guest among us
  tonight.

unter, zwischen

and [ænd; ənd; n]
∞ and so on

und
  und so weiter

∞ for miles and miles   meilenweit

∞ more and more   immer mehr

angel [ˈeɪndʒl]   Engel
⇔ devil

> *Liz:* My mother's an angel.
> *Trixie:* Mine is still alive.

angry [ˈæŋgrɪ]   ärgerlich, zornig
He's angry <u>with</u> me.   Er ist böse <u>auf</u> mich.
He was angry <u>at</u> what she said.   Er war ärgerlich <u>über</u> das, was sie sagte.

animal [ˈænɪml]   Tier

✎ **Animals**

anorak [ˈænəræk]   Anorak
✎ Clothes

another [əˈnʌðə]   noch ein(er); ein anderer
Would you like another piece of cake?   Möchtest du noch ein Stück Kuchen?
That's another story.   Das ist eine andere Geschichte.
∞ one another   einander
≈ each other   Sie können
They can't stand one another.   einander nicht ausstehen.

answer [ˈɑːnsə]   Antwort; (be)antworten
an answer <u>to</u> a question   eine Antwort <u>auf</u> eine Frage
Did she answer your letter?

any [ˈenɪ] → some   1. einige, welche
☞ *Any* steht in Fragen und verneinten Sätzen.
Have you got any peaches?   Haben Sie Pfirsiche?

– Sorry, I haven't got any fruit left.   – ..., ich habe kein Obst mehr.
∞ anybody/anyone   (irgend) jemand
Is anybody listening?   Hört jemand zu?
There isn't anybody here.   Es ist niemand da.
∞ anything   (irgend) etwas
Is there anything to do?   Gibt es etwas zu tun?
We haven't got anything to eat.   Wir haben nichts zu essen.
∞ anywhere   irgendwo(hin)
Did you go anywhere yesterday?   Bist du gestern irgendwohin gegangen?
I can't find my bag anywhere.   Ich kann meine Tasche nirgends finden.

2. jede(r/s) (beliebige)
They may arrive any minute now   Sie können jetzt jeden Augenblick ankommen.
∞ anybody/anyone   jeder (beliebige)
It's easy. Anyone can do it.
∞ anything   alles (egal was)
You can ask me anything.
∞ anywhere   überall (egal wo); irgendwo(hin)
You can sit anywhere.

anyway [ˈenɪweɪ]   trotzdem; sowieso; jedenfalls
Sorry I couldn't help you.
– Thank you, anyway.   ... Trotzdem, vielen Dank
Let's walk. We won't catch the bus anyway.   ... Wir erreichen den Bus sowieso nicht.
The party was great. Anyway, I enjoyed it.   ... Mir hat sie jedenfalls gefallen.

appear [əˈpɪə]   auftauchen, erscheinen
⇔ disappear

apple [ˈæpl] ✎ Fruit   Apfel

apply [əˈplaɪ]   sich bewerben; beantragen;
He applied <u>for</u> the job.   Er bewarb sich <u>um</u> die Stelle.
I've applied <u>for</u> a passport.   Ich habe einen Paß beantragt.

appointment [ə'pɔɪntmənt]
Termin, Verabredung
   I have an appointment with my dentist.

apprentice [ə'prentɪs]
Lehrling, Auszubildende(r)
↪ apprenticeship
   Lehre

April ['eɪprɪl]
April
✎ Months and seasons

architect ['ɑ:kɪtekt]
Architekt(in)
✎ Jobs

area ['eərɪə]
Gegend, Gebiet
   There's an amusement park in this area.

argument ['ɑ:gjʊmənt]
Grund (für/gegen); Streit
   There are many arguments against smoking. She had an argument with him because he had spent so much money.
↪ to argue
streiten, widersprechen
   Don't argue with me.
Widersprich mir nicht.

arm [ɑ:m]
Arm
✎ The human body
∞ armchair
Sessel
   ✎ Furniture
∞ arms ☛ immer in der Mehrzahl
Waffen
↪ armed
bewaffnet

around [ə'raʊnd]
um, herum
≈ round ✎ Place and direction
   a trip around the world
eine Reise um die Erde
   Don't run around in the church.
Lauft nicht in der Kirche herum.

arrive [ə'raɪv]
ankommen
⇔ leave/depart
   The train arrives at 7.40 pm.
↪ arrival ⇔ departure
Ankunft

art [ɑ:t]
Kunst (auch als Schulfach)
✎ School subjects
↪ artist ['ɑ:tɪst]
Künstler(in)

article ['ɑ:tɪkl]
Artikel
   There's an interesting article in the newspaper today.

as [æz; əz]
1. (genau)so
   He runs fast, but I can run just as fast.

2. wie
   as usual
wie gewöhnlich
∞ as … as
so … wie
   I'm as old as you.
Ich bin so alt wie du.
∞ as soon as
sobald
   As soon as he saw us, he ran away.
Sobald er uns sah, lief er weg.

3. als
   They keep a rattle snake as a pet.
Sie halten eine Klapperschlange als Haustier.

4. während, als
   As I was walking home, I met Jim.
Als ich nach Hause ging, traf ich Jim.

ask [ɑ:sk]
fragen; bitten
   ask s.o. a question
jdm. eine Frage stellen
   ask the way (to the station)
nach dem Weg (zum Bahnhof) fragen
   ask for help
um Hilfe bitten

be **asleep** [ə'sli:p]
schlafen
⇔ be awake
   Is Bob still asleep?
Schläft Bob noch?
∞ fall asleep
einschlafen

assistant [ə'sɪstənt]
Verkäufer(in); Assistent(in)
✎ Jobs
∞ shop assistant
Verkäufer(in)
∞ assistant manager
stellvertretende(r) Geschäftsführer(in)
↪ assist
helfen, assistieren

association [əsəʊsɪ'eɪʃn]
Verband, Organisation

at
✎ Place and direction
1. in Ortsangaben
   at home
zu Hause
   at school
in der Schule
   at the baker's
beim Bäcker
   at the corner
an der Ecke

✎ Expressions of time
at 5 o'clock
at night

at the weekend
at Christmas
at (the age of) 16

at work
at (a speed of) 70 mph

∞ at once
∞ not at all → all
∞ at last → last
∞ at least → least

attack [ə'tæk]

The settlers were attacked by Indians.
∞ a heart attack

attic ['ætɪk]
✎ House and flat
in the attic

attract [ə'trækt]
The park attracts lots of tourists.
⇨ attractive [ə'træktɪv]
⇨ attraction
Madame Tussaud's is one of the greatest attractions in London.

August
✎ Months and seasons

aunt [ɑːnt]
✎ Relatives
☛ Beachte die Groß- und Kleinschreibung:
my aunt
Aber: Aunt Mary

Australia [ɒ'streɪlɪə]
✎ Countries
⇨ Australian
→ American

2. in Zeitangaben
um 5 Uhr
in der Nacht, nachts
am Wochenende
zu Weihnachten
mit 16, im Alter von 16

3. in sonstigen Angaben
an/bei der Arbeit
mit (einer Geschwindigkeit von) 70 Meilen pro Stunde
sofort
überhaupt nicht
endlich
wenigstens, mindestens

angreifen; Angriff, Überfall; Anfall

Die Siedler wurden von Indianern angegriffen.
ein Herzanfall

Dachboden, Speicher
auf dem Dachboden

anziehen, anlocken

anziehend, attraktiv
Attraktion

August

Tante

Australien

australisch, Australier(in)

Austria ['ɔːstrɪə]
✎ Countries
⇨ Austrian
→ American

autumn ['ɔːtəm]
✎ Months and seasons

awake [ə'weɪk]
⇔ asleep
☛ *Awake* kann nur nach bestimmten Verben werden:
be awake
stay awake

away [ə'weɪ]
✎ Place and direction
Go away!
far away

awful ['ɔːfl]
≈ terrible

axe [æks] ✎ Tools

Österreich

österreichisch; Österreicher(in)

Herbst

wach

wach sein
wach bleiben

weg, fort

Geh weg!
weit weg

schrecklich

Axt, Beil

B [biː] is for

baby ['beɪbɪ]
∞ baby-sitter
⇨ baby-sit

back [bæk]
✎ The human body
My back hurts.

the back seats of the car
the back of the house
the back door
Come back!

bad [bæd] ⇔ good
☛ Steigerung: bad, worse [wɜːs], worst
bad weather
a bad mistake

bag [bæg]

a bag of apples
∞ school bag
✎ My school bag
∞ handbag
∞ sleeping bag
∞ bagpipe ✎ Musical instruments

Baby
Babysitter
babysitten

Rücken, Rückseite; zurück
Mein Rücken tut weh.
die Rücksitze des Wagens
die Rückseite des Hauses
die Hintertür
Komm zurück!

schlecht, schlimm

schlechtes Wetter
ein schlimmer Fehler

Tasche, Sack, Beutel, Tüte
eine Tüte Äpfel
Schultasche

Handtasche
Schlafsack
Dudelsack

baggage ['bægɪdʒ]
(AE) ≈ luggage *(BE)* — Gepäck

bake [beɪk] — backen
⇨ baker ✎ Jobs — Bäcker

balcony ['bælkənɪ] — Balkon
✎ House and flat

ball [bɔ:l] — Ball
∞ play ball/football/basketball (etc.) ✎ Sports and games — Ball/Fußball/Korbball(usw.) spielen

balloon [bə'lu:n] — (Luft)ballon
∞ hot air balloon ✎ Transport — Heißluftballon

banana [bə'nɑ:nə] — Banane
✎ Fruit

band [bænd] — Band, (Musik-)Kapelle
∞ jazz band
∞ rock band

bank [bæŋk] — 1. Bank (Geldinstitut)
✎ In town
∞ bank account — Bankkonto
∞ banknote — Geldschein
☛ Die Bank zum Sitzen heißt *bench*.

  — 2. Ufer
the banks of the Mississippi

bar [bɑ:] — 1. Bar, Lokal; Theke
∞ snackbar ≈ cafeteria — Snackbar, Imbißstube
She serves behind the bar. — Sie bedient hinter der Theke.

  — 2. Stange
an iron bar — eine Eisenstange
∞ a bar of chocolate — eine Tafel Schokolade

bark [bɑ:k] — bellen
The dog barked loudly when I went past.

basket ['bɑ:skɪt] — Korb
∞ wastepaper basket — Papierkorb
∞ basketball ✎ Sports and games — Korbball

baseball ['beɪsbɔ:l] — *Baseball* (amerikanisches Schlagballspiel)
✎ Sports and games

basic ['beɪsɪk] — grundlegend, Grund-
basic rules — Grundregeln
basic vocabulary [və'kæbjʊlərɪ] — Grundwortschatz

bath [bɑ:θ] — Bad; Badewanne
∞ take a bath — ein Bad nehmen
∞ bathroom — Badezimmer
✎ House and flat

✎ **In the bathroom**

⇨ bathing-suit ['beɪðɪŋ'su:t] ✎ Clothes — Badeanzug

battery ['bætərɪ] — Batterie
✎ Entertainment electronics

be [bi:] , **was/were, been** — sein
How much is this book? — Wieviel kostet dieses Buch?
What colour are her eyes? — Welche Farbe haben ihre Augen?

How are you? — Wie geht es dir?
Bob wants to be an electrician. — Bob möchte Elektriker werden.

beach [bi:tʃ] — Strand
We were lying on the beach the whole afternoon. — Wir lagen den ganzen Nachmittag am Strand.

bean [bi:n] — Bohne
✎ Vegetables

bear [beə] — Bär
✎ Animals
∞ polar bear — Eisbär

bear [beə], **bore** [bɔ:], **borne** [bɔ:n] — ertragen
I can't bear the noise any more.
⇨ (be) born — geboren (werden)
When were you born? — Wann bist du geboren?

beard [bɪəd]   Bart
✎ The human body

beautiful ['bjuːtɪfʊl]   schön
≈ pretty/lovely
⇔ ugly
a beautiful face
⇨ beauty   Schönheit

because [bɪ'kɒz]   weil
I couldn't come   …, weil ich
because I was ill.   krank war.
∞ because of   wegen
The plane
couldn't start
because of the   … wegen des
fog.   Nebels …

become [bɪ'kʌm],   werden
became [bɪ'keɪm],
become ≈ get
It's becoming   Es wird immer
colder and   kälter.
colder.
They soon be-   Sie wurden bald
came friends.   Freunde.
☛ Das englische
become ent-
spricht **nicht**
dem deutschen
bekommen:
He gets £5 an   Er bekommt £5
hour for the job.   pro Stunde …
German custom-
er in a restau-
rant: Waiter,
when will I be-
come a beef-
steak?
Waiter: I hope
you never do, sir.

bed [bed]   Bett
✎ Furniture
be in bed   im Bett sein
go to bed   ins Bett gehen
∞ bedroom   Schlafzimmer
✎ House and flat

∞ | **Bed & Breakfast**   Übernachtung
mit Frühstück

bee [biː] ✎ Animals   Biene

beef [biːf] ✎ Food   Rindfleisch
∞ beefsteak   *Beefsteak*
['biːfsteɪk]
∞ roast beef [rəʊst]   Rinderbraten

beer [bɪə] ✎ Drinks   Bier

before [bɪ'fɔː]   vor; bevor, ehe;
⇔ after   vorher, zuvor
✎ Expressions of time
before the party   vor der Party
She left before   Sie ging, bevor
we arrived.   wir ankamen.
The last test was   Der letzte Test
much easier than   war viel leichter
the one before.   als der zuvor.
∞ the day before   vorgestern
yesterday

beg [beg]   bitten, betteln
∞ I beg your   Ich bitte um
pardon.   Verzeihung.
⇨ beggar   Bettler(in)

begin [bɪ'gɪn], **be-**   anfangen
gan [bɪ'gæn], **begun**
[bɪ'gʌn] ≈ start
It's beginning to   Es fängt an zu
rain.   regnen.
⇨ beginning   Anfang
∞ at the beginning   am Anfang
∞ from the   von Anfang an
beginning
⇨ beginner   Anfänger(in)

behave [bɪ'heɪv]   sich verhalten, sich
≈ act   benehmen
He behaved very   Er benahm sich
badly.   sehr schlecht.

behind [bɪ'haɪnd]   hinter
⇔ in front of
✎ Place and direction
behind a tree   hinter einem
Baum

Belgium ['beldʒəm]   Belgien
✎ Countries
⇨ Belgian   belgisch;
→ American   Belgier(in)

believe [bɪ'liːv]   glauben
I believe he is   Ich glaube, er hat
right.   recht.
Do you believe in   Glaubst du an
ghosts?   Geister?

bell [bel]   Glocke, Klingel
Please ring the   Bitte klingeln.
bell.

belly ['belɪ]   Bauch
✎ The human body

belong [bɪ'lɒŋ]   gehören
This dictionary   Dieses Wörter-
belongs to the   buch gehört der
school library.   Schulbibliothek.

below [bɪ'ləʊ] — unter, unterhalb (von)
⇔ above ✎ Place and direction
  10 m below the ground — 10 m unter dem Erdboden

belt [belt] ✎ Clothes — Gürtel, Gurt
∞ seat-belt — Sicherheitsgurt

> Fasten your seat-belts, please. — Legen Sie bitte die Sicherheitsgurte an.

bench [bentʃ] — Bank (zum Sitzen)
✎ Furniture
  a park bench — eine Parkbank
  ☛ nicht *bank*!

beside [bɪ'saɪd] — neben
≈ next to ✎ Place and direction
  He was sitting beside the driver. — Er saß neben dem Fahrer.

besides [bɪ'saɪdz] — außerdem
  I haven't got time to go swimming today, and besides it's too cold.

best [best] → good — best(er), am besten
∞ Best wishes. — Viele Grüße.
∞ All the best. — Alles Gute.
∞ bestseller ['bestselə] — *Bestseller*, Verkaufsschlager
  What subject do you like best? — Welches Fach magst du am liebsten?

better ['betə] — besser(er)
→ good
  I like English better than maths. — Ich mag English lieber als Mathe.

between [bɪ'twi:n] — zwischen
✎ Place and direction
✎ Place and direction
  Tim is standing between his parents.
  between 8 and 9

bicycle ['baɪsɪkl] — Fahrrad
→ bike ✎ Transport

big [bɪg] ⇔ small, little — groß
  a big box
  my big brother
  a big surprise

bike [baɪk] — Fahrrad; Motorrad
→ bicycle
✎ Transport
∞ ride a bike — radfahren
∞ a bike ride — eine Spazierfahrt mit dem Rad
∞ motor-bike (Kurzform: bike) — Motorrad

bill [bɪl] — 1. Rechnung
  pay the bill — die Rechnung bezahlen
≈ (bank) note *(BE)* — 2. *(AE)* Geldschein
  a ten-dollar bill — ein Zehndollarschein

biology [baɪ'ɒlədʒɪ] — Biologie
✎ School subjects

bird [bɜ:d] — Vogel
✎ Animals
∞ a bird cage — ein Vogelkäfig

biro ['baɪrəʊ] — Kugelschreiber
✎ My school bag

birth [bɜ:θ] — Geburt
∞ birthday ['bɜ:θdeɪ] — Geburtstag
∞ place of birth — Geburtsort

biscuit ['bɪskɪt] — Keks
✎ Food

a bit [bɪt] ≈ a little — ein bißchen
  We're a bit late. — Wir kommen ein bißchen zu spät.
  I'll need a bit of time to finish this. — Ich werde ein bißchen Zeit brauchen, ...

bite [baɪt], **bit** [bɪt], **bitten** ['bɪtn] — beißen
  The boy bit into his cake. — Der Junge biß in seinen Kuchen.

bitter ['bɪtə] — bitter
⇔ sweet
  The tea tastes bitter.

black [blæk] — schwarz; Schwarze(r)
✎ Colours
  a black cloud
  the blacks and the whites — die Schwarzen und die Weißen
∞ blackout — *Blackout*; Stromausfall

blanket ['blæŋkɪt] — (Woll-/Bett-)Decke

block [blɒk] — Block, Klotz
∞ a block of flats — ein Wohnblock
  ✎ In town

blood [blʌd]   Blut
✎ The human body
⇨ bloody   blutig; verdammt
(Schimpfwort)
bloody hands   blutige Hände
a bloody idiot   ein verdammter
Idiot

blouse [blaʊz]   Bluse
✎ Clothes

blow [bləʊ], **blew**   blasen, wehen;
[blu:], **blown** [bləʊn]   Schlag, Hieb
The wind is   Der Wind weht
blowing from   von Norden.
the north.
∞ blow up   aufblasen
She blew up the
balloon.
He gave the   Er gab dem Ein-
burglar a blow   brecher einen
on the head.   Schlag auf den
Kopf.

blue [blu:] ✎ Colours   blau; traurig
a blue sky   blauer Himmel
I feel blue today.   Ich bin heute
traurig.

☛ "Blau" im Sinn
von "betrunken"
heißt *drunk*.

board [bɔ:d]   Tafel, Brett; Bord
The teacher
wrote the word
on the board.
∞ noticeboard   Schwarzes Brett
∞ surfboard   *Surfboard*
∞ keyboard´   *Keyboard;*
Tastatur
go on board a   an Bord eines
ship   Schiffes gehen

boat [bəʊt]   Boot, Schiff, Kahn
✎ Transport
∞ sailing boat   Segelboot
⇨ boating   Bootfahren

body ['bɒdɪ]   Körper

boil [bɔɪl]   kochen (lassen),
Boil the potatoes   sieden
for 20 minutes.
The water is
boiling.
☛cook a meal   eine Mahlzeit
kochen

bone [bəʊn]   Knochen
✎ The human body

book [buk]   Buch; buchen
∞ bookshop   Buchhandlung
✎ In town
∞ exercise-book   Heft
✎ My school bag
book a flight   einen Flug
buchen

boot [bu:t]   Stiefel; Kofferraum
✎ Clothes
He always wears
boots.
Put the suitcase
in the boot,
please.

border ['bɔ:də]   Grenze
the border
between the USA
and Canada

born [bɔ:n] → bear   geboren

boring ['bɔ:rɪŋ]   langweilig
⇔ interesting
a boring film

borrow ['bɒrəʊ]   (sich) ausborgen,
→ lend   (sich) ausleihen
He borrowed
two books from
me.

both [bəʊθ]   (alle) beide
Mary and John
have both won a
prize.
Hold this pot in
both hands.
☛Nach *the* steht
two:
the two brothers   die beiden/die
zwei Brüder

bottle ['bɒtl]   Flasche
a bottle of milk   eine Flasche
Milch

bottom ['bɒtəm]   unteres Ende,
⇔ top   Boden
at the bottom of   unten auf der
the stairs   Treppe

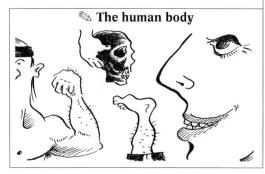
✎ **The human body**

bowl [bəʊl]
a bowl of fruit — Schüssel, Schale / eine Schale Obst

box [bɒks]
a box of matches — Schachtel, Kiste / eine Schachtel Streichhölzer

∞ post-box/letterbox — Briefkasten

∞ (tele)phone box/call box — Telefonzelle

boxing [ˈbɒksɪŋ]
✎ Sports and games — Boxen
➪ boxer ✎ Jobs — Boxer

boy [bɔɪ] — Junge
∞ boyfriend ['bɔɪfrend] — Freund (eines Mädchens)

brake [breɪk] — bremsen; Bremse
He braked suddenly.
The brakes didn't work.

branch [brɑːnʃ] — Ast; Zweigstelle, Filiale

the branch of a tree
the branch of a bank

bread [bred] ✎ Food — Brot

break [breɪk], **broke** [brəʊk], **broken** [ˈbrəʊkn] — (zer)brechen; Pause
The glass fell on the floor and broke. — Das Glas fiel auf den Boden und zerbrach.
break one's arm — sich den Arm brechen

∞ break down — versagen, stehenbleiben
Our car broke down on the motorway. — Wir hatten eine Panne auf der Autobahn.
➪ a breakdown — Panne, Maschinenschaden

tea break — Teepause

breakfast [ˈbrekfəst] — Frühstück
∞ have breakfast — frühstücken

bridge [brɪdʒ] — Brücke
✎ In town
∞ Tower Bridge — die Towerbrücke

bright [braɪt] — hell, strahlend; intelligent

a bright light
bright eyes
a bright child

bring [brɪŋ], **brought** [brɔːt], **brought** → take — (her)bringen
Bring me the paper, please.
☛ Take this letter to Mr Smith, please. — Bring bitte diesen Brief Mr Smith.

Britain [ˈbrɪtn] — Großbritannien
≈ Great Britain
✎ Countries
➪ British [ˈbrɪtɪʃ] — britisch
∞ the British Isles [aɪlz] — die Britischen Inseln
She is British. — Sie ist Britin.
∞ the British — die Briten
➪ Briton — Brite/Britin

broad [brɔːd] — breit
≈ wide
a broad street
∞ broadcast — (Rundfunk-/Fernseh-)Sendung; senden
∞ Broadway — der *Broadway* (in New York)

brother [ˈbrʌðə] — Bruder
✎ Relatives

brown [braʊn] — braun
✎ Colours

brush [brʌʃ] ✎ Tools — Pinsel; Bürste; bürsten
∞ paintbrush — Malerpinsel
∞ clothes brush — Kleiderbürste
∞ toothbrush ✎ In the bathroom — Zahnbürste
∞ brush one's teeth — sich die Zähne putzen

bubble [ˈbʌbl] — (Gas-)Blase
∞ a soap bubble — eine Seifenblase

bucket [ˈbʌkɪt] — Eimer

budgie [ˈbʌdʒɪ] — Wellensittich
✎ Animals

build [bɪld], **built** [bɪlt], **built** — bauen
The house was built in 1920. — Das Haus wurde 1920 gebaut.
➪ building — Gebäude
∞ building site — Baustelle

bulb [bʌlb] ✎ Electricity in the household — Glühbirne

bull [bʊl] ✎ Animals — Bulle, Stier

burglar [ˈbɜːglə] — Einbrecher(in)

burn [bɜːn], **burnt** [bɜːnt], **burnt** (oder: burned, burned)
✎ Danger and accidents
The house is burning.
She burnt all his letters.

brennen, verbrennen

Das Haus steht in Flammen.
Sie verbrannte all seine Briefe.

bury [ˈberɪ]
He was buried in the local churchyard.

The dog buried the bone in the garden.

begraben; vergraben
Er wurde auf dem örtlichen Friedhof begraben.
Der Hund vergrub den Knochen im Garten.

bus [bʌs] ✎ Transport
I met her <u>on</u> the bus.
You can go there <u>by</u> bus.

Bus
Ich traf sie <u>im</u> Bus.
Du kannst <u>mit dem</u> Bus hinfahren.

∞ bus station
∞ bus stop
  ✎ In town
∞ bus driver ✎ Jobs

Busbahnhof
Bushaltestelle

Busfahrer(in)

business

∞ businessman/-woman
∞ show business

Geschäft, Unternehmen
Geschäftsmann/-frau
Showbusiness, Unterhaltungsbranche

busy [ˈbɪzɪ]

She is always very busy.
All the telephone lines are busy.

beschäftigt, geschäftig; besetzt
Sie hat immer sehr viel zu tun.
Alle Telefonleitungen sind besetzt.

but [bʌt]
We invited her, but she didn't come.
He isn't English but Scottish.

aber; sondern
Wir luden sie ein, aber sie kam nicht.
Er ist kein Engländer, sondern Schotte.

butcher [ˈbʊtʃə]
✎ Jobs
I bought some ham at the butcher's.

Fleischer, Metzger

Ich habe beim Metzger etwas Schinken gekauft.

butter [ˈbʌtə]
✎ Food
∞ butterfly [ˈbʌtəflaɪ] ✎ Animals

Butter

Schmetterling

button [ˈbʌtn]
press/push a button

Knopf; *Button*
einen Knopf drücken

buy [baɪ], **bought** [bɔːt] **bought** ⇔ sell
We've bought her a CD for her birthday.

kaufen

by [baɪ] ≈ near
✎ Place and direction
by the window

1. in Ortsangaben

   am Fenster

✎ Expressions of time
Be back by 5 o'clock.
They must have arrived by now.

by day
by night

2. in Zeitangaben
   … bis (spätestens) 5 Uhr.
   Sie müssen inzwischen angekommen sein.
   bei Tag
   bei Nacht

He was bitten by a dog.

a film by Steven Spielberg

3. im Passiv, zur Angabe des Urhebers
   Er wurde von einem Hund gebissen.
   ein Film von Steven Spielberg

go by car/bus/train

4. bei Transportmitteln
   mit dem Auto/Bus/Zug fahren

Young man: Darling, how could I ever leave you?
Young girl: By bus, by train, by taxi …

People passed by without looking.

5. vorbei, vorüber
   Die Leute gingen vorbei, ohne hinzusehen.

∞ by the way

übrigens

By my watch it is seven now.

6. nach, laut
   Nach meiner Uhr ist es jetzt sieben.

bye [baɪ] ≈ bye-bye, goodbye

tschüs

C [si:] is for

cabbage ['kæbɪdʒ] Kohl
✎ Food

café ['kæfeɪ] Café, Imbißstube

cafeteria Cafeteria, Selbstbe-
[kæfɪ'tɪərɪə] dienungsrestaurant

cage [keɪdʒ] Käfig

cake [keɪk] ✎ Food Kuchen

calculator Taschenrechner
['kælkjʊleɪtə]
✎ My school bag

calendar ['kælɪndə] Kalender

calf [kɑːf], **calves** Kalb, Kälber
[kɑːvz] ✎ Animals

call [kɔːl] 1. rufen; Ruf
≈ shout/cry
He called for
help.
They heard a call
for help.
≈ (tele)phone/ring; 2. anrufen; Anruf
(tele)phone call
Can you answer
the phone if
anybody calls?
There's a call for
you from Leeds.
↪ caller Anrufer(in)
3. nennen
My friends call Meine Freunde
me Dick. nennen mich
Dick.
What do you call Wie heißt das auf
this in English? Englisch?

*Customer in a
restaurant (after
having paid the
bill):* Please, call
me a taxi.
Waiter: Okay,
you are a taxi.

camel ['kæml] Kamel
✎ Animals

camera ['kæmərə] Fotoapparat;
Kamera
∞ cameraman Kameramann
∞ video camera Videokamera
✎ Entertainment
electronics
↪ camcorder Kamerarekorder

camp [kæmp] zelten; (Zelt-)Lager
∞ go camping zelten gehen
∞ camping site Zeltplatz
∞ campfire Lagerfeuer

can [kæn; kən] können
≈ be able to
Can you swim? Kannst du
schwimmen?
We can't [kɑːnt]/ Wir können
cannot ['kænɒt] heute nicht
come today. kommen.
Could [kʊd] you Könntest du mir
help me, please? bitte helfen?
I couldn't Ich konnte sie
['kʊdnt] not nicht verstehen.
understand her.

can [kæn] ≈ tin Dose, Büchse;
Kanister
a can of beer eine Dose Bier
a can of petrol ein Kanister
Benzin
↪ canned food Konserven

candle ['kændl] Kerze

candy ['kændɪ] *(AE)* Bonbon; Süßig-
≈ sweet; sweets *(BE)* keiten
Would you like a Magst du ein
candy? Bonbon?
Candy is bad for Süßigkeiten sind
your teeth. schlecht für die
Zähne.

cap [kæp] ✎ Clothes Kappe, Mütze

capital ['kæpɪtl] Hauptstadt; groß
Rome is the
capital of Italy.
∞ capital letters Großbuchstaben

captain ['kæptn] Kapitän
✎ Jobs

car [kɑː] ✎ Transport Auto
∞ car park Parkplatz
✎ In town
∞ car mechanic Kfz-Mechani-
✎ Jobs ker(in)
∞ car wash Autowaschanlage

caravan ['kærəvən] Wohnwagen
✎ Transport

card [kɑːd] Karte
∞ postcard Postkarte
∞ Christmas card Weihnachtskarte
∞ phonecard Telefonkarte
∞ play cards Karten spielen
☛ticket Eintrittskarte;
Fahrkarte
☛map Landkarte

cardboard ['kɑːdbɔːd]
∞ a cardboard box — Kartonpapier, Pappe / ein Pappkarton

cardigan ['kɑːdɪgən]
✎ Clothes — Strickjacke

career [kəˈrɪə]
∞ careers office — berufliche Laufbahn / Berufsberatung(sstelle)

⇨ careers officer — Berufsberater(in)

careful ['keəfʊl]
⇔ careless
Be careful!
She's a careful worker./She works carefully. — vorsichtig; sorgfältig / Sei vorsichtig! / Sie arbeitet sorgfältig.

⇨ care — Sorge, Fürsorge; sich kümmern aufpassen

∞ take care
Can you take care of the dog for a while?
The Wilsons don't care for their cats properly.
Would you like coke or lemonade? – I don't care. — Kannst du eine Weile auf den Hund aufpassen? / Wilsons kümmern sich nicht richtig um ihre Katzen. / ... – Das ist mir egal.

careless ['keələs]
⇔ careful
a careless driver — unvorsichtig; nachlässig / ein unvorsichtiger Fahrer

a careless drawing — eine nachlässige Zeichnung

carpenter ['kɑːpɪntə] ✎ Jobs — Tischler(in), Zimmermann

carpet ['kɑːpɪt]
✎ House and flat — Teppich

carrot ['kærət]
✎ Vegetables — Karotte, Mohrrübe

carry ['kærɪ]
Shall I help you to carry your bag? — tragen
☛ wear jeans/a jacket/... — Jeans/eine Jacke/... tragen

cartoon [kɑːˈtuːn] — (gezeichneter) Witz; Zeichentrickfilm

case [keɪs]
∞ pencil case
✎ My school bag — Mappe, Etui / Federmäppchen
∞ suitcase ['suːtkeɪs] — Koffer

cash [kæʃ]
How much cash have you got on you? — Bargeld / Wieviel Bargeld hast du dabei?
∞ pay in cash — bar bezahlen

cassette [kəˈset]
✎ Entertainment electronics
∞ cassette recorder — Kassettenrekorder
∞ video cassette — Videokassette — Kassette

castle ['kɑːsl]
✎ In town — Schloß, Burg

cat [kæt] ✎ Animals — Katze

catalogue ['kætəlɒg] — Katalog

catch [kætʃ], **caught** [kɔːt], **caught**
The cat has caught a mouse. — fangen
∞ catch a train/bus/... — einen Zug/Bus/... erreichen
∞ catch a cold — sich erkälten

cathedral [kəˈθiːdrəl] — Kathedrale, Dom

cattle ['kætl]
✎ Animals — Vieh, Rinder
☛ The cattle look very healthy. — Das Viel sieht sehr gesund aus.

cauliflower ['kɒlɪflaʊə] ✎ Vegetables — Blumenkohl

cause [kɔːz]
The storm caused a lot of damage. — verursachen / Der Sturm richtete großen Schaden an.
⇨ because [bɪˈkɒz] — weil

ceiling ['siːlɪŋ]
⇔ floor
✎ House and flat — (Zimmer-)Decke

cellar ['selə]
✎ House and flat — Keller

cemetery ['semɪtrɪ]
≈ graveyard, churchyard
✎ In town — Friedhof

cent [sent] — Cent (= 1/100 Dollar)
⇨ per cent — Prozent

centimetre ['sentɪmiːtə]
15 centimetres (15 cm) — Zentimeter

centre ['sentə]	Zentrum, Mittelpunkt
∞ shopping centre	Einkaufszentrum
✎ In town	
∞ city centre	Stadtmitte
➪ central	zentral
∞ central station	Hauptbahnhof
✎ In town	
∞ central heating	Zentralheizung
✎ House and flat	
century ['sentʃərı]	Jahrhundert
the 20th century	
cereal ['sırıəl]	Getreide(produkt)
Cornflakes are the most popular breakfast cereal.	Cornflakes sind das beliebteste Frühstücksgetreideprodukt.
certain ['sɜːtn]	sicher, gewiß
≈ sure	
Can you come tonight? – I'm not quite certain.	... – Ich bin mir nicht ganz sicher.
a certain feeling	ein gewisses Gefühl
certificate [sə'tıfıkət]	Bescheinigung, Urkunde
∞ birth certificate	Geburtsurkunde
chain [tʃeın]	Kette
chair [tʃeə]	Stuhl
✎ Furniture	
∞ chairman ['tʃeəmən]/ chairperson	Vorsitzende(r)
∞ armchair ['ɑːmtʃeə]	Sessel
✎ Furniture	
champion ['tʃæmpjən]	Meister (im Sport)
∞ world champion	Weltmeister
➪ championship	Meisterschaft
championships	Meisterschaftskämpfe
chance ['tʃɑːns]	Chance, Gelegenheit; Zufall
We've got no chance of winning.	Wir haben keine Chance zu gewinnen.
I haven't had a chance to talk to him yet.	Ich habe noch keine Gelegenheit gehabt, mit ihm zu reden.
∞ by chance	zufällig
I met her by chance.	

change ['tʃeındʒ]	1. (sich) ändern; Änderung
The situation has changed.	Die Lage hat sich geändert.
We have to change our plans.	Wir müssen unsere Pläne ändern.
She has had her hair cut. – Oh, I didn't notice the change.	... – Oh, ich habe die Veränderung gar nicht bemerkt.
I got wet in the rain. I've got to change.	2. sich umziehen ... Ich muß mich umziehen.
It's not a direct train. We have to change at Crewe.	3. umsteigen Der Zug geht nicht durch. Wir müssen in Crewe umsteigen.
Can you change this pound note into two 50p pieces, please?	4. wechseln; Wechselgeld; Kleingeld Können Sie bitte diese Pfundnote in zwei 50-Pence-Stücke wechseln?
Here's your change.	Hier ist Ihr Wechselgeld.
Have you got any change on you? – No, only notes.	Hast du etwas Kleingeld dabei? – Nein, nur Scheine.
chase [tʃeıs]	jagen, verfolgen
The dog is chasing the cat again.	
cheap [tʃiːp]	billig
⇔ expensive	
check [tʃek]	überprüfen, kontrollieren; Überprüfung
I've got to check the air before we start.	
The car is at the garage for a check.	... zur Überprüfung ...
∞ check in	(Fluggäste/Fluggepäck) abfertigen, einchecken
∞ check-in	Abfertigung, Einchecken
∞ checklist	Checkliste, Kontrolliste
cheers [tʃıəz]	Beifallrufe
∞ Cheers!	Prost!

cheese [tʃiːz] Käse
✎ Food
∞ cheeseburger *Cheeseburger*
['tʃiːzbɜːgə]

chemist ['kemɪst] Apotheker(in)
✎ Jobs
at the chemist's in der Apotheke

cheque [tʃek] Scheck
∞ pay by cheque mit Scheck
bezahlen
∞ cheque card Scheckkarte
∞ Eurocheque Euroscheck
['juərəʊtʃek]
∞ traveller's cheque Reisescheck

cherry ['tʃerɪ] Kirsche
✎ Fruit

chess [tʃes] Schach
play chess Schach spielen

chest [tʃest] Brust(korb)
✎ The human body

chewing gum Kaugummi
['tʃuːɪŋ gʌm]

chicken ['tʃɪkn] Huhn, Hähnchen,
✎ Food; ✎ Animals Küken
Do you like Magst du
chicken? Hähnchen?
∞ Don't be a Sei kein Feigling.
chicken.

child [tʃaɪld], Kind, Kinder
children ['tʃɪldrən],
✎ People
∞ She's an only Sie ist ein
child. Einzelkind.

chimney ['tʃɪmnɪ] Schornstein, Kamin
✎ House and flat
∞ chimney sweep Schornsteinfe-
✎ Jobs ger(in)

China ['tʃaɪnə] China
✎ Countries
∞ Chinatown Chinesenviertel
⇨ Chinese chinesisch; Chi-
nesich; Chinese/
Chinesin
the Chinese die Chinesen
☛ ohne *s-*
Endung!

chips [tʃɪps] *(BE)* Pommes frites
≈ French fries *(AE)*
['frenʃfraɪz] ✎ Food
∞ fish and chips panierter Fisch
['fɪʃ'tʃɪps] mit Pommes
frites

Teacher: If I take
one potato and
divide it into two
parts and then
divide these two
parts again, what
would I have?
Pupil: Potato
chips.

☛ crips *(BE)* Kartoffelchips
= chips *(AE)*

chocolate ['tʃɒklɪt] Schokolade (auch
✎ Food; ✎ Drinks als Getränk)
∞ a bar of eine Tafel Scho-
chocolate kolade

choir ['kwaɪə] Chor
She sings in the Sie singt im
school choir. Schulchor.

choke [tʃəʊk] ersticken; erwürgen
He choked on a Er erstickte fast
fishbone. an einer Fisch-
gräte.

choose [tʃuːz], (aus)wählen
chose [tʃəʊz],
chosen ['tʃəʊzn]
You can choose Sie haben die
from 5 colours. Wahl zwischen
5 Farben.
⇨ choice [tʃɔɪs] (Aus)wahl

chop [tʃɒp] hacken; Kotelett
chop wood Holz hacken
∞ chop down a tree einen Baum
fällen
∞ pork chop Schweinekotelett
✎ Food

Christ [kraɪst] Christus
⇨ Christian christlich;
['krɪstʃən] Christ(in)
∞ Christian name Vorname
≈ first name

Christmas Weihnachten
['krɪsməs]
∞ Christmas carol Weihnachtslied
['kærəl]
∞ Christmas Eve Heiliger Abend
[iːv]
∞ Christmas Day 1. Weihnachtstag
∞ Father Christmas der Weihnachts-
mann
∞ Merry Christmas. Fröhliche Weihnachten!

church [tʃɜːtʃ] Kirche
✎ In town

∞ <u>in</u> church/
<u>at</u> church
    in der Kirche
    (= beim Gottes-
    dienst)

∞ go <u>to</u> church
    in die Kirche
    (= zum Gottes-
    dienst) gehen

cigar [sɪˈgɑː]   Zigarre

cigarette [sɪgəˈret]   Zigarette

cinema [ˈsɪnəmə]   Kino
✎ In town

city [ˈsɪtɪ]   Großstadt
∞ city centre   Stadtmitte,
    Innenstadt
⇨ citizen [ˈsɪtɪzn]   Staatsbürger(in);
    Einwohner(in)
∞ a British citizen   ein(e) britische(r)
    Staatsbürger(in)
   the citizens of   die Einwohner
   York   von York

class [klɑːs]   Klasse
∞ classmate   Klassenkame-
  [ˈklɑːsmeɪt]   rad(in)
∞ classroom   Klassenzimmer
  [ˈklɑːsruːm]
∞ school class   Schulklasse

clean [kliːn] ⇔ dirty   sauber; putzen,
    reinigen
  a clean shirt   ein sauberes
    Hemd
  clean the floor   den Boden
    putzen
∞ clean out (a   ausputzen
  cupboard, etc.)
∞ clean up   aufräumen,
    sauber machen
⇨ cleaner ✎ Jobs   Raumpfleger(in)
∞ vacuum cleaner   Staubsauger
  [ˈvækjʊəmkliːnə]
  ✎ Electricity in the
  household

clear [klɪə]   klar; (aus-/
    ab-)räumen
  a clear sky   ein klarer
    Himmel
  clear a building   ein Gebäude
    räumen
  clear snow from   Schnee von einer
  a street   Straße räumen

clerk [klɑːk] ✎ Jobs   Büroangestellte(r);
    Schalterbeamter/
    -beamtin

clever [ˈklevə]   klug, gescheit,
⇔ stupid   schlau

  a clever animal   ein kluges Tier
  a clever plan   ein schlauer Plan

climate [ˈklaɪmɪt]   Klima

climb [klaɪm]   klettern, steigen
  climb a mountain   einen Berg
    besteigen
⇨ (mountain)   Bergsteigen
  climbing ✎ Sports
  and games
⇨ (mountain)   Bergsteiger(in)
  climber

clock [klɒk]   (Turm-/Wand-/
    Stand-)Uhr
∞ alarm clock   Wecker
∞ clock radio   Radiowecker
∞ ten o'clock ✎ Ex-   zehn Uhr
  pressions of time
☛ watch   Armbanduhr

close [ˈkləʊz] ≈ shut   (sich) schließen
  Close the win-   Schließ bitte das
  dow, please.   Fenster.
  The door closed   Die Tür schloß
  suddenly.   sich plötzlich.

Closed	geschlossen

∞ close down a   ein Geschäft
  business   schließen
  The factory   Die Fabrik wurde
  closed down.   stillgelegt.

cloth [klɒθ]   Tuch; Stoff
  Polish with a soft   Mit einem
  cloth.   weichen Tuch
    polieren.
  a bag made of   eine Tasche aus
  cloth   Stoff

clothes [kləʊðz]   Kleider, Kleidung

✎ **Clothes**

cloud [klaʊd]   Wolke
⇨ cloudy ✎ The   wolkig, bewölkt
  weather

clown [klaʊn]   Clown

club [klʌb]   Club
∞ youth club   Jugendclub
∞ sports club   Sportclub

coach	Reisebus; Trainer(in)
∞ a coach tour	eine Busreise
∞ a football coach	ein(e) Fußball-
✎ Jobs	trainer(in)
coal [kəʊl]	Kohle
∞ a coal mine	ein Kohleberg-werk
coast [kəʊst]	Küste
∞ on the coast	an der Küste
coat [kəʊt]	Mantel
✎ Clothes	
∞ coat hanger	Kleiderbügel
coffee ['kɒfɪ]	Kaffee
∞ coffee shop	Café, Kaffeestube
✎ In town	
coin [kɔɪn]	Münze
cold [kəʊld] ⇔ hot, warm ✎ The weather ☞ We were/felt cold. Don't go out into the cold without a coat. have a cold	kalt; Kälte; Erkältung Uns war kalt. Geh nicht ohne Mantel hinaus in die Kälte. erkältet sein
∞ catch a cold	sich erkälten
collect [kə'lekt] collect stamps	(ein)sammeln Briefmarken sammeln
collect empty glasses	leere Gläser einsammeln

Boy: Mum, there's a man at the door. He says he is collecting for the new swimming pool. *Mother:* Well, give him a glass of water.

⇨ collection	Sammlung
a stamp collection	
colour ['kʌlə]	Farbe

✎ **Colours**

What colour is your new bike?	Welche Farbe hat dein neues Rad?
☞ paint	Farbe zum Anstreichen
comb [kəʊm]	Kamm; kämmen
✎ In the bathroom	
comb one's hair	sich die Haare kämmen
come [kʌm], **came** [keɪm], **come** [kʌm]	kommen
∞ come along	mitkommen
∞ Come on!	Komm schon!
∞ come to see s.o.	jdn. besuchen (kommen)
comfortable ['kʌmftəbl] a comfortable armchair make oneself comfortable be comfortable	bequem, behaglich ein bequemer Sessel es sich bequem machen sich wohl fühlen
comic ['kɒmɪk]	Comicheft
∞ comic strip	*Comic strip*
comment ['kɒment]	Bemerkung, Kommentar
∞ No comment.	Kein Kommentar
commercial [kə'mɜ:ʃl] watch the commercials on TV a commercial centre	Werbespot; Handels-die Werbespots im Fernsehen anschauen Handelszentrum
community [kə'mju:nɪtɪ]	Gemeinde; Gemeinschaft
company ['kʌmpənɪ] Miller & Co. (= Miller and Company) a company car We're expecting company tonight.	Firma; Gesellschaft, Gäste Miller & Co. ein Firmenwagen Wir erwarten heute abend Besuch.
compare [kəm'peə] Compare this picture with that one.	vergleichen Vergleicht dieses Bild mit dem da.
complain [kəm'pleɪn] She is complaining about a headache.	sich beschweren, klagen Sie klagt über Kopfschmerzen.

I'm going to complain to the manger about the bad service.

Ich werden mich beim Geschäftsführer über den schlechten Service beschweren.

complete [kəm'pli:t]

vollständig; vervollständigen; beenden

a complete list

eine vollständige Liste

complete a list

eine Liste vervollständigen

complete a job

eine Arbeit beenden

comprehensive (school) [kəmprɪ'hensɪv]

Gesamtschule

computer [kəm'pju:tə]

Computer

∞ personal computer

Personalcomputer

concert ['kɒnsət]

Konzert

confused [kən'fju:zd]

verwirrt

↪ confusing

verwirrend

↪ confusion [kən'fju:ʒn]

Verwirrung

congratulations [kən'grætjʊ'leɪʃnz]

Glückwunsch, Glückwünsche

Congratulations!

Herzlichen Glückwunsch!

connect [kə'nekt]

verbinden (z. B. telefonisch)

I'll connect you.

Ich verbinde.

↪ connection [kə'nekʃn]

Verbindung

construct [kən'strʌkt] ≈ build

bauen, konstruieren

construct a bridge

↪ construction

Bau, Konstruktion

∞ construction site ✎ In town

Baustelle

contain [kən'teɪn] This book contains some interesting stories.

enthalten

↪ container

Behälter; *Container*

continent ['kɒntɪnent]

Kontinent, Erdteil

∞ the Continent ⇔ Britain

das europäische Festland

↪ continental ⇔ British

(festland)europäisch

∞ continental breakfast

kleines Frühstück (Brot, Butter, Marmelade und Tee oder Kaffee)

continue [kən'tɪnju:] ≈ go on The rain continued for three days.

andauern; fortsetzen; weitermachen Der Regen dauerte drei Tage lang an.

After a short break they continued their journey.

Nach einer kurzen Pause setzten sie ihre Reise fort.

Let's continue with our work now.

Machen wir jetzt mit unserer Arbeit weiter.

∞ continued on page 20

Fortsetzung auf Seite 20

∞ to be continued

Fortsetzung folgt

control [kən'trəʊl]

kontrollieren, steuern; Kontrolle, Steuerung

control the quality of a product

die Qualität eines Produktes kontrollieren.

control the traffic

den Verkehr regeln

☛ Beachte das Doppel-L in: controlling, controlled

∞ keep s.th. under control

etwas unter Kontrolle halten

∞ remote control ✎ Entertainment electronics

Fernsteuerung, Fernbedienung

conversation [kɒnvə'seɪʃn] ≈ talk

Gespräch, Unterhaltung

cook [kʊk] ✎ Jobs

kochen; Koch, Köchin

cook a meal

ein Essen kochen

☛ boil potatoes

Kartoffeln (ab-)kochen (= in kochendem Wasser garen)

She is a good cook.

Sie ist eine gute Köchin.

↪ cooking

Kochen

∞ home cooking

Hausmannskost

↪ cooker ✎ Electricity in the household

Herd, Kocher

↪ cookery ['kʊkərɪ]

Kochen, Koch-

∞ cookery club

Kochclub

∞ cookery book/ cookbook — Kochbuch

cool [ku:l] ⇔ warm — kühl; abkühlen
✎ The weather

It's cool outside. — Es ist kühl draußen.

The soup has cooled. — Die Suppe ist abgekühlt.
They cooled their hands in the river. — Sie kühlten sich die Hände im Fluß.

copy ['kɒpɪ] — abschreiben, kopieren; Kopie

I've copied this sentence from a book. — Ich habe diesen Satz aus einem Buch abgeschrieben.

Can you make me a copy of this letter? — Können Sie mir eine Kopie von diesem Brief machen?

∞ photocopy ['fəʊtəʊkɒpɪ] — fotokopieren; Fotokopie
⇨ photocopier — Fotokopiergerät

corn [kɔ:n] ✎ Food — BE: Getreide; AE: Mais

∞ a cornfield — ein Kornfeld
∞ cornflakes — Cornflakes

corner ['kɔ:nə] — Ecke
at the corner of the street

correct [kə'rekt] — richtig, korrekt; korrigieren

a correct answer — eine richtige Antwort

correct a mistake — einen Fehler korrigieren

corridor ['kɒrɪdɔ:] — Gang, Korridor
✎ House and flat

cost [kɒst], **cost, cost** — kosten; Kosten

This T-shirt only cost £5. — Dieses T-shirt kostete nur £5.
The cost of our trip was higher than we had thought. — Die Kosten für die Reise waren höher, als wir gedacht hatten.

cotton ['kɒtn] — Baumwolle; Faden
a cotton shirt — ein Baumwollhemd

I need some cotton to sew on a button. — Ich brauche etwas Faden, um einen Knopf anzunähen.

couch [kaʊt] ≈ sofa — Couch, Sofa
✎ Furniture

count [kaʊnt] — zählen
count one's money — sein Geld zählen
count to ten — bis zehn zählen
∞ countdown — Countdown

counter ['kaʊntə] — Theke; Ladentisch; (Bank-/Post-) Schalter

country ['kʌntrɪ] — Land

✎ Countries

a European country — ein europäisches Land
live in the country — auf dem Land leben
∞ countryside — Landschaft

cousin ['kʌzn] — Cousin, Cousine
✎ Relatives

cover ['kʌvə] — zudecken, bedecken; Decke, Deckel, Einband

She covered her face with her hands. — Sie deckte ihr Gesicht mit den Händen.
Dust covered all the furniture.
He put a cover over the bed.
When the water boils, take the cover from the pot.
the cover of a book/magazine

cow [kaʊ] ✎ Animals — Kuh
∞ cowboy — Cowboy

crash [kræʃ] — aufprallen, krachen; Aufprall, Unfall, Krachen

The car crashed into a tree. — Der Wagen fuhr auf einen Baum auf.

The thunder crashed.	Der Donner krachte.	**cupboard** ['kʌbəd] ✎ House and flat	Schrank
a car crash	ein Autounfall		
a plane crash	ein Flugzeugabsturz	**curtain** ['kɜ:tn] ✎ House and flat	Vorhang
a loud crash	ein lautes Krachen	draw the curtains	die Vorhänge zuziehen

crazy ['kreɪzɪ] ≈ mad — verrückt
  What a crazy idea!

cream [kri:m] — Sahne; Creme (Speise-)Eis
∞ ice-cream ✎ Food
∞ face cream — Gesichtscreme

crime [kraɪm] — Verbrechen
⇨ criminal ['krɪmɪnl] — kriminell; Verbrecher(in)

crisps [krɪsps] ✎ Food — (Kartoffel-)Chips

crocodile ['krɒkədaɪl] ✎ Animals — Krokodil

cross [krɒs] — Kreuz; kreuzen, überqueren
∞ the Red Cross — das Rote Kreuz
  cross the road — eine Straße überqueren
∞ crossword (puzzle) ['krɒswɜ:d 'pʌzl] — Kreuzworträtsel

crowd [kraʊd] ✎ People — (Menschen-)Menge
  There were crowds of people in the streets.
⇨ crowded — überfüllt, voll
  The bus was crowded.

crown [kraʊn] — Krone
∞ the Crown Jewels ['kraʊn 'dʒu:əlz] — die Kronjuwelen

cry [kraɪ] ≈ shout — schreien; weinen; Schrei
  "Stop!" he cried.
  He was so unhappy that he started to cry.
  a cry of fear — ein Angstschrei

cucumber ['kjʊkʌmbə] ✎ Vegetables — Gurke

cup [kʌp] — Tasse
✎ Laying the table
  a cup of tea — eine Tasse Tee

---

cushion ['kʊʃn] — Kissen
  Put the cushions on the couch.

customer ['kʌstəmə] — Kunde, Kundin
  She's one of our best customers. — Sie ist eine unserer besten Kundinnen

customs ['kʌstəmz] — Zoll
  to go through customs (at the airport) — durch den Zoll gehen

cut [kʌt], **cut, cut** — schneiden; Schnitt, Platzwunde
  Don't cut yourself with that knife.
∞ cut down a tree — ein Baum fällen
  How did you get that cut on your hand?
∞ a power cut — ein Stromausfall

cycle ['saɪkl] ≈ go by bike, ride a bike — radfahren
⇨ cyclist — Radfahrer(in)

D [di:] is for

dad [dæd] ≈ father — Papa, Vati
✎ Relatives

daily ['deɪlɪ] — täglich
  a daily walk — ein täglicher Spaziergang
∞ a daily paper — eine Tageszeitung
  I telephone her daily. — Ich rufe sie täglich an.
⇨ day — Tag

damage ['dæmɪdʒ] — beschädigen; Schaden
  The fire damaged a large part of the building. — Das Feuer beschädigte einen großen Teil des Gebäudes.
  The storm did a lot of damage. — Der Sturm richtete großen Schaden an.

Damn! [dæm] — Verdammt!

damp [dæmp]   feucht
⇔ dry
✎ The weather

dance [dɑ:ns]   tanzen; Tanz
⇨ dancer   Tänzer(in)

Dane → Denmark   Däne/Dänin

danger ['deɪndʒə]   Gefahr

✎ **Danger and accidents**

⇨ dangerous   gefährlich

Danish   dänisch; Dänisch
→ Denmark

dark [dɑ:k]   dunkel; Dunkelheit
It's too dark to
read.
My little brother
is afraid of the
dark.
∞ dark-blue, dark-   dunkelblau,
red, etc.   dunkelrot usw.

date [deɪt]   Datum; Verabre-
    dung
What's the date   Welches Datum
today?   haben wir heute?
∞ date of birth   Geburtsdatum
∞ up-to-date   *up-to-date*, auf
    dem neuesten
    Stand
I have a date   Ich habe heute
with my girl-   abend eine Ver-
friend tonight.   abredung mit
    meiner Freundin.

day [deɪ]   Tag

✎ **Days of the week**

It happened <u>on</u>   Es geschah <u>am</u>
the first day after   ersten Tag nach
the holidays.   den Ferien.

It all happened   Es geschah alles
<u>in</u> one day.   <u>an</u> einem Tag.
∞ by day ✎ Expres-   tagsüber
sions of time
∞ day by day   Tag für Tag
∞ day and night/   Tag und Nacht
night and day
∞ the day after   übermorgen
tomorrow
∞ the day before   vorgestern
yesterday
∞ one day   eines Tages
One day a circus
came to our town
…
One day you will
understand.
∞ the other day   neulich
The other day
something funny
happened at
school …
∞ these days   heutzutage
These days
everybody has a
colour TV.
∞ time of day   Tageszeit
⇨ daily   täglich

dead [ded] ⇔ alive,   tot
living

Teacher: What
can you tell me
about the Dead
Sea?
Pupil: I didn't
even know it was
ill.

⇨ death [deθ]   Tod

deaf [def]   taub, gehörlos

dear [dɪə]   liebe(r)
Dear Peter, …   Lieber Peter, …
∞ Oh dear!   Du meine Güte!

December   Dezember
[dɪ'sembə] ✎ Months
and seasons
    in December   <u>im</u> Dezember

decide [dɪ'saɪd]   sich entschließen,
    beschließen
We've decided to   Wir haben
go to Austria this   beschlossen,
summer.   diesen Sommer
    nach Österreich
    zu fahren.
⇨ decision [dɪ'sɪʒn]   Entschluß

declare [dɪ'kleə] — (beim Zoll) angeben, verzollen

Have you anything to declare? — Haben sie etwas zu verzollen?

deep [di:p] — tief
a deep voice
a deep lake

degree [dɪ'gri:] — Grad
∞ 30 degrees centigrade = 86 degrees Fahrenheit ['færənhaɪt] — 30 Grad Celsius = 86 Grad Fahrenheit
✎ The weather

deliver [dɪ'lɪvə] — liefern, ausliefern
The milkman delivers the milk at six every morning.

Denmark ['denmɑ:k] ✎ Countries — Dänemark
⇨ Dane [deɪn] — Däne/Dänin
⇨ Danish ['deɪnɪʃ] — dänisch; Dänisch
∞ the Danish/the Danes — die Dänen

dentist ['dentɪst] ✎ Jobs — Zahnarzt, Zahnärztin
I have to go to the dentist's next week.

department [dɪ'pɑ:tmənt] — Abteilung
The food department is downstairs. — Die Lebensmittelabteilung ist unten.
∞ department store ✎ In town — Kaufhaus, Warenhaus

departure [dɪ'pɑ:tʃə] ⇔ arrival — Abfahrt, Abflug

describe [dɪ'skraɪb] — beschreiben
Can you describe the man? — Können Sie den Mann beschreiben?
⇨ description [dɪ'skrɪpʃn] — Beschreibung

desert ['dezət] — Wüste

design [dɪ'zaɪn] — entwerfen; Entwurf, *Design*

I've designed and made this model plane myself. — Ich habe dieses Modellflugzeug selbst entworfen und hergestellt.

This is a design of the new sports centre.
I don't like the design of this car. — Dies ist ein Entwurf des neuen Sportzentrums. Mir gefällt das Design dieses Wagens nicht.
⇨ designer ✎ Jobs — Designer(in) Modezeichner(in)
∞ fashion designer

desk [desk] — Schreibtisch
✎ Furniture
∞ cash-desk — Kasse (in Geschäften)
Please pay at the cash-desk.

dessert [dɪ'zɜ:t] — Nachtisch
What's for dessert? — Was gibt es zum Nachtisch?

detective [dɪ'tektɪv] — Kriminalbeamtin/-beamter; Detektiv
✎ Jobs
∞ private detective — Privatdetektiv
∞ detective story — Kriminalgeschichte

develop [dɪ'veləp] — (sich) entwickeln
develop a film — einen Film entwickeln
∞ a developing country — ein Entwicklungsland
⇨ development — Entwicklung

devil ['devl] — Teufel
⇔ angel

dial ['daɪəl] — (Telefonnummer) wählen
You've dialled the wrong number. — Sie haben die falsche Nummer gewählt.

dialogue ['daɪəlɒg] — Dialog, Zwiegespräch

diary ['daɪərɪ] — Tagebuch
keep a diary — ein Tagebuch führen

dictation [dɪk'teɪʃn] — Diktat
⇨ dictate [dɪk'teɪt] — diktieren

dictionary ['dɪkʃənrɪ] — Wörterbuch
look up a word in a dictionary — ein Wort in einem Wörterbuch nachschlagen

die [daɪ] — sterben
☛ dying — sterbend, im Sterben
⇨ dead [ded] — tot

different ['dɪfrənt]   anders, verschieden
⇔ the same
   Mary is quite   Mary is ganz
   different <u>from</u>   anders <u>als</u> Judy.
   Judy.
   two different   zwei verschie-
   colours   dene Farben
⇨ difference   Unterschied

difficult ['dɪfɪkəlt]   schwierig
⇔ easy, simple
   It's difficult to
   answer this
   question.

dinner ['dɪnə]   Mittagessen/Abend-
   essen (als Haupt-
   mahlzeit)
   It's time for
   dinner.
⇨ dining-room   Eßzimmer
   ✎ House and flat

direct [dɪ'rekt/   direkt
'daɪrekt]
   a direct flight   ein Direktflug
∞ direct speech   wörtliche Rede

direction [dɪ'rekʃn]   Richtung; Himmels-
   richtung
   You're going in   Du gehst in die
   the wrong   falsche Richtung.
   direction.

director [dɪ'rektə]   Direktor(in),
   Leiter(in)

dirty ['dɜːtɪ]   schmutzig
⇔ clean

disadvantage   Nachteil
['dɪsədvɑːntɪdʒ]
⇔ advantage

disappear [dɪsə'pɪə]   verschwinden
⇔ appear
   He disappeared   Er verschwand
   as suddenly as he   genauso plötz-
   had appeared.   lich, wie er auf-
      getaucht war.

disappointed   enttäuscht
[dɪsə'pɔɪntɪd]
   Bob was dis-
   appointed that
   Sue didn't come
   to his party.
⇨ disappoint s.o.   jdn. enttäuschen

disc [dɪsk] ✎ Enter-   (runde) Scheibe;
tainment electronics   Schallplatte
∞ compact disc   *CD*
   (CD)

∞ CD player   *CD*-Platten-
   ✎ Entertainment   spieler
electronics
∞ disc jockey   *Diskjockey*
⇨ disco ['dɪskəʊ]   *Disko(thek)*

discover [dɪs'kʌvə]   entdecken
   Columbus
   discovered
   America in 1492.

dishes ['dɪʃɪz]   Geschirr
∞ wash the dishes   das Geschirr
   ≈ wash up   spülen
∞ dishwasher   Spülmaschine
   ✎ Electricity in the
household

distance ['dɪstəns]   Entfernung
   What's the   Wie groß ist die
   distance between   Entfernung zwi-
   London and   schen London
   Glasgow?   und Glasgow?
∞ in the distance   in der Ferne

disturb [dɪ'stɜːb]   stören

| Please, do not disturb. | Bitte nicht stören. |

dive [daɪv]   tauchen
⇨ diving ✎ Sports   Tauchen
   and games
⇨ diver   Taucher(in)

divorce [dɪ'vɔːs]   Scheidung
⇔ marriage
∞ get a divorce   sich scheiden
      lassen
⇨ divorced   geschieden

do [duː], **did** [dɪd] ,   tun, machen
done [dʌn]
☛he/she/it <u>does</u>
   [dʌz]
   What does your   Was macht deine
   aunt do?   Tante (beruf-
      lich)?
   What do you do   Was machst du
   in your free   in deiner
   time?   Freizeit?
∞ do a room   ein Zimmer
      putzen
∞ do the washing   (die Wäsche)
      waschen
∞ do the cooking   kochen

docks [dɒks]   Hafenanlagen
⇨ docker   Hafenarbeiter(in)

doctor ['dɒktə]   Arzt, Ärztin
✎ Jobs

at the doctor's
Dr (= Doctor)
Smith

beim Arzt
(Herr/Frau) Dr.
Smith

dog [dɒg] ✎ Animals
∞ sheepdog

Hund
Schäferhund

dollar ['dɒlə]
a hundred
dollars ($100)

Dollar
hundert Dollar

donkey ['dɒŋkɪ]
✎ Animals

Esel

door [dɔː]
✎ House and flat
∞ front door
∞ back door
∞ doorbell
∞ stay indoors
[ɪn'dɔːz]
∞ be outdoors
[aʊt'dɔːz]
∞ an indoor swim-
ming pool ['ɪndɔː]
∞ an outdoor
swimming pool
['aʊtdɔː]
∞ next door
✎ Place and
direction
She lives next door.

Tür

Haustür
Hintertür
Türklingel
im Haus bleiben

im Freien sein

ein Hallenbad

ein Freibad

nebenan

double ['dʌbl]
a double whisky

He bought an old
car and sold it at
double the price.
∞ double-decker
✎ Transport

doppelt
ein doppelter
Whisky
... und verkaufte
ihn zum doppel-
ten Preis.
Doppeldek-
ker(bus)

down [daʊn] ⇔ up

herunter, hinunter,
nieder; unten

We walked down
the hill.
Put your bag
down.
David is down by
the lake.
∞ sit down
∞ break down
→ break
∞ turn (the radio)
down → turn

Wir gingen den
Hügel hinunter.
Stell deine
Tasche ab.
David ist unten
am See.
sich setzen
versagen,
stehenbleiben
(das Radio) leiser
stellen

downstairs
[daʊn'steəz]
✎ Place and direction
Come down-
stairs.

die Treppe herun-
ter/hinunter; unten
(einen Stock tiefer)
Komm herunter.

The toilet is
downstairs.

Die Toilette ist
unten.

draw [drɔː], **drew**
[druː], **drawn** [drɔːn]
The coach was
drown by four
horses.
Can you draw a
map of the
British Isles?

ziehen; zeichnen

Die Kutsche
wurde von vier
Pferden gezogen.
Kannst du eine
Landkarte der
Britischen Inseln
zeichnen?

⇨ drawing

Zeichnung

dream [driːm]
Do you dream
every night?
I had a funny
dream last night.

träumen; Traum

dress [dres]
✎ Clothes
She was wearing
a beautiful dress.
When I had
washed and
dressed, I went
down for
breakfast.
∞ dressmaker
✎ Jobs
⇨ (salad) dressing
✎ Food

Kleid; sich
anziehen

Damenschnei-
der(in)
(Salat-)Soße

drill [drɪl] ✎ Tools
∞ an electric drill

drill for oil
⇨ drilling machine

Bohrer; bohren
ein elektrischer
Bohrer
nach Öl bohren
Bohrmaschine

drink [drɪŋk], **drank**
[dræŋk], **drunk**
[drʌŋk]

trinken; Getränk(e)

✎ **Drinks**

Let's have
something to eat
and drink.
I've brought
some food and
drink.
⇨ be drunk

betrunken sein

drive [draɪv], **drove** [drəʊv], **driven** ['drɪvn]
   1. (Auto) fahren (= selbst fahren)

Don't drive so fast.
Lady Emily drives a Rolls Royce.
☛ When does the bus go?   Wann fährt der Bus?
⇨ driver   Fahrer(in)
∞ driving licence ['laɪsns]   Führerschein
∞ a drive-in restaurant   ein *Drive-in*-Restaurant

   2. (an)treiben

This car is driven by solar energy.
The cowboys drove the cattle into the field.

drop [drɒp]   Tropfen; fallen lassen; fallen
a drop of water   ein Wassertropfen
Don't drop that plate, or it will break.
The temperature dropped by 10°.   Die Temperatur fiel um 10°.

drugs [drʌgz]   Drogen, Rauschgift; Medikamente

drum [drʌm] ✎ Musical instruments   Trommel
⇨ drummer   Schlagzeuger(in)

dry [draɪ] ⇔ wet   trocken; trocknen
✎ The weather
a dry cloth
He dried his hands with a clean towel.
The clothes will dry quickly in this wind.
⇨ dryer ✎ Electricity in the household   (Wäsche-)Trockner
∞ hair dryer ✎ In the bathroom   Haartrockner, Fön
∞ dry-cleaning   chemische Reinigung

duck [dʌk]   Ente
✎ Animals

dumb [dʌm]   stumm; dumm, doof
∞ deaf and dumb   taubstumm

during ['djuːrɪŋ]   während
✎ Expressions of time
during the week   während der Woche, die Woche über

☛ *During* steht nur vor Hauptwörtern, die eine Zeitspanne angeben:
Did anyone call while I was away?   Hat jemand angerufen, während ich weg war?

dust [dʌst]   Staub
⇨ dusty   staubig

duty [djuːtɪ]   Pflicht; Zoll
∞ duty-free   zollfrei
∞ duty-free shop

E [iː] is for

each [iːtʃ]   jede(r/s)
Each of the children got a present.
Each present was different.
∞ each other ≈ one another   einander
Tom and Jane love each other.

ear [ɪə]   Ohr
✎ The human body

early ['ɜːlɪ] ⇔ late   früh
an early lunch
early in the morning

earn [ɜːn]   verdienen
She earns £2,000 a month.

earth [ɜːθ]   Erde
The earth is round.   Die Erde ist rund.
all the children on earth   all Kinder auf der Erde
How on earth did it happen?   Wie um alles in der Welt ist es passiert?
a hut made of wood and earth   eine Hütte aus Holz und Erde

east [iːst] ✎ Place and direction   Ost-; Osten; östlich; nach Osten
East Africa   Ostafrika

The wind is blowing from the east. — Der Wind blast von Osten.

They live east of Manchester. — Sie wohnen östlich von Manchester.

We are travelling east. — Wir reisen nach Osten.

Easter [ˈiːstə] — Ostern
∞ at Easter ✎ Expressions of time — zu Ostern

easy [ˈiːzɪ] — leicht, einfach
⇔ difficult
This text is easy to understand.

eat [iːt], **ate** [et], **eaten** [ˈiːtn] — essen; fressen
Why don't you eat your cake?
What do you give your dog to eat?

education [edjʊˈkeɪʃn] — Erziehung, Ausbildung
∞ religious education (R. E.) — Religion(sunterricht)
✎ School subjects —)

e.g. [ˈiː ˈdʒiː] ≈ for example — z. B. (zum Beispiel)
fruit, e.g. apples

egg [eɡ] ✎ Food — Ei

either [ˈaɪðə] — entweder; auch (nicht)
You can either have fish or chicken. — Du kannst entweder Fisch oder Hähnchen haben.

☛ Nach *not* steht niemals *too*, sondern *either*: — Das Essen ist gut, und es ist auch nicht teuer.
The food is good, and it isn't expensive either.

elbow [ˈelbəʊ] — Ellbogen
✎ The human body

elect [ɪˈlekt] — wählen
They elected him president. — Sie wählten ihn zum Präsidenten.
⇨ election [ɪˈlekʃn] — Wahl

electric [ɪˈlektrɪk] — elektrisch
electric light — elektrisches Licht
⇨ electrician [ɪlekˈtrɪʃn] ✎ Jobs — Elektriker(in)

⇨ electricity [ɪlekˈtrɪsɪtɪ] — Strom, Elektrizität

✎ **Electricity in the household**

⇨ electronic [ɪlekˈtrɒnɪk] — elektronisch
⇨ electronics — Elektronik
✎ Entertainment electronics

elephant [ˈelɪfənt] — Elefant
✎ Animals

else [els] — sonst
What else have you got? — Was hast du sonst noch?
Anything else? — Sonst noch etwas?

∞ someone else — jemand anders
∞ something else — etwas anderes
∞ somewhere else — anderswo(hin)

emergency [ɪˈmɜːdʒənsɪ] — Notfall
∞ emergency call — Notruf

∞ | EMERGENCY EXIT | — Notausgang

emigrate [ˈemɪɡreɪt] — auswandern
⇔ immigrate
⇨ emigrant — Auswanderer, Auswanderin

employ [ɪmˈplɔɪ] — beschäftigen
⇨ employer [ɪmˈplɔɪə] — Arbeitgeber(in)
⇨ employee [emplɔɪˈiː] — Arbeitnehmer(in)
⇨ employment — Anstellung, Arbeit
⇨ unemployment — Arbeitslosigkeit

empty [ˈemptɪ] — leer; leeren
⇔ full; fill
The bottle is empty.
I've emptied the wastepaper-basket.

end [end] ⇔ start: beginning; begin — Ende; enden

at the end of the year

∞ at the weekend — am Wochenende
∞ in the end — am Ende
How did the story end?
↪ ending — Ende, Ausgang
a story with a happy ending

energy [ˈenədʒɪ] — Energie, Kraft
∞ atomic energy [əˈtɒmɪk] — Atomkraft
∞ solar energy [ˈsəʊlə] — Sonnenkraft

engine [ˈendʒɪn] — Motor, Maschine
↪ engineer [ˈendʒɪnɪə] ✎ Jobs — Ingenieur(in)

England [ˈɪŋglənd] — England
✎ Countries
↪ English — englisch; Englisch (Sprache)
∞ the English — die Engländer
↪ Englishman, Englishwoman — Engländer, Engländerin

enjoy [ɪnˈdʒɔɪ] — genießen, Spaß haben (an)

We are enjoying our stay at the seaside very much. — Wir genießen unseren Aufenthalt am Meer sehr.
I enjoy swimming in the sea. — Ich schwimme sehr gern im Meer.

Enjoy yourselves. — Amüsiert euch gut! / Viel Spaß!

enough [ɪˈnʌf] — genug, genügend
You're not fast enough to catch him.
Have we got enough money for the tickets?
∞ I've had enough! — Mir reicht es!

enter [entə] — eintreten, hineingehen, hereinkommen
≈ go/come in
He entered the room without knocking.
↪ **ENTRANCE** — Eingang, Eintritt
[ˈentrəns]
∞ entrance fee — Eintrittsgebühr
↪ entry — Eingang, Zutritt
∞ **NO ENTRY** — Zutritt verboten

entertainment [entəˈteɪnmənt] — Unterhaltung, Vergnügen
∞ entertainment electronics — Unterhaltungselektronik

✎ **Entertainment electronics**

envelope [ˈenvələʊp] — Briefumschlag

environment [ɪnˈvaɪərənmənt] — Umwelt

equal [ˈiːkwəl] — gleich
Equal pay for equal work! — Gleiche Bezahlung für gleiche Arbeit!

equipment [ɪˈkwɪpmənt] — Ausrüstung
camping equipment

escape [ɪˈskeɪp] — entfliehen, entweichen; Flucht

They managed to escape from the burning house.
All the air has escaped from the tyre.
an escape from prison

etc [ɪt ˈsetrə] — usw. (und so weiter)
≈ and so on
I've bought some biros, pencils, etc.

Europe [ˈjʊərɒp] — Europa
↪ European [jʊərəˈpiːən] — europäisch, Europäer(in)
∞ the European Union (EU) — die Europäische Union

even [ˈiːvn] — sogar, noch
He wasn't angry at the joke. He even laughed.
Today it's even colder than it was yesterday.

evening ['iːvnɪŋ] Abend
✎ Expressions of time
∞ <u>in</u> the evening <u>am</u> Abend,
abends
∞ this evening heute Abend
∞ Good evening. Guten abend.

event [ɪ'vent] Ereignis
an important
event

ever ['evə] schon einmal;
✎ Expressions of time jemals
Have you ever Warst du schon
been to York? einmal in York?
Will I ever see Werde ich dich
you again? jemals wiedersehen?
∞ for ever für immer, ewig
We can't stay
here for ever.

every ['evrɪ] jeder, jede, jedes
I see him every Ich sehe ihn
day. jeden Tag.
∞ everyday use Alltagsgebrauch
∞ everybody/ jeder(mann)
everyone
Everybody
knows him.
∞ everything alles
Is everything
alright?
∞ everywhere überall
I looked for my
keys everywhere,
but I couldn't
find them.

exact(ly) genau
[ɪg'zækt(lɪ)]
What's the exact
time?
It's exactly eleven
o'clock.

exam [ɪg'zæm] Prüfung, Examen
≈ examination
∞ take an exam eine Prüfung
ablegen
∞ pass an exam eine Prüfung
bestehen

example [ɪg'zɑːmpl] Beispiel
∞ for example zum Beispiel

except [ɪk'sept] außer, mit Ausnahme von
The museum is
open every day
except Monday.

exchange Umtausch
[ɪks'tʃeɪndʒ]
∞ exchange rate Wechselkurs

excited [ɪk'saɪtɪd] aufgeregt
⇨ exciting aufregend,
spannend
an exciting book

excuse [ɪk'skjuːs] entschuldigen; Ent-
schuldigung, Aus-
rede
Excuse me, Entschuldigen
please. Sie bitte.
You're late. What
excuse have you
got ?

exercise ['eksəsaɪz] Übung
∞ exercise book Heft
✎ My school bag

exist [ɪg'zɪst] existieren, dasein

exit ['eksɪt] EXIT Ausgang
≈ way out
⇔ entrance

expect [ɪk'spekt] erwarten
I'm expecting a Ich erwarte einen
phone call. Anruf.

expensive [ɪk'spen- teuer
sɪv] ⇔ cheap

experience Erfahrung
[ɪk'spɪərɪəns]
a doctor with ten
years' experience

expert ['ekspɜːt] Experte, Expertin

explain [ɪk'spleɪn] erklären
Could you ex- ... Könntest du es
plain it <u>to us</u>? <u>uns</u> erklären?

explosion [ɪk- Explosion
'spləʊʒn] ✎ Danger
and accidents
⇨ explode explodieren
[ɪk'spləʊd]

expresssion Ausdruck
[ɪk'spreʃn]
✎ Expressions of time

extra ['ekstrə] extra, zusätzlich
I have some extra
work to do today.
Transport costs
£2 extra.

eye [aɪ] ✎ The Auge
human body

F [ef] is for

face [feɪs]   Gesicht
✎ The human body
∞ make faces   Grimassen schneiden

fact [fækt]   Tatsache
Just tell us the facts.

factory ['fæktərɪ]   Fabrik
✎ In town
∞ factory worker   Fabrikabeiter(in)
   ✎ Jobs

fair [feə]   fair, gerecht; blond; Jahrmarkt; Messe
a fair mark (for a test)   eine gerechte Note
play fair   fair spielen
a girl with fair hair   ein Mädchen mit blonden Haaren
∞ fun fair ✎ In town   Jahrmarkt
∞ the Frankfurt Book Fair   die Frankfurter Buchmesse

fall [fɔ:l], **fell** [fel], **fallen** ['fɔ:ln]   fallen
Don't fall off the ladder!
∞ fall over   umfallen
∞ fall asleep   einschlafen
∞ fall in love   sich verlieben

false [fɔ:ls] ≈ wrong   falsch, unecht, trügerisch
⇔ true, right
a false answer
false teeth
a false smile

family ['fæmɪlɪ]   Familie
the Smith family   die Familie Smith
∞ family name   Nachname
≈ surname ['sɜ:neɪm]

famous ['feɪməs]   berühmt
She is a famous tennis player.

fan [fæn]   Fan, Anhänger(in)
He's a football fan.   Er ist Fußballfan

fantastic [fæn'tæstɪk]   fantastisch, großartig, toll
a fantastic film

far [fɑ:]   weit (weg), fern
☛ Steigerung: far, further ['fɜ:ðə], furthest

We didn't travel far.
How far is it to the station?
The supermarket isn't far away.
a far country
∞ so far   bis jetzt, bisher
I haven't had a traffic accident so far.

fare [feə]   Fahrpreis
How much is the train fare to York?

farm [fɑ:m]   Bauernhof, Farm
∞ farmhouse   Bauernhaus
∞ farmland   Ackerboden, Ackerlandland
⇨ farmer ✎ Jobs   Bauer, Bäuerin, Landwirt(in)

fascinate ['fæsɪneɪt]   faszinieren, fesseln
a fascinating show
⇨ fascination   Faszination

fashion ['fæʃn]   Mode
Fashion changes every year.   Die Mode ändert sich jedes Jahr.
∞ fashion designer   Modezeichner(in)
   ✎ Jobs
∞ the latest fashion   die neueste Mode
∞ out of fashion   unmodern
∞ old-fashioned   altmodisch
⇨ fashionable   modisch

fast [fɑ:st]   schnell
≈ quick(ly) ⇔ slow
a fast driver
She drives very fast.
∞ a fast train   ein Schnellzug
∞ fast food   *Fast food*

fasten ['fɑ:sn]   befestigen, fest-machen
He fastened the keys to his belt.   Er befestigte die Schlüssel an seinem Gürtel.

> Fasten your seat-belts, please.

Legen Sie bitte ihre Sicher-heitsgurte an.

fat [fæt]   dick; fett; Fett
You're getting fat.   Du wirst dick. ...
You should stop eating so much.

☛ Das Wort *thick*
verwendet man
nur bei Dingen,
nicht bei
Personen:
a thick book   ein dickes Buch
Cheese contains   Käse enthält viel
a lot of fat.   Fett.

father [ˈfɑːðə]   Vater
✎ Relatives

favourite [ˈfeɪvrɪt]   Lieblings-
Geography is my   ... mein Lieb-
favourite subject.   lingsfach.

fear [fɪə]   Angst, Furcht;
    (be)fürchten
His face was   Sein Gesicht war
white with fear.   blaß vor Angst.
We have nothing   Wir haben nichts
to fear.   zu befürchten.

February [ˈfebruəri]   Februar
✎ Months and seasons

fee [fiː]   Gebühr
∞ pay an entrance   Eintrittsgebühr
fee   bezahlen

feed [fiːd], **fed** [fed],   füttern
fed
Don't forget to
feed the fish.
∞ be fed up with   etwas satt haben
something

feel [fiːl], **felt** [felt],   fühlen, spüren; sich
felt   fühlen
I felt the wind on
my face.
I feel ill.   Ich fühle mich
    krank.
∞ I feel cold.   Mir ist kalt.
∞ feel frightened   sich fürchten
➪ feeling   Gefühl

feet [fiːt] → foot   Füße

fellow [ˈfeləʊ]   Kerl; Mit-; -kollege/
    -kollegin
a nice fellow   ein netter Kerl.
a fellow   eine(e) Mit-
passenger   reisende(r)
a fellow student   ein(e) Studien-
    kollege/–kollegin

female [ˈfiːmeɪl]   weiblich; Weibchen
⇔ male   (bei Tieren)
The club has 22
female and 25
male members.

Is your cat a male
or a female?

fence [fens]   Zaun
✎ House and flat

ferry [ˈferɪ]   Fähre
✎ Transport

festival [ˈfestɪvl]   Fest; Festspiele,
    Festival
Christmas and
other festivals
a rock festival
∞ the Edinburgh
Festival

fetch [fetʃ] ≈ get   (herbei)holen
Could you fetch
some more
chairs, please?

fever [ˈfiːvə]   Fieber
☛ She has a high   Sie hat hohes
fever.   Fieber.

few [fjuː] ≈ not   wenige
many
He has few   Er hat wenig
friends.   Freunde.
☛ a few ≈ some   einige, ein paar
Let's invite a few   Laden wir doch
friends.   ein paar Freunde
    ein.
∞ the next few   die nächsten
weeks   Wochen
∞ the last few years   die letzten Jahre

field [fiːld]   Feld, Weide, Wiese
☛ cows in a field   Kühe auf einer
    Weide
∞ cornfield   Kornfeld
∞ football field   Fußballplatz
✎ Sports and
games
∞ playing field(s)   Sportplatz
☛ at the playing   auf dem
fields   Sportplatz

fight [faɪt], **fought**   (be)kämpfen;
[fɔːt], **fought**   Kampf
fight for one's   für seine Rechte
rights   kämpfen
fight (against)   Verbrechen
crime   bekämpfen
a fight between   ein Kampf
two gangs   zwischen zwei
    Banden

fill [fɪl]   füllen
Fill this pot with
water, please.

∞ fill up   auffüllen
We must fill up
the water tank.
∞ filling station   Tankstelle
≈ petrol/gas
station ✎ In town
∞ fill in a form   ein Formular
                   ausfüllen
⇨ filling   Füllung
⇨ full   voll

film [fɪlm] ≈ movie   Film
(AE)
∞ a film star   ein *Filmstar*

final ['faɪnl] ≈ last   letzte(r/s); Finale,
                   Endspiel
'Z' is the final
letter in the
alphabet.
Our team is
playing in the
final.
∞ semi-final   Halbfinale
[semɪ'faɪnl]
∞ quarter final   Viertelfinale
⇨ finally ≈ at last   schließlich, end-
                   lich
Finally our guests
arrived.

find [faɪnd], **found**   finden
[faʊnd], **found**
⇔ lose
Have the police
found the
missing child?
∞ find out   herausfinden
I won't tell you –
you must find
out for yourself.

fine [faɪn]   schön, gut, fein;
                   Geldstrafe
a fine day   ein schöner Tag
How are you? –   Wie geht's? –
Fine, thank you.   Danke, gut.
fine hair   feines Haar
He had to pay a   Er mußte £100
£100 fine for   Strafe zahlen,
driving too fast.   weil er zu schnell
                   fuhr.

finger ['fɪŋə]   Finger
✎ The human body
∞ Good luck! I'm   Viel Glück. Ich
keeping my fin-   halte dir die
gers crossed for   Daumen.
you.

finish ≈ stop, end   (be)enden, auf-
⇔ start   hören; Ende,
                   Abschluß
He finishes work   Er hört um 16.45
at 4.45 p.m.   mit der Arbeit
                   auf.
School finishes   Die Schule endet
at 3.15.   um 15.15.
∞ finish up   austrinken, auf-
                   essen
Finish up your
potatoes.
He fought to the   Er kämpfte bis
finish.   zum Schluß.
∞ finish line   Ziellinie

fire ✎ Danger and   Feuer; feuern,
accidents   schießen
∞ be on fire   in Brand sein,
                   brennen
The house is on
fire.
∞ fire alarm   Feuermelder
∞ fire brigade   Feuerwehr
∞ fireman   Feuerwehrmann
∞ firewood   Brennholz
fire a rocket   eine Rakete
                   abschießen

firm [fɜːm]   Firma; fest
☛ run a firm   eine Firma leiten
a firm decision   ein fester
                   Entschluß

first [fɜːst]   erste(r/s); zuerst,
                   als erste(r/s)
the first of April
(1st April)
∞ first aid ✎ Danger   Erste Hilfe
and accidents
∞ first class   erste(r) Klasse
∞ first name *(AE)*   Vorname
I'll help you in a   …, aber ich muß
minute, but I   zuerst diesen
have to finish   Brief fertig-
that letter first.   schreiben.
Who arrived   Wer kam zuerst
first?   an?
∞ at first   zuerst (= am An-
                   fang), zunächst
I didn't believe it
at first, but then I
saw it was true.

fish [fɪʃ] ✎ Animals,   Fisch, Fische;
✎ Food   fischen
☛ Einzahl und
Mehrzahl sind
gleich: one fish –
three fish

∞ fish and chips

∞ fisherman ✎ Jobs — Fischer

∞ go fishing — fischen gehen

∞ fishing boat — Fischerboot
  ✎ Transport

∞ fishing village — Fischerdorf

fit [fɪt] — passen; passend, geeignet; *fit*, in Form

These jeans don't fit me any more. — Diese Jeans passen mir nicht mehr.

Ann isn't fit for this job, she's too slow. — Ann ist für diese Aufgabe nicht geeignet, …

My father goes jogging every day to keep fit. — Mein Vater geht jeden Tag joggen, um fit zu bleiben.

⇨ fitness — Fitneß, Kondition

∞ fitness training — Fitneßtraining
  ✎ Sports and games

fix [fɪks] — reparieren; befestigen, anbringen

My alarm doesn't work any more. Could you fix it for me?
Shall I fix this shelf to the wall?

flag [flæg] — Fahne, Flagge

∞ national flag — Nationalflagge

flame [fleɪm] — Flamme

∞ be in flames — in Flammen stehen

flash [flæʃ] — Blitz; blitzen

flat [flæt] — flach, platt; (Etagen-)Wohnung
  ✎ House and flat
  a flat area
  a flat tyre
  We live in a small flat.

flea [fliː] ✎ Animals — Floh

∞ flea market — Flohmarkt

flight [flaɪt] — Flug

∞ charter flight — Charterflug

⇨ fly — fliegen

floor [flɔː] — Fußboden; Stockwerk
  ✎ House and flat
  The glass fell to the floor. — Das Glas fiel auf den Boden.
  We live <u>on</u> the first floor. — Wir wohnen <u>im</u> ersten Stock.

∞ ground floor — Erdgeschoß

∞ top floor — oberstes Stockwerk

flour ['flaʊə] ✎ Food — Mehl

flower ['flaʊə] — Blume
  flowerbed — Blumenbeet

fly [flaɪ], **flew** [fluː], **flown** [fləʊn] — fliegen; Fliege
  ✎ Animals

∞ a flying saucer — eine fliegende Untertasse

⇨ flight — Flug

Waiter, what's that fly doing in my soup? – It looks like it's swimming.

fog [fɒg] — Nebel
  ✎ The weather

⇨ foggy — neblig

folder ['fəʊldə] — Ordner, Schnellhefter
  ✎ My school bag

⇨ fold — falten

folk [fəʊk] — Volks-

∞ folk dance — Volkstanz

∞ folk music — Volksmusik

follow ['fɒləʊ] — folgen
  The visitors followed the guide down the stairs.

food [fuːd] — Essen, Nahrung(smittel), Futter

✎ **Food**

⇨ feed [fiːd] — ernähren, füttern

∞ food-poisoning ['fuːdpɔɪznɪŋ] — Lebensmittelvergiftung

fool [fuːl] — Dummkopf, Narr

foot [fʊt], **feet** — Fuß, Füße; Fuß (als Längenmaß = 30,48 cm)
✎ The human body

go on foot ≈ walk — zu Fuß gehen
∞ football ✎ Sports and games — Fußball
∞ football team — Fußballmannschaft
∞ footpath ['fʊtpɑ:θ] — Fußweg
The lake is 5 feet (10 ft.) deep. — Der See ist 5 Fuß tief.

for [fɒ:; fə] — 1. für, zu, nach, wegen (Ziel, Zweck, Grund)

This is for you. — Das ist für dich.
We had fried eggs for lunch. — Wir aßen Spiegeleier zum Mittagessen.
He's leaving for Australia. — Er geht weg nach Australien.
The town is famous for its cathedral. — Die Stadt ist berühmt wegen ihrer Kathedrale.
∞ for the first/ second/… time — zum ersten/zweiten/… Mal

✎ Expressions of time — 2. seit, … lang, … weit (Zeitspanne, Wegstrecke)

We have known each other for five years. — Wir kennen uns schon seit fünf Jahren.
He stayed for two days. — Er blieb zwei Tage lang.
They walked for miles and miles. — Sie gingen meilenweit.

force [fɔ:s] — Gewalt, Kraft, Stärke

∞ armed forces — Streitkräfte

forehead ['fɒrɪd] — Stirn
✎ The human body

foreign ['fɒrən] — fremd, ausländisch
a foreign country
➭ foreigner — Fremde(r), Ausländer(in)

forest ['fɒrɪst] — Wald, Forst
➭ forester ≈ forest ranger (AE) — Förster(in)
✎ Jobs

forget [fə'get], **forgot** [fə'gɒt], **forgotten** [fə'tɒtn] — vergessen
⇔ remember

Don't forget us!
∞ Forget it! — Schon gut!

fork [fɔ:k] — Gabel
✎ Laying the table

form [fɔ:m] — Form, Gestalt; Klasse; Formular
an invitation in the form of a letter — eine Einladung in Form eines Briefs
She's in the third form. — Sie ist in der dritten Klasse.
fill in a form — ein Formular ausfüllen

a **fortnight** ['fɔ:tnaɪt] (BE) ≈ two weeks — vierzehn Tage
✎ Expressions of time

forward ['fɔ:wəd] — vorwärts, nach vorn
✎ Place and direction
come forward — nach vorn kommen
∞ look forward to — sich freuen auf
I'm looking forward to seeing you again. — Ich freue mich darauf, dich wiederzusehen.

France [frɑ:ns] — Frankreich
✎ Countries
➭ French [frentʃ] → English — französisch; Französisch
➭ Frenchman ['frentʃmən] — Franzose
➭ Frenchwoman ['frentʃwʊmən] — Französin
∞ the French — die Franzosen

free [fri:] — frei; kostenlos, gratis; befreien
Do you have a room free? — Haben Sie ein Zimmer frei?
∞ free time ≈ spare time — Freizeit
∞ set s.o. free — jdn. freilassen
free meals — kostenlose Mahlzeiten
∞ go free — umsonst mitfahren
Terrorists attacked the prison and freed the prisoners. — Terroristen griffen das Gefängnis an und befreiten die Gefangenen.
➭ freedom ['fri:dəm] — Freiheit

freeze [fri:z], **froze** [frəʊz], **frozen** ['frəʊzn] — (ge)frieren
The lake is frozen. — Der See ist zugefroren.

I'm freezing. | Mir ist eiskalt.
⇨ freezer ✎ Electricity in the household | Gefrierschrank, Kühltruhe

French → France

fresh [freʃ] | frisch
fresh fruit

Friday [fraɪdɪ]) | Freitag
✎ Days of the week
on Friday | am Freitag
on Fridays | freitags

fridge [frɪdʒ] | Kühlschrank
✎ Electricity in the household

friend [frend] | Freund(in)
∞ boyfriend | Freund (eines Mädchens)
∞ girlfriend | Freundin
⇨ friendly | freundlich

frighten ['fraɪtn] | erschrecken, Angst einjagen

Did the noise frighten you?
⇨ frightened | verängstigt, erschrocken

a frightened child
∞ be/feel frightened (of) ≈ be afraid | Angst haben (vor)

frog [frɒg] | Frosch
✎ Animals

from [frɒm; frəm] | von (weg), aus
✎ Place and direction
Where are you from? –I'm from London. | Woher kommst du? – Ich komme aus London.
Oxford is 100km from London. | ... ist 100 km von London entfernt.
∞ from … to | von … bis
from Glasgow to Edinburgh
from 3 to 4

front ⇔ back | vorderer Teil, Vorderseite

the front of a building
∞ front seat | Vordersitz
∞ front door | Haustür
∞ front wheel | Vorderrad
∞ in front of ⇔ behind ✎ Place and direction | vor (in Ortsangaben)
There's a tree in front of the house.

frost [frɒst] | Frost
✎ The weather
⇨ frosty | frostig

fruit [fru:t] | Obst

✎ **Fruit**

fry [fraɪ] | braten
∞ fried eggs ✎ Food | Spiegeleier
∞ fried potatoes ✎ Food | Bratkartoffeln
∞ frying pan | Bratpfanne

fun [fʌn] | Spaß
Dancing is fun. | Tanzen macht Spaß.
∞ fun fair → fair | Jahrmarkt
⇨ funny | lustig, komisch, seltsam

fur [fɜ:] | Fell, Pelz
∞ a fur coat | ein Pelzmantel
✎ Clothes

furniture ['fɜ:nɪtʃə] | Möbel
✎ House and flat

✎ **Furniture**

☛This **is** our new furniture. | Dies **sind** unsere neuen Möbel.

further [fɜ:ðə] → far | weiter
He was too tired to walk any further.

future ['fju:tʃə] | Zukunft; zukünftig
Have you got any plans for the future?
my future job

G [dʒi:] is for

gallon ['gælən] — Gallone (Hohlmaß: 1 Gallone = 4,546 l)

game [geɪm] — Spiel
- ∞ play a game — ein Spiel machen
- ∞ a video game — ein Videospiel
- ∞ games ✎ School subjects — Mannschaftsspiele als Schulfach
  My favourite subject is games.
- ∞ the Olympic Games — die Olympischen Spiele

gangster ['gæŋstə] — *Gangster,* Verbrecher
- ⇨ gang — Bande, Gruppe

garage ['gærɪdʒ] *(BE)*/['gærɑːʒ] *(AE)* ✎ In town — Tankstelle, Autowerkstatt; Garage

garden ['gɑːdn] ✎ House and flat — Garten
- ⇨ gardener — Gärtner(in)
- ⇨ gardening — Gartenarbeit
- ∞ gardening tools — Gartengeräte

gas [gæs] → petrol — *Gas; AE* auch: Benzin
- ∞ gas stove — Gasherd
- ∞ gas station *(AE)* ≈ petrol station *(BE)* — Tankstelle

gate [geɪt] — Tor
✎ House and flat
- ∞ garden gate — Gartentor

geese [giːs] → goose — Gänse
✎ Animals

general ['genərəl] — General; generell, allgemein
- ∞ in general — im allgemeinen

gentleman ['dʒentlmən] ✎ People — Herr, *Gentleman*
  Ladies and gentlemen, … — Meine Damen und Herren, …
  He is a real gentleman. — Er ist ein echter Gentleman.

geography [dʒɪˈɒgrəfɪ] ✎ School subjects — Geographie, Erdkunde

Germany ['dʒɜːmənɪ] ✎ Countries — Deutschland
- ∞ the Federal Republic of Germany (FRG) — die Bundesrepublik Deutschland

- ⇨ German — deutsch;
  → English — Deutsch; Deutsche(r)

get [get], **got** [gɒt], **got** ≈ receive — 1. bekommen, erhalten
  I got a letter from my pen-friend today.
- ∞ I didn't get that. → understand — Das habe ich nicht verstanden.
- ∞ have got ≈ have — haben
  Have you got a computer?
- ∞ have got to ≈ have to — müssen
- ≈ I've got to leave now.

- ≈ fetch — 2. holen
  Could you get some glasses from the kitchen, please?

- ≈ become — 3. werden
  It's getting dark.

  — 4. (hin)kommen, (hin)gelangen
  We got to the station by bus.
- ∞ get up — aufstehen
- ∞ get on (a bus) — einsteigen
- ∞ get off — aussteigen
- ∞ get to know s.o. — jdn. kennenlernen
- ∞ get married — heiraten
- ∞ get on/along with s.o. — sich mit jdm. verstehen

ghost [gəʊst] — Geist, Gespenst

Patient: Doctor, can you help me? I think I'm a ghost.
Doctor: I thought so when you walked through the wall.

giant ['dʒaɪənt] — Riese; riesig

gift [gɪft] ≈ present — Geschenk, Gabe
☛ poison ['pɔɪzn] — Gift

giraffe [dʒɪˈrɑːf] — Giraffe
✎ Animals

girl [gɜːl] ✎ People — Mädchen
- ∞ girlfriend — Freundin

give [gɪv], **gave** [geɪv], **given** ['gɪvn]   geben
   Give me that book, please.
   Give this letter to your mother.
   Pat was given a moped for her birthday.   Pat bekam zum Geburtstag ein Moped.
∞ give s.o. a hand   jdm. helfen
∞ give s.o. a ride/a lift   jdn. im Auto mitnehmen
∞ Give him my love.   Grüße ihn von mir.
∞ give up   aufgeben
   My parents have both given up smoking.   Meine Eltern haben beide das Rauchen aufgegeben.

glad [glæd] ≈ happy, pleased   froh, erfreut
   I'm glad to see you.

glass [glɑːs]   Glas
✎ Laying the table
   a glass of milk   ein Glas Milch
✎ Drinks
   a glass door   eine Glastür
∞ glasses   Brille
  ☛ immer Mehrzahl:
   Where <u>are</u> my glasses?   Wo <u>ist</u> meine Brille?

glide [glaɪd]   gleiten
↪ glider ✎ Transport   Segelflugzeug
↪ gliding ✎ Sports and games   Segelfliegen
∞ hang-gliding   Drachenfliegen

globe [gləʊb]   Globus, Erdkugel

glove [glʌv]   Handschuh
✎ Clothes

go [gəʊ], **went** [went], **gone** [gɒn]   1. gehen, fahren, reisen
∞ go by car/train/bus   mit dem Auto/Zug/Bus fahren
∞ go by plane ≈ fly   fliegen
∞ go on foot ≈ walk   zu Fuß gehen
∞ go and see ≈ visit   besuchen (gehen)
∞ go shopping/swimming/fishing/…   einkaufen/schwimmen/fischen/… gehen
∞ go for a walk   spazierengehen
∞ go for a ride   eine Spazierfahrt machen

∞ go on   weitergehen, weitermachen; geschehen, vorgehen
   Now we've had a rest, let's go on.   …, gehen wir weiter.
   What's going on?   Was geht hier vor?
≈ get, become   2. werden
   His face went red.   Sein Gesicht wurde rot.

God [gɒd]   Gott
   pray to God   zu Gott beten
∞ Thank God!   Gott sei Dank!

gold [gəʊld]   Gold
✎ Colours
   a gold watch   eine goldene Armbanduhr
↪ golden   golden
∞ the Golden Gate Bridge   Brücke über das „Goldene Tor" bei San Francisco

golf [gɒlf]   Golf
✎ Sports and games
∞ golf course [kɔːs]   Golfplatz
∞ crazy golf, mini-golf   Minigolf

good [gʊd] ⇔ bad   gut
☛ Steigerung: good, better, best
   He is good <u>at</u> maths.   Er ist gut <u>in</u> Mathe.
∞ Good morning.   Guten Morgen.
∞ Goodbye.   Auf Wiedersehen.
∞ Good luck!   Viel Glück!
∞ good-looking   gutaussehend
↪ Goodness!   Du liebe Güte!

goose [guːs], **geese** [giːs] ✎ Animals   Gans, Gänse

government ['gʌvmənt]   Regierung

gram [græm]   Gramm
   200 grams (200 g)   200 g

grammar ['græmə]   Grammatik

grand… [grænd]   Groß-, Enkel-
✎ Relatives
   grandmother   Großmutter
   ≈ grandma, granny
   grandfather   Großvater
   ≈ grandpa, granddad(dy)

grandparents	Großeltern	∞ ground floor	Erdgeschoß
grandchild,	Enkelkind,	✎ House and flat	
grandchildren	Enkelkinder	∞ the Underground	die Untergrund-
granddaughter	Enkeltochter	✎ Transport	bahn
grandson	Enkelsohn	∞ background	Hintergrund
∞ great-grand...	Urgroß-, Ur-enkel-		

group [gru:p] — Gruppe
a group of people

grow [grəʊ], **grew** [gru:], **grown** [grəʊn] — wachsen; züchten, anbauen; werden
Grass grows fast after it has rained.
He grows his own vegetables.
It is growing colder and colder.
∞ grow up — aufwachsen
↪ grown-up ≈ adult — erwachsen; Er-wachsene(r)
✎ People
children and grown-ups

guarantee [ˌgærən'ti:] — Garantie; garan-tieren
There's a two-year guarantee on this watch. — Für diese Uhr besteht eine Garantie von zwei Jahren.
I can't guarantee that the plan is going to work. — Ich kann nicht garantieren, daß der Plan funk-tioniert.

guard [gɑ:d] — Wache, Wach-posten; bewachen
∞ the Changing of the Guard — die Wachab-lösung (vor dem Buckingham-palast)
The house was guarded by the police. — Das Haus wurde von der Polizei bewacht.

guess [ges] — (er)raten; AE auch: vermuten, schätzen
Guess what I found today. — Rate mal, was ich heute gefunden habe.
Can you answer the phone? It's your boyfriend, I guess. (AE) — ... Ich vermute es ist dein Freund.

guest [gest] ≈ visitor — Gast
∞ guesthouse — Gästehaus, Pension

---

great-grand-parents — Urgroßeltern

great-grandchild — Urenkel
great-grand-mother, etc. — Urgroßmutter, usw.
great-great-grandparents, etc. — Ururgroßeltern, usw.

grapes [greɪps] — Weintrauben
✎ Fruit

grapefruit ['greɪpfru:t] ✎ Fruit — *Grapefruit*, Pampelmuse

grass [grɑ:s] — Gras

grave [greɪv] — Grab
∞ graveyard ≈ cemetery — Friedhof

great [greɪt] — groß, großartig
a great artist — ein(e) große(r) Künstler(in)
That's great! — Das ist toll!
∞ Great Britain — Großbritannien
∞ great-grandpar-ents → grand... — Urgroßeltern

Greece [gri:s] — Griechenland
✎ Countries
↪ Greek — griechisch; Grie-chisch; Grieche, Griechin
→ German

green [gri:n] — grün
✎ Colours
∞ greengrocer — Obst- und Ge-müsehandler(in)
✎ Jobs

grey [greɪ] ✎ Colours — grau

grill [grɪl] — Grill; grillen
grilled sausages — gegrillte Würst-chen

grocer ['grəʊsə] — Lebensmittelhänd-ler(in)
✎ Jobs
at the grocer's — im Lebensmittel-laden

ground [graʊnd] — (Erd)boden, Ge-lände, Grund
∞ football ground — Fußballplatz
✎ Sports and games

guide [gaɪd] ✎ Jobs

Our guide told us some interesting facts about the castle.
I've bought a guide to the Alps.

(Fremden)führer(in); (Reise)führer

guinea pig [ˈgɪnɪ pɪg] ✎ Animals

Meerschweinchen

guitar [gɪˈtɑː] ✎ Musical instruments
∞ play the guitar
➪ guitarist

Gitarre

Gitarre spielen
Gitarrist(in)

gum [gʌm] → chewing gum

Gummi, Kaugummi

gun [gʌn]

Schußwaffe

guy [gaɪ]
Who's the guy over there?

Kerl, Typ
Wer ist der Typ dort drüben?

gym [dʒɪm] → gymnasium, gymnastics
∞ gym shoes
✎ Clothes

Turnhalle; Gymnastik, Turnen
Turnschuhe

gymnasium [dʒɪmˈneɪzɪəm]
☛grammar school

Turnhalle

Gymnasium

gymnastics [dʒɪmˈnæstɪks]
✎ Sports and games

Gymnastik

H [eɪtʃ] **is for**

hair [heə]
✎ The human body
☛Immer Einzahl:
Your hair <u>has</u> grown very long.

Haare

Deine Haare <u>sind</u> sehr lang geworden

∞ hairbrush
✎ In the bathroom
∞ hair dryer

Haarbürste

Fön, Haartrockner

∞ hairdresser, hairstylist ✎ Jobs
∞ hairdo, hairstyle

Friseur(in)

Frisur

half [hɑːf], **halves** [hɑːvz]
He cut the cake in two halves. Of course he took the bigger half.

Hälfte, Hälften; halb, Halb-

half an hour
a mile and a half
at half past three
✎ Expressions of time

eine halbe Stunde
1 1/2 Meilen
um halb vier

hall [hɔːl]
✎ House and flat
∞ concert hall
∞ church hall
∞ town hall

Diele, Flur; Halle, Saal
Konzertsaal
Gemeindesaal
Rathaus

ham [hæm] ✎ Food
∞ hamburger [ˈhæmbɜːgə]

Schinken
Hamburger

hammer [ˈhæmə] ✎ Tools

Hammer

hamster [ˈhæmstə] ✎ Animals

Hamster

hand [ˈhænd]
✎ The human body
∞ Hands off!
∞ Hands up!
∞ handball
✎ Sports and games
∞ handbag
✎ Clothes
∞ handbrake
∞ give s.o. a hand
Could you hand me that book, please?
∞ hand in

Please hand in this form by 1st May.

Hand; reichen, geben
Hände weg!
Hände hoch!
Handball

Handtasche

Handbremse
jdm. helfen
Könntest du mir bitte dieses Buch reichen?
abgeben, einreichen
Bitte reichen Sie dieses Formular bis zum 1. Mai ein.

hang [hæŋ], **hung** [hʌŋ], **hung**
A big lamp hung above the table.
∞ hang up

I've hung up your coat in the hall.
I've got to hang up now. Mum wants to use the phone.
☛*Hang* in der Bedeutung „erhängen" hat die Formen *hang, hanged, hanged:*
He was hanged for murder.

hängen

aufhängen; (den Hörer) auflegen

Er wurde wegen Mordes erhängt.

happen ['hæpn]
How did the accident happen?

geschehen, passieren

happy ['hæpɪ]
⇔ unhappy, sad
∞ Happy birthday.

glücklich

Alles Gute zum Geburtstag.

harbour ['hɑːbə]
There are some big ships in the harbour.

(See-)Hafen

hard ['hɑːd] ≈ difficult; ⇔ easy; soft
It's hard to understand.
a hard chair
⟳ hardly
☛ She works hard.
She hardly works.

hart, schwer, schwierig
Es ist schwer zu verstehen.
ein harter Stuhl
kaum
Sie arbeitet hart.
Sie arbeitet kaum.

hat [hæt] ✎ Clothes

Hut

hate [heɪt] ⇔ love

Billy hates school.
I hate washing up.

hassen, nicht leiden können
Billy haßt die Schule.
Ich wasche sehr ungern ab.

have [hæv], **had** [hæd], **had**
☛ he/she/it has [hæz]
≈ have got
Paul has (got) a new girlfriend.

We had tea and biscuits in the break.
∞ have breakfast
∞ have lunch

have a break

have a bath
have a look at

∞ have (got) to
→ must
You've got to hurry.
We had to walk because we missed the bus.

1. haben, besitzen

2. essen, trinken

frühstücken
zu Mittag essen
3. machen, unternehmen
(eine) Pause machen
ein Bad nehmen
ansehen, nachsehen
müssen

∞ I'd better
You'd better shut up.

ich sollte lieber
Du solltest lieber den Mund halten.

he [hiː]

er

head [hed]
✎ The human body
∞ headlight ['hedlaɪt]
∞ headline ['hedlaɪn]
∞ headmaster ['hedmɑːstə]
∞ headphone
✎ Entertainment electronics

Kopf

Scheinwerfer

Schlagzeile

Schulleiter, Rektor
Kopfhörer

health [helθ]
∞ in good health

∞ health insurance [ɪnˈʃɔːrəns]
⟳ healthy ['helθɪ]

Gesundheit
gesund, bei guter Gesundheit
Krankenversicherung
gesund

Reporter to a 99-year-old woman: I hope I can return next year to celebrate your 100th birthday. *Old lady:* Why not? You look healthy enough to me.

hear [hɪə], **heard** [hɜːd], **heard**
Speak louder, please. I can't hear very well.
☛ listen
listen to the radio

hören

zuhören, anhören
Radio hören

heart [hɑːt]
✎ The human body
∞ learn/know s.th. by heart

Herz

etw. auswendig lernen/können

heat [hiːt]

Let's go inside, I can't bear the heat any more.
I'll heat the milk for you.
⟳ heater

⟳ heating
∞ central heating

Hitze, Wärme; erhitzen

Heizgerät; Heizkörper
Heizung
Zentralheizung

heavy [ˈhevɪ] ⇔ light
a heavy bag
heavy rain
schwer (von Ge-
wicht), stark

helicopter [ˈheli-
kɒptə] ✎ Transport;
✎ Danger and accidents
Hubschrauber

hello [heˈləʊ]
Hello, Tim. How
are you?
Say hello to your
family.
hallo, guten Tag

Schöne Grüße an
deine Familie.

helmet [ˈhelmɪt]
✎ Danger and accidents
Helm

help [help]
Can you help me
with my home-
work?
Can I help you?

∞ help oneself
Here are some
sandwiches.
Help yourselves.
Tell me if you
need help.
☛ first aid
helfen; Hilfe
Kannst du mir
bei den Hausauf-
gaben helfen?
Kann ich etwas
für Sie tun?
sich bedienen

Sag mir, wenn du
Hilfe brauchst
Erste Hilfe

hen [hen] ✎ Animals
Henne, Huhn

here [hɪə]
Come here!
∞ in here
∞ out here
∞ up here
∞ near here
∞ Here you are.
Can I have an-
other piece of
cake, please? –
Of course, here
you are.
hier, hierher
Komm hierher
hier drinnen
hier draußen
hier oben
hier in der Nähe
(Hier,) bitteschön.

Hi! [haɪ] ≈ Hello!
Hallo!

hide [haɪd], **hid**
[hɪd], **hidden** [ˈhɪdn]
Let's hide behind
that tree.
He hid the
money in the
garden.
(sich) verstecken

high [haɪ] ⇔ low
a high mountain
high prices
∞ high school [ˈhaɪ
skuːl] (AE)
hoch
ein hoher Berg
hohe Preise
Gesamtschule
Klasse 7–12

∞ highway [ˈhaɪweɪ]

∞ high fidelity (hi-fi
[haɪ ˈfaɪ])
Landstraße;
Hauptverkehrs-
straße (AE)
Hi-Fi

hike [haɪk]
∞ go hiking
∞ hitchhike
[ˈhɪtʃhaɪk]
wandern
wandern gehen
per Anhalter
fahren

hill [hɪl]
Hügel

history [ˈhɪstərɪ]
✎ School subjects
She is good at
history.
☛ She told us a
funny story.
Geschichte (auch
als Schulfach)
Sie ist gut in
Geschichte
... eine komische
Geschichte.

hit [hɪt], **hit, hit**

She hit the
burglar on the
head with a stick.

He was hit by a
rock.

The car came off
the road and hit
a tree.
Her new song is
a hit.
schlagen; treffen;
aufprallen auf;
Treffer, Schlager

Sie schlug dem
Einbrecher mit
einem Stock auf
den Kopf.
Er wurde von
einem Stein
getroffen.
Der Wagen ...
fuhr gegen einen
Baum.
Ihr neues Lied ist
ein Hit.

hitchhike [ˈhɪtʃhaɪk]
→ hike
per Anhalter fahren

hobby [ˈhɒbɪ]
Hobby

hockey [ˈhɒkɪ]
✎ Sports and games
Hockey

hold [ˈhəʊld], **held**
[held], **held**
She held a
candle in her
hand.
The festival will
be held in August
this year.
halten, haben; ab-
halten, veranstalten
Sie hielt eine
Kerze in der
Hand.
Das Fest wird die-
ses Jahr im August
veranstaltet.

hole [həʊl]
There's a hole in
my left sock.
Loch

holidays [ˈhɒlɪdeɪz]
∞ the summer
holidays
∞ go/be on holiday
Ferien, Urlaub
die Sommer-
ferien
in Urlaub
gehen/sein

55

home [həʊm]   Heim, Zuhause; heim, nach Hause

Do you like your new home?   Gefällt dir dein neues Zuhause?
∞ s.o.'s home town   jds. Heimatstadt
∞ homework   Hausaufgaben
∞ at home   zu Hause
I'm going home now.   Ich gehe jetzt nach Hause.

honest ['ɒnɪst]   ehrlich
an honest person
an honest answer

honey ['hʌnɪ]   Honig
✎ Food

hope [həʊp]   hoffen; Hoffnung
I hope everything is alright.
She hopes to find a job soon.
Let's hope for the best.
You are my last hope.

horoscope ['hɒrəskəʊp]   Horoskop

horror ['hɒrə]   Entsetzen, Grauen
∞ a horror film   eine Horrorfilm
⇨ horrible ['hɒrɪble]   schrecklich
⇨ horrific [hə'rɪfɪk]   entsetzlich

horse [hɔ:s]   Pferd
✎ Animals

hose [həʊs]   (Wasser)schlauch
✎ Danger and accidents

hospital ['hɒspɪtl]   Krankenhaus
✎ In town
Pete broke his leg and had to go to hospital.   … und mußte ins Krankenhaus (gehen).
Is your father still in hospital?   Liegt dein Vater noch im Krankenhaus?

hostel ['hɒstl]   (Wohn)heim
∞ youth hostel   Jugendherberge

hot ['hɒt] ⇔ cold   heiß, warm
hot water   heißes/warmes Wasser

hotel [həʊ'tel]   Hotel
✎ In town

hour ['aʊə]   Stunde
✎ Expressions of time
half an hour   eine halbe Stunde
∞ opening hours   Öffungszeiten

house [haʊs]   Haus

✎ **House and flat**

∞ housewife   Hausfrau
∞ housework   Hausarbeit
∞ household   Haushalt
✎ Electricity in the household

hovercraft ['hɒvəkrɑ:ft] ✎ Transport   Luftkissenboot

how [haʊ]   wie
How did you get here?   Wie bist du hierher gekommen?
How old are you?   Wie alt bist du?
How much is this T-shirt?   Wieviel kostet dieses T-Shirt
How many times have you been here?   Wie oft warst du schon hier?
How are you?   Wie geht es dir?
How do you do?   Angenehm. (bei Vorstellungen)
How nice.   Wie nett!
How about …?   Was ist mit …?/
→ about   Wie ist es/Wie wär's mit …?

human ['hju:mən]   menschlich
✎ The human body

humour ['hju:mə]   Humor
a sense of humour   Sinn für Humor

hungry ['hʌŋgrɪ]   hungrig
→ thirsty
be hungry   Hunger haben
⇨ hunger ['hʌŋgə]   Hunger

hunt [hʌnt]   jagen
∞ go hunting   jagen, auf die Jagd gehen
⇨ hunter ✎ Jobs   Jäger(in)

hurry ['hʌrɪ]   sich beeilen; Eile
We needn't hurry, there's plenty of time.

He is always in a hurry. | Er ist immer in Eile

hurt [hɜːt], **hurt, hurt** ≈ injure | verletzen; schmerzen, weh tun
He hurt his hand with a saw. | Er verletzte sich die Hand mit einer Säge.

My back hurts. | Mein Rücken tut weh.

husband ⇔ wife | (Ehe)mann
✎ Relatives

hut [hʌt] | Hütte

hymn [hɪm] | Kirchenlied

I [aɪ] is for

I [aɪ] ☛ immer groß geschrieben: | ich
What shall I do? | Was soll ich tun?
☛ Für betontes *ich* sagt man *me:*
Who's that? – It's me.

ice [aɪs] | Eis
∞ ice hockey | Eishockey
✎ Sports and games
∞ ice skating | Eislaufen
✎ Sports and games
∞ ice-cream ✎ Food | Speiseeis, Eiskrem

idea [aɪˈdɪə] | Idee, Vorstellung
That's a good idea. | Das ist eine gute Idee.
What's your idea of a nice holiday? | Was stellst du dir unter einem schönen Urlaub vor?
What's this? – I've no idea. | Was ist das? – Ich habe keine Ahnung.

ideal [aɪˈdɪəl] | ideal; Ideal

if [ɪf] | wenn, falls; ob
If you break that window, you'll have to pay for it. | Wenn du dieses Fenster zerbrichst, …
I don't know if that's true. | Ich weiß nicht, ob das stimmt.
∞ as if | als ob
He walked past us as if he hadn't seen us. | Er ging vorbei, als ob er uns nicht gesehen hätte.

ill [ɪl] | krank
She can't come – she's ill.
∞ fall ill | krank werden
☛ Vor Hauptwörtern benutzt man *sick:*
a sick child | ein krankes Kind
↪ illness | Krankheit

imagine [ɪˈmædʒɪn] | sich vorstellen
Imagine you are a millionaire … | Stell dir vor, du bist Millionär …
↪ imagination [ɪmædɪˈneɪʃn] | Phantasie, Vorstellungskraft

important [ɪmˈpɔːtnt] | wichtig, bedeutend
It's important to get good training.
an important city

impossible [ɪmˈpɒsəbl] ⇔ possible | unmöglich
It's impossible to read and watch TV at the same time.

in [ɪn] | 1. in Orts- und Richtungsangaben
✎ Place and direction
in York | in York
in Oxford Street | in der Oxford Street
in the street | auf der Straße
in town | in der Stadt
in the country | auf dem Land
in a field | auf einer Weide
in a tree | auf einem Baum
in the world | auf der Welt
in a picture | auf einem Bild
in bed | im Bett
in here | hier drinnen; hier hinein
∞ in front of → front | vor
✎ Place and direction
go in | hineingehen
come in | hereinkommen

✎ Expressions of time | 2. in Zeitangaben
in 1999 | (im Jahre) 1999
in the 1970s | in den Siebzigern
in January | im Januar
in the morning/afternoon/evening | am Morgen/Nachmittag/Abend
(just) in time | (gerade noch) rechtzeitig
in two hours | in zwei Stunden
in the end | am Ende

in English
in a friendly way

in bad weather

inch [ɪntʃ]

include [ɪnˈkluːd]

The price includes meals and entrance fees.

indeed [ɪnˈdiːd]
Did you enjoy your holidays?
– Yes, indeed.

Indian [ˈɪndɪən]

∞ the Indian Ocean

⇨ India ✎ Countries

indoor [ˈɪndɔː]
⇔ outdoor
∞ an indoor swimming pool
⇨ indoors ✎ Place and direction

industry [ˈɪndəstrɪ]

inform [ɪnˈfɔːm]

Have you informed the police of/about the accident yet?
⇨ information [ɪnfəˈmeɪʃn]
☛ immer in der Einzahl:
Further information is to be found in the leaflet.

∞ | TOURIST INFORMATION |

injure [ˈɪndʒə]
≈ hurt
Three people were injured in the accident.
⇨ injury [ˈɪndʒərɪ]

3. in sonstigen Angaben
auf Englisch
auf freundliche Weise, freundlich
bei schlechtem Wetter

Zoll (Längenmaß = 2,54 cm)

einschließen, einbeziehen

tatsächlich, wirklich

1. indianisch; Indianer(in)
2. indisch; Inder(in)
der Indische Ozean
Indien

Innen-

ein Hallenbad

drinnen, im Haus

Industrie; Gewerbe

informieren, benachrichtigen

Information(en), Auskunft

Weitere Informationen sind in dem Prospekt zu finden.

(Fremden)verkehrsbüro

verletzen

Verletzung

ink [ɪŋk]
write in ink

inside [ɪnˈsaɪd]
⇔ outside
✎ Place and direction
inside the house
Let's wait inside.

install [ɪnˈstɔːl]
Have the new heaters been installed yet?

instead [ɪnˈsted]
Sorry, I haven't got any ice-cream. How about chocolate pudding instead?
∞ instead of
I bought apples instead of pears by mistake.
Why don't you help me instead of criticizing me?

instrument [ˈɪnstrʊmənt]
∞ musical instrument

Tinte
mit Tinte schreiben

in, (drinnen); innen, drinnen

im Haus drinnen
Laßt uns drinnen warten.

installieren
Sind die neuen Heizkörper schon installiert?

statt dessen

… Wie wär's statt dessen mit Schokoladepudding?
statt, anstatt
Ich habe aus Versehen Äpfel statt Birnen.

… statt mich zu kritisieren?

Instrument

Musikinstrument

✎ **Musical Instruments**

insurance [ɪnˈʃɔːrəns]
∞ life insurance

∞ health insurance

⇨ insure [ɪnˈʃɔː]
The house is insured against fire.

intelligent [ɪnˈtelɪdʒənt] ⇔ stupid
⇨ intelligence

Versicherung

Lebensversicherung
Krankenversicherung
versichern

intelligent

Intelligenz

interest ['ɪntrɪst]   interessieren; Interesse

Computer games don't interest me.   Computerspiele interessieren mich nicht.

She didn't manage to interest her friends <u>in</u> the project.   Es gelang ihr nicht, Ihre Freunde <u>für</u> das Projekt zu interessieren.

He didn't show much interest <u>in</u> my stamp collection.   Er zeigte kein großes Interesse <u>an</u> meiner Briefmarkensammlung.
↪ interesting   interessant
↪ interested   interessiert
Are you interested <u>in</u> sports?   Interessierst du dich <u>für</u> Sport?

international [ɪntəˈnæʃnəl]   international
an international organization

interview ['ɪntəvju:]   Interview; interviewen, befragen

a TV interview   ein Fernsehinterview

∞ a job interview   ein Vorstellungsgespräch

Our reporter has interviewed some people in the street.

into ['ɪntʊ]   in (hinein)
✎ Place and direction
Let's go into the living room.   Gehen wir ins Wohnzimmer.
Turn right into King Street.   Biegen Sie nach rechts in die King Street ein.

Translate this sentence into English.   Übersetzt diesen Satz ins Englische.

invent [ɪnˈvent]   erfinden
The telephone was invented by Alexander Graham Bell in 1872.
↪ invention   Erfindung
↪ inventor   Erfinder(in)

iron ['aɪən]   Eisen; Bügeleisen; bügeln

an iron mine   ein Eisenbergwerk
an electric iron   ein elektrisches Bügeleisen
✎ Electricity in the household

Do you know how to iron a shirt?   Kannst du ein Hemd bügeln?

ironical [aɪˈrɒnɪkl]   ironisch
an ironical remark

island ['aɪlənd]   Insel
Britain is an island.
↪ isle [aɪl]   Insel (in Eigennamen)
∞ the Isle of Man   die Insel Man

it [ɪt]   es/sie/er
↪ its   sein/ihr
☛ Verwechsle nicht *it's (it is/it has)* und *its*.
<u>It's</u> five o'clock.   Es ist fünf Uhr.
<u>It's</u> stopped raining.   Es hat aufgehört zu regen.
the town and <u>its</u> inhabitants   die Stadt und ihre Einwohner

Italy ['ɪtəli]   Italien
✎ Countries
Italian → German   italienisch; Italienisch; Italiener(in)

J [dʒeɪ] **is for** + *k*

jacket ['dʒækɪt]   Jacke
✎ Clothes

jam [dʒæm] ✎ Food   Marmelade; Gedränge

strawberry jam   Erdbeermarmelade
☛ marmalade ['mɑ:məleid]   Orangenmarmelade
∞ traffic jam   Verkehrstau

January ['dʒænjʊəri]   Januar
✎ Months and seasons

jazz [dʒæz]   *Jazz*

jeans [dʒi:nz]   *Jeans*
✎ Clothes
∞ blue jeans   *Bluejeans*
∞ a pair of jeans   ein Paar Jeans

jewel ['dʒu:əl]   Edelstein; Juwel, Schmuckstück

∞ the Crown Jewels   die Kronjuwelen
↪ jewel(le)ry ['dʒu:əlri]   Schmuck
↪ jeweller ✎ Jobs   Juwelier(in)

job [dʒɒb] — Arbeit, Stelle, Job; Aufgabe

✎ **Jobs**

He has got a good job in a bank.
I've got a few jobs to do this afternoon.

jog [dʒɒg] — *joggen*, Dauerlauf machen
⇨ jogging ✎ Sports and games — *Jogging*, Dauerlauf

join [dʒɔɪn] — sich anschließen
join a club — einem Klub beitreten

We're going for walk. Come and join us. — … Komm doch mit.

joke [dʒəʊk] — Witz; Spaß/Witze machen

Is that a joke or is it true?
Don't believe him, he's only joking!

journey ['dʒɜːnɪ] — Reise
a journey to France — eine Reise nach Frankreich
∞ go on a journey — eine Reise machen

joy [dʒɔɪ] — Freude, Vergnügen
⇨ enjoy — genießen
Enjoy yourselves. — Viel Spaß!
∞ joystick ✎ Entertainment electronics — *Joystick*

juice [dʒuːs] — Saft
✎ Drinks
∞ apple juice — Apfelsaft
∞ orange juice — Orangensaft

July [dʒuːˈaɪ] — Juli
✎ Months and seasons

jump [dʒʌmp] — springen, hüpfen
He jumped over the fence.

June [dʒuːn] — Juni
✎ Months and seasons

jungle ['dʒʌŋgl] — Dschungel

just [dʒʌst] — gerade, soeben; genau; enfach, nur

Where's Pat? – She's just left.
These jeans are just the right size. — … Sie ist gerade weggegangen. Diese Jeans haben genau die richtige Größe.

Try on this hat, just for fun.
Just a moment, please. — …, nur zum Spaß. Einen Moment, bitte.

K [keɪ] is for

kangaroo [kæŋɡəˈruː] — Känguruh
✎ Animals

karate [kəˈrɑːtɪ] — Karate
✎ Sports and games

keep [kiːp], **kept** [kept], **kept** — behalten; halten; bleiben
Can I keep this leaflet? — Kann ich diesen Prospekt behalten?

Keep the door closed, please.
Keep quiet, please. — Haltet bitte die Tür geschlossen. Bleibt bitte ruhig.
∞ keep (on) doing s.th. — etw. weiterhin tun; etw. ständig tun

We kept (on) walking although we were tired.
Some customers keep (on) complaining. — Wir gingen weiter, obwohl wir müde waren. Manche Kunden beschweren sich ständig.
∞ Keep smiling.

ketchup ['ketʃəp] — *Ketchup*
✎ Food

key [kiː] — Schlüssel; Taste
Here's the key to the front door.
the keys of a piano/typewriter/computer keybord

∞ keyboard
✎ Entertainment electronics

Tastatur; *Keyboard*

kick [kɪk]
He kicked the ball into the goal.
Stop kicking me!
∞ kick-off

kicken, treten (gegen)

Anstoß, Anpfiff (zu Beginn eines Spiels)

kid [kɪd] ≈ child
∞ kidnap ['kɪdnæp]

Kind
entführen, *kidnappen*

kill [kɪl]

töten

kilometre ['kɪləmiːtə]
50 kilometres (50 km)

Kilometer

50 Kilometer

kind [kaɪnd] ≈ sort

What kinds of fruit have you got?
She served us a kind of pudding.
It was very kind of you to help us.

Art, Sorte; freundlich

Welche Obstsorten haben Sie?
Sie servierte uns eine Art Pudding.
Es war sehr freundlich von Ihnen, uns zu helfen.

kindergarten ['kɪndəɡɑːtn]
∞ kindergarten teacher ✎ Jobs

Kindergarten

Kindergärtner(in)

king [kɪŋ]
⇨ kingdom ['kɪŋdəm]
∞ the United Kingdom (U.K.) (= England, Scotland, Wales and Northern Ireland)

König
Königreich

das Vereinigte Königreich

kiss [kɪs]
She kissed him on the cheek.
They kissed and said goodbye.
a kiss on the mouth

(sich) küssen; Kuß

kit [kɪt]

∞ repair kit

Ausrüstung, Werkzeug(kasten)
Flickzeug

∞ first-aid kit
✎ Danger and accidents

Verbandszeug

kitchen ['kɪtʃɪn]
✎ House and flat

Küche

kite [kaɪt]
∞ fly a kite

(Papier-)Drachen
einen Drachen steigen lassen

knee [niː]
✎ The human body

Knie

knife [naɪf], **knives** [naɪvz]
✎ Laying the table

Messer

knit [nɪt]
She is knitting a pullover.

stricken

knock [nɒk]

knock at the door
a loud knock
∞ knock over
Don't knock your glass over.
∞ knock down

They are going to knock down the old school.
A cyclist was knocked down by a car.

klopfen, stoßen (gegen); Klopfen, Stoß, Schlag
an die Tür klopfen
ein lauter Schlag
umstoßen

(Gebäude) abreißen; überfahren, umwerfen

knot [nɒt]
∞ tie/untie a knot

Knoten
einen Knoten machen/lösen

know [nəʊ], **knew** [njuː], **known** [nəʊn]
She didn't know what to do.
Do you know Alan?
∞ get to know
I don't know French.
He doesn't know how to swim.
∞ know-how ['nəʊhaʊ]
⇨ knowledge ['nɒlɪdʒ]

wissen; kennen; können

kennenlernen
Ich kann kein Französisch.
Er kann nicht schwimmen
Know-how, (Fach)wissen
Wissen, Kenntnis(se)

L [el] is for

ladder ['lædə]   Leiter
✎ Danger and accidents

lady ['leɪdɪ]   Dame; *Lady*
→ gentleman
∞ landlady   (Haus)wirtin

lake [leɪk]   (der) See
∞ the Great Lakes   die Großen Seen (in Amerika)
∞ Lake Michigan   der Michigansee

lamb [læm]   Lamm
✎ Animals

lamp [læmp]   Lampe
✎ Furniture

land [lænd]   Land; landen
After 10 days at sea one of the sailors saw land. They bought a piece of land to plant vegetables.
∞ landlady   (Haus)wirtin
∞ landlord   (Haus)wirt
The plane has just landed.
☛ a European country   ein europäisches Land
live in the country   auf dem Land leben

language ['læŋgwɪdʒ]   Sprache
∞ foreign language   Fremdsprache

large [lɑːdʒ] ≈ big   groß
⇔ small
a large room
a large T-shirt

last [lɑːst]   letzte(r/s); (an)dauern
our last chance   unsere letzte Chance
last week   letzte Woche
∞ last night ✎ Expression of time   gestern abend; letzte Nacht
∞ at last   endlich
The meeting lasted until ten.   Die Versammlung dauerte bis zehn.

late [leɪt] ⇔ early   spät
a late visitor   ein später Gast
∞ be late   zu spät kommen
She is always late.

∞ sooner or later   früher oder später
∞ the latest news   die neuesten Nachrichten

laugh [lɑːf]   lachen
laugh at s.o.   über jdn. lachen

law [lɔː]   Gesetz
∞ break the law   das Gesetz brechen
⇨ lawyer ['lɔːjə]   Rechtsanwalt/Rechtsanwältin
✎ Jobs

lay [leɪ], **laid** [leɪd], **laid** ≈ put   legen
He laid the baby on the couch.
∞ lay eggs   Eier legen
∞ lay the table   den Tisch decken

✎ **Laying the table**

∞ layout   Gestaltung, Anordnung

lazy ['leɪzɪ]   faul
a lazy pupil

lead [liːd], **led** [led], **led**   führen, leiten
The guide led us down the stairs. Where does this road lead to?
⇨ leading   führend
a leading company
⇨ leader   (An)führer(in)

leaf [liːf], **leaves** [liːvz]   Blatt, Blätter

leaflet ['liːflɪt]   Prospekt

learn [lɜːn]   lernen
learn a language   eine Sprache lernen
learn (how) to write   schreiben lernen
∞ learn s.th. by heart   etwas auswendig lernen
⇨ learner   Lernende(r), Anfänger(in)
∞ learner driver   Fahrschüler

lease [li:s] ≈ rent

We have leased the car, it's not our own.

mieten, pachten, *leasen;* Pacht

least [li:st] → little

weniste(r/s), am wenigsten

∞ at least

wenigstens, mindestens

The food wasn't good, but at least it was cheap.
The tickets will cost at least £5.

leather ['leðə]
a leather jacket

Leder
eine Lederjacke

leave [li:v], **left** [left], **left**

weggehen, abfahren, abfliegen; verlassen; (übrig-/zurück-)lassen

I've got to leave for school now.
The train leaves at 15:15.
Don't leave the house until I'm back, please.
Don't eat all the cake. Leave some for Jean and Bill.
⇨ left

übrig(geblieben)

Are there any sandwiches left?
I left my coat on the bus.
Leave the door open, please.

∞ leave s.o. alone

jdn. in Ruhe lassen

∞ school leaver

Schulabgänger(in)

left [left] ⇔ right

linke(r/s); (nach) links; linke Seite

my left leg
turn left

mein linkes Bein
nach links abbiegen

on the left

links, auf der linken Seite

on your left

links von dir

leg [leg]
✎ The human body

Bein

lemon ['lemən]
✎ Fruit
⇨ lemonade [lemə-'neɪd] ✎ Drinks

Zitrone

Limonade

lend [lend], **lent** [lent], **lent** → borrow
Can you lend me some money?
☛ I borrowed some money from a friend.

(jdm. etw.) leihen

Ich lieh (mir) etwas Geld von einem Freund.

less [les] → little

weniger

lesson ['lesn]

an English lesson

Unterrichtsstunde; Lektion
eine Englischstunde

∞ teach s.o. a lesson

jdm. eine Lektion erteilen

let [let], **let, let**

lassen; etw. zulassen, erlauben

Let's go.
let s.o. or s.th. in/out/down/etc.

Laßt uns gehen.
jdn. oder etw. herein-/hinaus-/herunterlassen usw.

He let the rope down.
My parents don't let me go to discos.
☛ Our teacher makes us write a lot of tests.
→ make
☛ I've left the book on the table.
→ leave

Er ließ das Seil herunter.
Meine Eltern lassen mich nicht in Diskos gehen.
Unser Lehrer läßt uns viele Tests schreiben.
(Er veranlaßt es.)
Ich habe das Buch auf dem Tisch gelassen.

letter ['letə]
write a letter
∞ capital letters ['kæpɪtl]
∞ small letters
∞ block letters

Brief; Buchstabe

Großbuchstaben

Kleinbuchstaben
Blockschrift

lettuce ['letɪs]
✎ Vegetables
☛ salad ['sæləd]

Kopfsalat

(angemachter) Salat (als Gericht)

liberty ['lɪbətɪ]
≈ freedom
∞ the Statue of Liberty
→ statue

Freiheit

die Freiheitsstatue (in New York)

library ['laɪbrərɪ]

Bücherei, Bibliothek

lie [laɪ], **lay** [leɪ], **lain** [leɪn]
A lot of books and papers were lying around.
∞ lie down

liegen

sich hinlegen

lie [laɪ], **lied** [laɪd], **lied** — lügen; Lüge
He lied when he said that. — Er log, als er das sagte.
That's a lie! — Das ist eine Lüge!
∞ tell a lie/tell lies — lügen

life [laɪf], **lives** [laɪvz] — Leben
She saved <u>his</u> life. — Sie rettete <u>ihm</u> <u>das</u> Leben.
☞ She saved <u>their</u> lives. — Sie rettete <u>ihnen</u> <u>das</u> Leben.
⇨ live [lɪv] — leben
⇨ live [laɪv] → live — lebend; *live, direkt*
⇨ alive [ə'laɪv] — am Leben

lift [lɪft] — (hoch)heben; *Lift,* Aufzug
Can you help me to lift this box into the car?
Shall we walk up the stairs or take the lift?
∞ give s.o. a lift — jdn. im Auto mitnehmen

light [laɪt], **lit** [lɪt], **lit** — Licht; beleuchten; anzünden; hell; leicht
a bright light — ein helles Licht
∞ traffic lights — Verkehrsampel
∞ by daylight — bei Tageslicht
The room was lit by candles. — Das Zimmer war von Kerzen beleuchtet.
He lit a match. — Er zündete ein Streichholz an.
⇨ lighter ['laɪtə] — Feuerzeug
light colours — helle Farben
⇔ dark
∞ light blue/green/ etc. — hellblau/-grün usw.
a light bag — eine leichte Tasche
⇔ heavy
a light meal — eine leichte Mahlzeit

like [laɪk] — mögen; (so) wie
She likes you. — Sie mag dich.
He likes swimming. — Er schwimmt gern.
What would you like to drink? — Was möchtest du trinken?
I'd like to see New York. — Ich würde gern New York sehen.
He is a sailor, like his father. — Er ist Seemann, wie sein Vater.

What's your new teacher like? — Wie ist dein neuer Lehrer?
☞ How's your new teacher? — <u>Wie geht es deinem neuen Lehrer?</u>
∞ like this — so, auf diese Weise
⇨ likely [laɪklɪ] — wahrscheinlich
He's (most) likely to come. — Er kommt (höchst)wahrscheinlich.

line [laɪ] — Zeile; Linie; Leitung
Read the first two lines.
∞ draw a line — eine Linie ziehen
∞ a railway line — ein Bahnlinie
∞ a telephone line — eine Telefonleitung

lion ['laɪən] — Löwe
✎ Animals

lip [lɪp] — Lippe
✎ The human body
∞ upper/lower lip — Ober-/Unterlippe
∞ lipstick — Lippenstift

list [lɪst] — Liste
∞ shopping list — Einkaufsliste

listen ['lɪsn] → hear — zuhören
listen to s.o. — jdm. zuhören; auf jdn. hören
Everybody was listening to the speaker.
I warned you but you didn't listen to me.
listen to music — Musik (an)hören

litre ['li:tə] — Liter
2 litres of water (2 l water) — 2 Liter Wasser

litter ['lɪtə] — Abfall
∞ litter bin — Abfalleimer

little ['lɪtl] ≈ small — 1. klein
☞ Steigerung: smaller, smallest
a little boy
the smallest boy of all
≈ not much — 2. wenig
☞ Steigerung: less, least
There's very little room in here. — Hier drinnen ist sehr wenig Platz.
I earn less than you. — Ich verdiene weniger als du.

∞ a little ≈ a bit (of); → a few — ein wenig, ein bißchen
There' a little tea left.
I'm a little nervous.
Please wait a little.

live [lɪv] — leben, wohnen
How long do cats live? — Wie lange leben Katzen?
Does Ann still live <u>with</u> her parents? — Wohnt Ann noch <u>bei</u> Ihren Eltern?
⇨ life [laɪf] — Leben
⇨ alive [ə'laɪv] — am Leben
⇨ live [laɪv] — lebend; *live*, direkt

a live animal ≈ a living animal — ein lebendes Tier
The show will be broadcast live on TV. — Die Show wird direkt im Fernsehen übertragen.
a live programme — eine *Live*sendung
⇨ lively — lebhaft, lebendig
a lively discussion
∞ living room — Wohnzimmer
✎ House and flat

local ['ləʊkl] — örtlich, Orts-, lokal
the local newspaper — die Lokalzeitung
local people — Einheimische, Ortsansässige

lock ['lɒk] — (ab-/zu)schließen; Schloß
Lock the door when you leave.
I've lost the key to this lock.

lonely ['leʊnlɪ] — einsam

long [lɒŋ] ⇔ short — lang; lange
long hair — lange Haare
How long have you been here? — Wie lange bist du schon hier?
It won't take long. — Es dauert nicht lange.
∞ a long-playing record (an LP) — eine Langspielplatte

look [lʊk] — schauen; Blick; aussehen
Look, it's snowing. — Schau mal, es schneit.
∞ look at s.o./s.th. — jdn./etw. anschauen

∞ look for s.o./s.th. — jdn./etw. suchen
∞ look after s.o. — sich um jdn. kümmern
∞ look round — sich umschauen
∞ look up a word — ein Wort nachschlagen
∞ look forward to (doing) s.th. → forward — sich auf etw. freuen
∞ look out (for) — achtgeben (auf)
a quick look — ein kurzer Blick (nach)schauen
∞ have a look
These sandwiches look nice. — Diese Sandwiches sehen gut aus. …
I'll have one.
<u>What</u> does your boyfriend look <u>like</u>? — <u>Wie</u> sieht dein Freund aus?

lorry ['lɒrɪ] (BE) ≈ truck (AE) — Lastwagen
✎ Transport
∞ lorry driver — Lastwagenfahrer(in)
✎ Jobs

lose [luːs], **lost** [lɒst], **lost** ⇔ find; win — verlieren
She has lost her new ring.
We lost the match 1:2.
∞ Get lost! — Hau ab!
⇨ loser — Verlierer(in)

a lot [ə 'lɒt] — viel, viele, eine Menge
a lot <u>of</u> work — viel Arbeit
a lot <u>of</u> people — viele Leute
Did you take any photos? – Yes, a lot. — … – Ja, eine Menge.
∞ lots (of) ≈ a lot (of) — viel, viele, eine Menge
She's got lots of CDs.

loud [laʊd] — laut
loud music
∞ loudspeaker — Lautsprecher
✎ Entertainment electronics

love [lʌv] — lieben; Liebe; (liebe) Grüße
He loves his wife very much. — Er liebt seine Frau sehr.
I'd love to come, but I can't. — Ich würde sehr gerne kommen, …
true love — wahre Liebe

∞ a love story	eine Liebes-geschichte
∞ a love letter	ein Liebesbrief
∞ be in love (with)	verliebt sein (in)
∞ fall in love (with)	sich verlieben (in)
Love, Alan	Liebe Grüße, Alan
Give my love to your parents!	Liebe Grüße an Deine Eltern!
⇨ lovely ['lʌvlɪ]	wunderschön

low [ləʊ] ⇔ high — niedrig
a low wall

luck [lʌk] — Glück (= glück-licher Zufall)
→ happiness
∞ wish s.o. good luck — jdm. viel Glück wünschen
∞ bad luck — Pech
⇨ lucky — Glücks-
a lucky number — eine Glückszahl
be lucky/unlucky — Glück/Pech haben
⇨ luckily — zum Glück

lunch [lʌnʃ] — Mittagessen
∞ have lunch — zu Mittag essen
We had sausages <u>for</u> lunch. — Wir aßen Würst-chen <u>zum</u> Mittag-essen.

M [em] is for

machine [mə'ʃi:n] — Maschine; Automat
∞ washing machine — Waschmaschine
✎ Electricity in the household
∞ ticket machine — Fahrkartenauto-mat

mad [mæd] ≈ crazy — verrückt

madam ['mædəm] — meine Dame *(wird meist gar nicht übersetzt)*
→ sir
Can I help you, madam? — Kann ich etwas für Sie tun?

magazine [mægə'zi:n] — Zeitschrift

mail [meɪl] ≈ post — Post
send s.th. by mail — etw. mit der Post schicken
∞ airmail — Luftpost

main [meɪn] — hauptsächlich, Haupt-
main entrance — Haupteingang
main course — Hauptgericht, Hauptgang

make [meɪk], **made** [meɪd], **made** — machen; (veran-)lassen
make tea — Tee kochen
∞ make money — Geld verdienen
∞ make sense — einen Sinn ergeben
This doesn't make sense.
∞ make up one's mind (to do s.th.) — sich entschließen (etw. zu tun)
∞ make use of s.th. — etw. (aus)nutzen
a model plane made of paper — ein Modellflug-zeug aus Papier
∞ make it — es schaffen
We've made it! — Wir haben es geschafft!
make s.o. come → let — jdn. kommen lassen (= jdn. herbestellen)

man [mæn], **men** [men] ✎ People — Mann, Männer; Mensch(en)
men and women — Männer und Frauen
Man cannot live without food. — Der Mensch kann nicht ohne Nahrung leben.

manage ['mænɪdʒ] — etw. schaffen, fertig-bringen; etw. füh-ren, leiten
Can you manage all that work? — Schaffst du die ganze Arbeit?
How did you manage to find us? — Wie hast du es fertiggebracht, uns zu finden?
Jane Baxter man-ages the food department. — … leitet die Lebensmittel-abteilung.
⇨ manager ['mænɪdʒə] — Geschäftsfüh-rer(in)
⇨ manageress [mænɪdʒə'res] — Geschäftsführerin

many ['menɪ] ≈ a lot (of) → much — viele
I don't know many people.
☛ Steigerung: more, most
∞ how many → how — wie viele
∞ too many → too — zu viele

map [mæp] — Landkarte
✎ My school bag

March [mɑːtʃ] — März
✎ Months and seasons

mark [mɑːk]
She always gets
good marks in
her English tests.

Note, Zensur

market ['mɑːkɪt]
✎ In town
∞ market place
∞ flea market
['fliːmɑːkɪt]

Markt

Marktplatz
Flohmarkt

marmalade ['mɑːmə-
leɪd] → jam ✎ Food

Orangenmarmelade

marry ['mærɪ]
She married a
schoolfriend.
⊅ married
a married man
∞ get married
They are going to
get married.
⊅ marriage ['mærɪdʒ]

heiraten

verheiratet

heiraten

Heirat, Ehe

match [mætʃ]
a football match
a box of matches

Spiel; Streichholz

eine Schachtel
Streichhölzer

material [mə'tiːrɪəl]

Material, Stoff

mathematics
[mæθə'mætɪks]
✎ School subjects
⊅ maths [mæθs]

Mathematik

Mathe

matter ['mætə]

Angelegenheit,
Sache; eine Rolle
spielen
Was ist los?

∞ What's the
matter?
What colour
would you like?
– It doesn't
matter.

... – Das ist egal.

May [meɪ]
✎ Months and seasons

Mai

may [meɪ], **might**
[maɪt]
May I come in?

He may/might be
right.

⊅ maybe ≈ perhaps
Maybe I'm wrong.

dürfen, (vielleicht)
können

Darf ich herein-
kommen?
Er kann/könnte
Recht haben./Er
hat vielleicht
Recht.
vielleicht

me [miː]
Can you help me,
please?

mir, mich, ich

Is this for me?
That's me. → I

meal [miːl]
We had one hot
meal a day.

∞ meals-on-wheels

Essen, Mahlzeit
Wir bekamen
eine warme
Mahlzeit pro Tag.
„Essen auf
Rädern"

mean [miːn], **meant**
[ment], **meant**
What does that
sign mean?
I don't know
what you mean.

bedeuten; meinen

meat [miːt] ✎ Food

Fleisch

mechanic [mɪ'kænɪk]
✎ Jobs
∞ car mechanic

Mechaniker(in)

Kfz-Mechani-
ker(in)

medicine ['medsn]
You must take
your medicine if
you want to get
well soon.

Medizin, Arznei

meet [miːt], **met**
[met], **met**
I met an old
friend today.
⊅ meeting

∞ meeting point
Do you know my
sister? – No, but
I'd like to meet
her.
We'll meet you at
the station when
you arrive.

treffen; kennenler-
nen; abholen

Treffen, Ver-
sammlung
Treffpunkt

member ['membə]
She's a member
of the swimming
club.

Mitglied

mend [mend]
≈ repair
mend a machine/
a fence/clothes

reparieren, ausbes-
sern, flicken

mention ['menʃn]
The accident
wasn't men-
tioned in the
newspaper.

erwähnen

menu ['menjuː]

Speisekarte

message ['mesɪdʒ] | Mitteilung, Nachricht, Botschaft
∞ take a message | etwas ausrichten
Mrs Bell is not in. Can I take a message?

metal ['metl] | Metall

metre ['miːtə] | Meter
10 metres (10 m) | 10 Meter

Mexico ['meksɪkəʊ] | Mexiko
✎ Countries
⇨ Mexican | mexikanisch;
→ American | Mexikaner(in)

micro ['maɪkrəʊ] | Mikro-
∞ microphone | Mikrofon
['maɪkrəfəʊn]
✎ Entertainment electronics
∞ microscope | Mikroskop
['maɪkrəskəʊp]
∞ microwave (oven) | Mikrowellenherd
✎ Electricity in the household

middle ['mɪdl] | Mitte, Mittel-, mittlere(r/s)
in the middle of | mitten auf der
the road | Straße
∞ the Middle Ages | das Mittelalter

midnight ['mɪdnaɪt] | Mitternacht
at midnight ✎ Expressions of time | um Mitternacht

might → may

mile [maɪl] | Meile (= 1,6 km)
20 miles | 20 Meilen

milk [mɪlk] ✎ Drinks | Milch
∞ milkman | Milchmann
['mɪlkmən]

million ['mɪlɪən] | Million
30 million people | 30 Millionen Menschen
millions of | Millionen von
people | Menschen
⇨ millionaire | Millionär(in)

mind [maɪnd] | Geist, Verstand; achten auf, sich kümmern um
She must have | Sie muß den Verlost her mind! | stand verloren haben!
∞ make up one's | sich entscheiden
mind → make

| Mind the step! | Achtung, Stufe!

Do you mind if I | Macht es dir
open the window? | etwas aus, wenn ich ...?

mine [maɪn] | Bergwerk, Mine
coal mine | Kohlebergwerk
⇨ miner ✎ Jobs | Bergmann

mineral water | Mineralwasser
['mɪnərəl 'wɔːtə]
✎ Drinks

minute ['mɪnɪt] | Minute; Augenblick
It's two minutes to ten.
Just a minute. | Einen Augenblick!

mirror ['mɪrə] | Spiegel
✎ In the bathroom

Miss [mɪs] (Taylor/ | Fräulein (Taylor/
Smith/...) | Smith/...)
∞ Miss World

miss [mɪs] | verpassen, verfehlen; vermissen
You'll miss the train if you don't hurry.
The post office is on your way. You can't miss it.
Good bye. We'll miss you.
⇨ missing | vermißt, verschwunden

Is there any news about the missing boy?
My purse is missing.

missis → Mrs

mist [mɪst] ≈ fog | (feiner) Nebel,
✎ The weather | Dunst

mistake [mɪs'teɪk] | Fehler
You've made a mistake.

mister → Mr

mix [mɪks] | (ver)mischen, verrühren
Mix the eggs with the butter, add the flour ...
∞ mixing bowl [bəʊl] | Rührschüssel
⇨ mixer ✎ Electricity | Mixer, Rührgerät
in the household
⇨ mixture ['mɪkstʃə] | Mischung

model ['mɒdl] Modell; Mannequin
∞ a model railway eine Modell-
  eisenbahn

  She is a (fashion)
  model.

modern ['mɒdən] modern
↪ modernize modernisieren
  ['mɒdənaɪz]

moment ['məʊmənt] Moment, Augenblick
  Just a moment, Einen Augen-
  please. blick bitte.
∞ at the moment im Augenblick

Monday ['mʌndɪ] Montag
✎ Days of the week

money ['mʌnɪ] Geld
∞ make money Geld verdienen
  I like my job and … und ich be-
  the money is komme einen
  good. guten Lohn.

monkey ['mʌŋkɪ] Affe
✎ Animals

monster ['mɒnstə] Ungeheuer, Monster

month [mʌnθ] Monat
  in the month of im Monat Mai
  May

✎ **Months and seasons**

---

moon [muːn] Mond
  The moon is up. Der Mond ist
  aufgegangen.
∞ full moon Vollmond
  It's full moon Heute nacht ist
  tonight. Vollmond.
∞ half-moon Halbmond
∞ moonlight Mondlicht

moped ['məʊped] Moped
✎ Transport

more [mɔː] → many, mehr
→ much
  We want more Wir wollen mehr
  money. Geld.

He works more Er arbeitet mehr
than the others. als die anderen.
∞ more and more immer mehr
  more modern/ moderner/wich-
  important/ex- tiger/teurer/…
  pensive/…
∞ not … any more nicht mehr
  They don't live
  here any more.
∞ some more noch etwas, noch
  einige

  We need some
  more coffee, and
  some more cups.
∞ once more noch einmal
  Let's try once
  more.

morning ['mɔːnɪŋ] Morgen, Vormittag
→ evening
✎ Expressions of time
∞ Good morning. Guten Morgen.
☛ in the morning am Morgen, am
  Vormittag, mor-
  gens, vormittags
∞ this morning heute morgen,
  heute vormittag
∞ tomorrow morgen früh,
  morning morgen vormittag

most [məʊst] die meisten, das
→ many, much meiste, am meisten;
  äußerst, sehr
  Most people like Die meisten Leute
  music. mögen Musik.
  We stayed at Wir blieben die
  home most of meiste Zeit zu
  the time. Hause.
  the most mod- das modernste/
  ern/important/ wichtigste/be-
  famous/... rühmteste/...
  building Gebäude
  What I hate Was ist am mei-
  most at school is sten an der Schu-
  … le hasse, ist …
  Do you think
  they will come? … – Es ist sehr
  – It's most likely. wahrscheinlich.

mother ['mʌðə] Mutter
✎ Relatives

motor ['məʊtə] Motor
∞ motor-bike Motorrad
  ✎ Transport
∞ motorcycle Motorrad
  ['məʊtəsaɪkl]
∞ motor-boat Motorboot
∞ motorway (BE) Autobahn

mountain ['maʊntɪn]
  mountains
∞ the Rocky
  Mountains

Berg
Berge; Gebirge
(Gebirge im Nord-
westen der USA)

mouse [maʊs], **mice**
[maɪs] ✎ Animals

Maus, Mäuse

mouth [maʊθ]
✎ The human body

Mund

move [mu:v]

  Stay where you
are – don't move.
My arm hurts, I
can't move it.
They moved to
Bristol last year.

(sich) bewegen;
umziehen
… – beweg dich
nicht.
…, ich kann ihn
nicht bewegen.
Sie sind letztes
Jahr nach Bristol
umgezogen.

⇨ movement

Bewegung

Mr (Smith) ['mɪstə]

Herr (Smith)

Mrs (Miller) ['mɪsɪz]

Frau (Miller)

much [mʌtʃ] ≈ a lot
(of) → many
  We didn't spend
much money.
I didn't do much
today.
This T-shirt is
much nicer than
that.

viel

∞ how much
∞ too much
∞ Thank you very
much.
☛ Steigerung: more,
most

wieviel
zuviel
Vielen Dank.

mud [mʌd]
⇨ muddy

Schlamm, Matsch
schlammig,
matschig

muesli ['mju:zlɪ]
✎ Food

Müsli

Mum [mʌm]

Mutti, Mama

museum [mju:'zɪəm]
✎ In town

Museum

mushroom ['mʌʃ-
rʊm] ✎ Vegetables

Pilz

music ['mju:zɪk]
✎ School subjects
⇨ musician
[mju:'zɪʃn] ✎ Jobs
⇨ musical [mju:zɪkl]
✎ Musical instru-
ments

Musik

Musiker(in)

musikalisch,
Musik-; *Musical*

must [mʌst]
≈ have (got) to
  We must leave
now.
☛ must not
We mustn't miss
the train.

müssen

Wir müssen jetzt
gehen.
nicht dürfen
Wir dürfen den
Zug nicht verpas-
sen.

my [maɪ]
  my parents
⇨ mine [maɪn]
This is your glass
and that's mine.

mein(e)
meine Eltern
meine(r/s)
Das ist dein Glas,
und das ist mei-
nes.

⇨ myself

mir/mich/ich
(selbst)

  I have hurt my-
self with a knife.

Ich habe mich
mit einem Messer
verletzt.

  I can do that
myself.

Ich kann das
selbst tun.

N [en] is for

nail [neɪl]
  Have you got a
hammer and a
nail?
I want to nail
this picture to
the wall.

Nagel; nageln

∞ fingernail

Fingernagel

name [neɪm]
  What's your
name?
∞ first name,
Christian name
∞ second name,
family name,
surname

Name
Wie heißt du?

Vorname

Nachname,
Familienname

narrow ['nærəʊ]
⇔ wide, broad
  a narrow river
a narrow street
☛ a small gate

schmal, eng

ein kleines Tor
(nicht „schmal"!)

nation ['neɪʃn]
∞ the United
Nations (UN)
⇨ national ['næʃənl]
∞ national park
∞ national anthem
['ænθəm]
⇨ nationality
[næʃə'nælɪtɪ]

Nation, Volk
die Vereinten
Nationen
national
Nationalpark
Nationalhymne

Staatsangehörig-
keit, Nationalität

nature ['neɪtʃə] — Natur
➪ natural ['neɪtʃrəl] — natürlich, Natur-
a natural flower — eine natürliche Blume

➪ naturally — natürlich
≈ of course
Are you looking forward to your holidays? – Naturally.

near [nɪə] — nahe; in die/der Nähe von
⇔ far (from)
✎ Place and direction
the near future — die nahe Zukunft
The post office is near the station. — Die Post ist in der Nähe des Bahnhofs.
Don't go near the fire. — Geh nicht in die Nähe des Feuers.
∞ near here — hier in der Nähe

nearly ['nɪəlɪ] — fast, beinahe
≈ almost
Is it still far to walk? – No, we're nearly there.

necessary ['nesəsrɪ] — notwendig, nötig
Shall we help you? – No, that's not necessary.

neck [nek] — Hals
✎ The human body
∞ necklace ['neklɪs] — (Hals)kette

need [ni:d] — brauchen
I need new boots. — Ich brauche neue Stiefel.
☞needn't — nicht müssen, nicht (zu tun) brauchen

☞mustn't — nicht dürfen
We needn't run, we've got lots of time. — Wir brauchen nicht zu rennen …
You mustn't run across the road without looking out for traffic. — Ihr dürft nicht über die Straße laufen, ohne auf den Verkehr zu achten.

needle [ni:dl] — Nadel
∞ knitting needle — Stricknadel
☞pin — Stecknadel

neighbour ['neɪbə] — Nachbar(in)
➪ neighbourhood ['neɪbəhʊd] — Nachbarschaft

neither ['naɪðə] — keine(r/s) von beiden; auch nicht
Neither of my two sisters can swim. — Keine meiner beiden Schwestern kann schwimmen.
I don't like coffee. – Neither do I. — Ich mag keinen Kaffee. – Ich auch nicht.
→ nor.

nerve [nɜ:v] — Nerv
➪ nervous ['nɜ:vəs] — nervös

net [net] — Netz
a fishing net — ein Fischernetz
∞ netball ✎ Sports and games — Netzball

never ['nevər] — nie; noch nie
⇔ often, always
✎ Expressions of time
I never lie. — Ich lüge nie.
I've never been to Paris. — Ich war noch nie in Paris.

new [nju:] — neu
∞ the New Year — das neue Jahr
Happy New Year! — Ein gutes neues Jahr!
∞ New Year's Day — Neujahrstag
∞ New Year's Eve — Silvester

news [nju:z] — Nachricht(en); Neuigkeit(en)
Be quiet! I'm listening to the news. — Seid still! Ich höre gerade die Nachrichten.
Bob told me some interesting news about Sally today. — Bob hat mir heute ein paar interessante Neuigkeiten … erzählt.

☞ Immer in der Einzahl:
The news begins at eight. — Die Nachrichten beginnen um acht.

☞ Nie mit *a*:
That's good news. — Das ist eine gute Nachricht.
∞ newspaper ['nju:zpeɪpə] — Zeitung
∞ news agency ['eɪdʒənsɪ] — Nachrichten-agentur

next [nekst] — nächste(r/s); als nächste(r/s)
We have to get out at the next stop. — Wir müssen an der nächsten Haltestelle aussteigen.

He came the next day.	Er kam am nächsten Tag.
☞ the <u>next few</u> days/weeks/months/…	die <u>nächsten</u> Tage/Wochen/Monate/…
What shall we do next?	Was sollen wir als nächstes tun?
∞ next door	nebenan
She lives next door.	
∞ next to ≈ beside	neben
✎ Place and direction	
the table next to the window	

nice [naɪs] — nett, schön, gut
Be nice to him. — Seid nett zu ihm.
The weather is nice. — Das Wetter ist schön.
That cake tastes nice. — Dieser Kuchen schmeckt gut.

night [naɪt] — Nacht, Abend
✎ Expressions of time
at night — nachts
Good night. — Gute Nacht.
∞ last night — heute (= vergangene) Nacht;
I slept very badly last night.
∞ tonight [təˈnaɪt] — heute (= kommende) nacht; heute abend

no [nəʊ] — nein; kein(e)
Would you like some more tea? – No, thanks. — Nein Danke.
no traffic — kein Verkehr
no buses — keine Busse
∞ no one/nobody [ˈnəʊbodɪ] — niemand
There's no one home.
∞ nothing [ˈnʌθɪŋ] — nichts
Have you got nothing to do?
∞ nowhere [ˈnəʊweə] — nirgends, nirgendwo(hin)
Tom is nowhere in the house.
⇨ none [nʌn] — keine(r/s)
How much money have you got? – None at all. — … – Überhaupt keines.
None of my friends could help me. — Keiner meiner Freunde konnte mir helfen.

noise [nɔɪz] — Lärm, Geräusch
Don't make so much noise. — Macht nicht solchen Lärm.
⇨ noisy — laut, lärmend, geräuschvoll
a noisy street/machine/child

non- [nɒn] — Nicht-
∞ non-smoker — Nichtraucher(in)
∞ non-stop — ohne Unterbrechung
a non-stop flight

none [nʌn] → no — keine(r/s)

nor [nɔː] ≈ neither — auch nicht
I can't play tennis. – Nor can I. — … – Ich auch nicht.

normal [ˈnɔːml] ≈ ordinary ⇔ special — normal

north [nɔːθ] — Norden; nördlich, Nord-; nach Norden
in the north of the USA — im Norden der USA
∞ north of — nördlich von
Scotland is north of England.
∞ the North Pole — der Nordpol
go north — nach Norden gehen
∞ north-east — (nach) Nordosten, nordöstlich
∞ north-west — (nach) Nordwesten, nordwestlich
⇨ northern — nördlich, Nord-
the northern part of the country

Norway [ˈnɔːweɪ] — Norwegen
✎ Countries
⇨ Norwegian [nɔːˈwiːdʒn] — norwegisch; Norwegisch; Norweger(in)

nose [nəʊz] — Nase
✎ The human body

not [nɒt] — nicht
Are you hungry? – Not really. — … – Nicht besonders.
☞ Die Kurzform *n't* wird an Hilfsverben angehängt:
It isn't (= is not) raining.
I don't (= do not) know.

∞ not at all → all überhaupt nicht
∞ not yet → yet noch nicht
∞ not ... either auch nicht
  → either

note [nəʊt] Notiz; (Musik-/
  Bank-)Note

  Jane has left a
  note for you.
∞ notebook Notizbuch
  ✎ My school bag
∞ a pound note eine Pfundnote

nothing [nʌθɪŋ] nichts
  → no

notice [ˈnəʊtɪs] bemerken; Notiz,
  Anzeige, Mitteilung

  Nobody noticed Niemand bemerk-
  the mistake. te den Fehler.
  Have you read Hast du diese
  that notice at the Mitteilung an der
  door? Tür gelesen?
∞ notice board Notizbrett

November November
[nəʊˈvembə]
✎ Months and seasons

now [naʊ] jetzt
✎ Expressions of time
∞ Bye for now. Tschüs für heute.
∞ now and then ab und zu
  Do you feel
  better now?

number [ˈnʌmbə] Zahl, Nummer
  2,000,000 is a 2.000.000 ist eine
  large number. große Zahl.
  room number 10 Zimmer Nr. 10
  (N° 10)
∞ telephone number Telefonnummer

nurse [nɜːs] ✎ Jobs Krankenschwester

nut [nʌt] ✎ Fruit Nuß

O [əʊ] is for

oak [əʊk] Eiche

ocean [ˈəʊʃn] ≈ sea Ozean
∞ the Atlantic der Atlantische
  Ocean Ozean

o'clock [əˈklɒk] Uhr (bei Uhrzeit-
✎ Expressions of time angaben)
  nine o'clock neun Uhr

of [ɒv; əv] von
  most of us die meisten von
  uns

the colour of the die Farbe des
dress Kleides
a cup of tea eine Tasse Tee
the first of April der erste April
∞ of course natürlich
  Could you help
  me, please? –
  Yes, of course.
∞ because of wegen
  The plane can't ... wegen des
  land because of Nebels ...
  the fog.

off [ɒf] ✎ Place and ab, weg (von)
direction
  The car came off Der Wagen kam
  the road. von der Straße ab.
  Off with you! Weg mit dir!/Hau
  ab!
∞ set off aufbrechen, losfahren
∞ take off starten; aus-
  ziehen, absetzen;
  wegnehmen
  (von), entfernen

  The plane has
  taken off.
  He took off his
  coat and his hat.
  She took the lid Sie nahm den
  off the pot and Deckel vom Topf
  looked in. ...
∞ We're off. Wir gehen jetzt.

offer [ˈɒfə] anbieten; Angebot
  They offered her
  $50,000 for that
  picture.
  a special offer

office [ˈɒfɪs] Büro
∞ office worker Büroangestell-
  ✎ Jobs te(r)
∞ post office Postamt
  ✎ In town
∞ lost property Fundbüro
  office
↪ officer ✎ Jobs Beamter, Beam-
  tin; Offizier
∞ (police) officer Polizeibeamter/
  -beamtin
∞ careers officer Berufsberater(in)
↪ official offiziell, amtlich

often [ˈɔːfn] oft
⇔ seldom, rarely
✎ Expressions of time
  How often have
  you been here?

oil [ɔɪl] Öl
∞ oil company Ölgesellschaft
∞ oil tanker Öltanker
➪ oily ölig

okay, OK [əʊˈkeɪ] in Ordnung
≈ alright

old [əʊld] ⇔ new, alt
young
    an old car
    How old are you?

on [ɒn] 1. auf, an, in
    The book is on ... auf deinem
    your desk. Schreibtisch.
    a town on the ... an der Küste
    coast
    I left my bag <u>on</u> ... <u>im</u> Bus/<u>im</u>
    the bus/<u>on</u> the Zug ...
    train.
∞ on the left/on the links/rechts
right
    on Sunday am Sonntag
∞ on time pünktlich
    We arrived on
    time.
∞ be on holiday Ferien machen
    on the phone am Telefon
    on the radio im Radio
    on television im Fernsehen

  2. weiter
    He walked on. Er ging weiter.
∞ pass s.th. on etw. weitergeben
∞ go on/keep on etw. weiter tun
    doing s.th.
    He didn't look
    up when we
    entered but went ..., sondern las
    on reading his weiter seine
    paper. Zeitung.
∞ Come on! Komm schon!
∞ and so on und so weiter

once [wʌns] einmal
    I have only been Ich war erst
    there once. einmal dort.
    once a week einmal pro
      Woche
∞ once more noch einmal
    She was a Sie war (früher)
    famous singer einmal eine
    once, but nobody berühmte Sän-
    knows her now. gerin, ...
∞ once upon a time vor langer Zeit
    Once upon a Es war einmal
    time there was a eine wunder-
    beautiful princess schöne Prinzes-
    ... sin ...

one [wʌn] eins; ein(e/r/s)
    number one
    one pound
    fifteen
    How many post-
    cards do you
    need? – Only
    one.
    He bought three ... einen blauen
    envelopes: a blue und zwei weiße.
    one and two
    white ones.
∞ one day → day eines Tages
∞ one another einander
    → another
∞ one-way street Einbahnstraße

onion [ˈʌnjən] Zwiebel
✎ Vegetables

only [ˈəʊnlɪ] nur; erst; einzige(r/s)
    It won't take Es dauert nicht
    long, only five lange, nur fünf
    minutes. Minuten.
    She is only Sie ist erst
    fifteen. fünfzehn.
    He has only just Er ist eben erst
    arrived. angekommen.
    You're my only Du bist meine
    hope. einzige Hoffnung.
    There were no
    other visitors. We ... Wir waren die
    were the only einzigen.
    ones.
∞ an only child ein Einzelkind

open [ˈəʊpn] aufmachen, (sich)
⇔ shut, ⇔ close/ öffnen; offen
closed
    Can I open the
    window, please?
    The door
    opened, and they
    went in.
➪ tin opener Dosenöffner
∞ opening hours Öffnungszeiten
    Are the shops Haben die Läden
    still open? noch offen?
∞ an open-air ein *Open-air-*
    festival *Festival*

operate [ˈɒpəreɪt] operieren; (ein
      Gerät) bedienen
    The doctors Die Ärzte be-
    decided to schlossen, <u>sie</u>
    operate <u>on her</u> at sofort zu
    once. operieren.
➪ operation Operation
    operate a com- einen Computer
    puter bedienen

⇨ operator
∞ computer oper-
ator
∞ (telephone) oper-
ator

Operateur(in)
Bildschirm-
arbeiter(in)
Telefonver-
mittlung

opposite ['ɒpəzɪt]
✎ Place and direction
The post office is
opposite the
station.
"Hot" is the op-
posite of "cold".

gegenüber; Gegen-
teil
Die Post ist
gegenüber dem
Bahnhof.
„Heiß" ist das
Gegenteil von
„kalt".

or [ɔ:]
Would you like
tea or coffee?
∞ either ... or
→ either

oder

entweder ... oder

orange ['ɒrɪndʒ]
✎ Fruit, ✎ Colours

Orange; orange(far-
ben)

order ['ɔ:də]

bestellen; Bestel-
lung; befehlen;
Befehl; Ordnung,
Reihenfolge

Who ordered the
fish and chips?
The waiter came
to take our order.

... um unsere
Bestellung ent-
gegenzunehmen.

The police or-
dered everybody
to leave the
building.
The soldiers had
to follow the the
general's orders.
Put these words
in the right order.

ordinary ['ɔ:dnrɪ]
≈ normal; ⇔ special
ordinary people

gewöhnlich, normal

organize ['ɔ:gənaɪz]

organisieren, veran-
stalten

Who is going to
organize the
festival?
⇨ organization

Organisation

other ['ʌðə]
They live on the
other side of the
town.
He doesn't care
about other
people.

andere(r/s)

∞ on the other
hand
∞ the other day
→ day
∞ the other way
round
∞ each other
→ each
⇨ others ≈ other
ones/people
Some of the cus-
tomers got angry,
others laughed.

andererseits

neulich

umgekehrt

einander

andere

our ['aʊə]
⇨ ourselves

We painted our
house ourselves.

unser(e)
uns (selbst); wir
selbst

out [aʊt]

Is Billy at home?
– No, he is out.
The fire has gone
out.
Let's go out into
the garden.
Please come out.
∞ out of

unterwegs; aus, hin-
aus, heraus
... – Nein, er ist
unterwegs.
Das Feuer ist
ausgegangen.

aus (heraus/hin-
aus); außer(halb
von)

come out of the
house
look out of the
window
be out of work
a model made
out of paper
∞ outside ⇔inside

arbeitslos sein
ein Modell aus
Papier
draußen; hinaus;
außerhalb von,
vor

The children were
playing outside.
Let's go outside.
We had to wait
outside the house.
∞ outdoor(s)
→ door
∞ outback

... vor dem
Haus ...
im Freien

australisches
Hinterland

oven ['ʌvn] ✎ Elec-
tricity in the household

Backofen

over ['əʊvə]
✎ Place and direction;
✎ Expressions of time
a bridge over a
river

über; herüber,
hinüber;
vorüber, vorbei

jump over a fence   ... hier herüber.
Come over here.   ... dort hin-
Let's go over   über ...
there.   ... vorbei.
The party is over.
∞ fall over   umfallen
∞ knock/push s.th.   etwas umstoßen
over
∞ all over the   überall im Land
country → all
∞ overnight   übernacht
→ night
∞ work overtime   Überstunden
['əʊvətaɪm]   machen
∞ overall   *Overall*
∞ overhead   *Overhead*pro-
projector   jektor

own [əʊn]   eigene(r/s); besitzen
That was my own   Das war meine
idea.   eigene Idee.
☛ Vor *own* steht
immer ein besitz-
anzeigendes Für-
wort (*my, your,
his,* usw.):
We have our own   Wir haben ein
room. *Oder:*   eigenes Zimmer.
We have a room
of our own.
∞ on one's own   allein

Father: Do you
need any help
with your home-
work?
Son: No, thank
you, Dad. I can
get it wrong on
my own.

Who owns this   Wem gehört
house?   dieses Haus?
⇨ owner   Besitzer(in)

ox [ɒks], **oxen**   Ochse, Ochsen
['ɒksn] ✎ Animals

P [pi:] is for

p [pi:] → penny,   britische Geldein-
pence   heit

pack [pæk]   packen
Have you packed   Hast du (deinen
(your suitcase)?   Koffer) gepackt?

packet ['pækɪt]   Packung, Päckchen
a packet of   eine Packung
biscuits   Kekse

a packet of   eine Schachtel
cigarettes.   Zigaretten

page [peɪdʒ]   (Buch-/Heft-/
   Zeitungs-)Seite
Continued on   Fortsetzung Seite
page 10.   10.
☛ the other <u>side</u> of   die andere
the road   Straßen<u>seite</u>

pain [peɪn] ≈ ache   Schmerz(en)
He was crying   Er schrie vor
with pain.   Schmerzen.

paint [peɪnt]   (an)malen, (an)strei-
   chen; Farbe (zum
   Streichen)
He painted the
door red.
a tin of paint   eine Dose Farbe

| Wet paint! | Vorsicht, frisch
   gestrichen!
∞ paintbrush   Pinsel
✎ Tools
☛ What <u>colour</u> are   Welche <u>Farbe</u> ha-
her eyes?   ben ihre Augen?
⇨ painter   Maler(in)
⇨ painting   Gemälde

pair [peə]   Paar
a pair of jeans   ein Paar Jeans
two pairs of   zwei (Paar) Hosen
trousers

palace ['pælɪs]   Palast
∞ Buckingham
Palace

pan [pæn]   Pfanne; Topf mit
   Stiel
∞ pancake ✎ Food   Pfannkuchen

paper   Papier; Zeitung
a sheet of paper   ein Blatt Papier
∞ paperback   Taschenbuch,
   Paperback
Have you read
the (news)paper?
∞ paperboy   Zeitungsjunge

paradise ['pærədaɪz]   Paradies
<u>in</u> paradise   <u>im</u> Paradies

parcel ['pɑ:sl]   Paket
send a parcel by
post

pardon ['pɑ:dn]   Verzeihung
I beg your   Verzeihen Sie
pardon.   bitte.
(I beg your)   Wie bitte?
pardon?

parents ['pærənts] Eltern
✎ Relatives

park [pɑːk] parken; Park

> **Do not park
> in front of
> the gates.**

| No parking | Parken verboten

∞ car park Parkplatz
  ✎ In town
∞ national park Nationalpark
∞ caravan park Campingplatz für
  Wohnwagen

parliament Parlament
['pɑːləmənt]
∞ Member of Abgeordnete(r)
  Parliament des britischen
  (MP [emˈpiː]) Unterhauses

parrot ['pærət] Papagei
✎ Animals

part [pɑːt] Teil
  the parts of a die Teile einer
  machine Maschine
  Only part of the Nur ein Teil der
  story is true. Geschichte ist
  wahr.
∞ take part <u>in</u> s.th. <u>an</u> etw. teilnehmen
∞ be part of s.th. ein Teil von etw.
  sein, zu etwas
  gehören

  You're part of the
  family now.
∞ a part-time job eine Teilzeit-
  beschäftigung

partner ['pɑːtnə] Partner(in)

party ['pɑːtɪ] *Party*, Fest, Feier
∞ birthday party

pass [pɑːs] vorbeigehen/-kom-
  men (an); über-
  holen; (Prüfung)
  bestehen

  The days passed
  quickly.
  He waited for an
  hour, but no taxi
  passed.
  We passed some
  shops on our
  way.
  The car passed
  the bus at high
  speed.

Did your sister
pass her exam?
∞ pass s.o. or s.th. an jdm. oder etw.
  by vorübergehen
∞ pass s.th. on etw. weitergeben

passenger Passagier, Fahr-/
['pæsɪndʒə] Fluggast

passport ['pɑːspɔːt] Reisepaß
∞ passport control Paßkontrolle

past [pɑːst] nach; vorbei (an);
✎ Expressions of time vergangene(r/s);
✎ Place and direction Vergangenheit
  quarter past ten Viertel nach zehn
  half past three halb vier
  He walked past Er ging schnell
  (the house) (am Haus) vorbei.
  quickly.
  I've been work- Ich habe in den
  ing hard for the vergangenen Wo-
  past few weeks. chen hart ge-
  arbeitet.
  Forget the past Vergiß die Ver-
  and think of the gangenheit und
  future. denke an die
  Zukunft.
∞ past tense Vergangen-
  heit(sform)

path [pɑːθ] Pfad, Fußweg

patient ['peɪʃnt] Patient(in);
  geduldig
  There were a lot
  of patients in the
  doctor's waiting-
  room.
  Thank you for
  being so patient
  with me.
⇨ patience Geduld

pay [peɪ], **paid** (be)zahlen
  [peɪd], **paid**
  She paid £12 for
  that CD.
  They pay the Sie zahlen den
  workers £10 an Arbeitern £10
  hour. pro Stunde.
∞ pay <u>for</u> s.th. etw. (das man
  kauft) bezahlen
  Have you paid Hast du dein
  <u>for</u> your meal Essen schon
  yet? bezahlt?

pea [piː] Erbse
✎ Vegetables

peace [piːs] ⇔ war Friede
⇨ peaceful friedlich, ruhig

peach [piːtʃ] ✎ Fruit   Pfirsich

pear [peə] ✎ Fruit   Birne

pedestrian
[pɪ'destrɪən]
∞ pedestrian area   Fußgängerzone
∞ pedestrian cross-   Fußgängerüber-
   ing ✎ In town   weg

pen [pen]   Füller, Füllfeder-
✎ My school bag   halter
∞ pen-friend   Brieffreund(in)

pence → penny

pencil ['pensl]   Bleistift
✎ My school bag
∞ pencil case   Federmäppchen

penny ['penɪ],   Penny, Pence
pence   (= 1/100 Pfund)
   one penny
   (1p [piː])
   ten pence (10 p)

people [piːpl]   Leute; Volk
≈ persons; nation

✎ People

There weren't
many people at
the meeting.
The Chinese are
a people with a
long history.

pepper ['pepə]   Pfeffer; Papri-
✎ Food; ✎ Vegetables   ka(schote)
   pepper and salt
   two green peppers

per [pɜː]   pro; je
   50 miles per hour   50 Meilen pro
   (50 mph   Stunde
   ['empiː'eɪtʃ])
∞ per cent [pə'sent]   Prozent
   10 per cent (10%)

percussion [pə'kʌʃn]   Schlagzeug
✎ Musical instruments
▷ percussionist   Schlagzeuger(in)

perfect ['pɜːfɪkt]   perfekt, vollkommen
∞ Practice makes   Übung macht
   perfect.   den Meister.

perform [pə'fɔːm]   (vor Publikum) auftreten, aufführen
   The band per-
   formed in 20
   European cities.
   Our theatre
   group is perform-
   ing a play on
   Friday night.
▷ performance   Aufführung, Auftritt

perhaps [pə'hæps]   vielleicht
≈ maybe
   Perhaps she's   Vielleicht hat sie
   right.   recht.

period (of time)   Zeitabschnitt, Zeit-
['pɪərɪəd]   spanne

person ['pɜːsn]   Person
▷ personal ['pɜːsnl]   persönlich
   a very personal
   letter

pet [pet] ✎ Animals   Haustier

petrol ['petrəl] *(BE)*   Benzin
≈ gas *(AE)*
∞ petrol station   Tankstelle

phone [fəʊn]   Telefon; anrufen
≈ telephone
∞ on the phone   am Telefon
∞ phone call   Anruf
   He phoned his
   friend.

photo ['fəʊtəʊ]   Foto
∞ take a photo   ein Foto machen
▷ photographer   Fotograf(in)
   [fə'tɒgrəfə]

physics ['fɪzɪks]   Physik
✎ School subjects
▷ physical ['fɪzɪkl]   physikalisch;
   körperlich
∞ physical educa-   Sportunterricht
   tion

piano [pɪ'ænəʊ]   Klavier
✎ Musical instruments

pick [pɪk]   pflücken
   pick flowers
∞ pick up   aufheben;
   abholen
   He picked up all
   the pieces of
   broken glass.
   I'll pick you up at
   the hotel at seven.
▷ pick-up (truck)   Kleinlastwagen

picnic ['pɪknɪk]   Picknick; picknicken

picture ['pɪktə]   Bild
∞ picture book   Bilderbuch

pie [paɪ] ✎ Food   Pastete
∞ steak and kidney   Fleischpastete
   pie   mit Nieren

piece [pi:s]   Stück
   a piece of cake   ein Stück Kuchen
∞ fall to pieces   zerfallen

pig [pɪg] ✎ Animals   Schwein

pill [pɪl] ≈ tablet   Pille

pillow ['pɪləʊ]   Kopfkissen

pilot ['paɪlət] ✎ Jobs   Pilot(in)
∞ helicopter pilot   Hubschrauber-
     pilot(in)

pin [pɪn]   Stecknadel, Stift

pink [pɪŋk]   rosa, pink
✎ Colours

pint [paɪnt]   Maßeinheit für
BE: 0.568 litre   Flüssigkeiten
AE: 0.473 litre

pipe [paɪp]   (Tabaks)pfeife;
     Rohr, Leitung
   smoke a pipe   Pfeife rauchen
   water pipe   Wasserrohr
∞ bagpipe ✎ Musi-   Dudelsack
   cal instruments
∞ pipeline   *Pipeline*, Rohr-
     leitung

pity ['pɪtɪ]   Mitleid; bedauern,
     bemitleiden
∞ What a pity!   Wie schade!
∞ It's a pity (that) …   Es ist schade,
     daß …
➪ pitiful   bedauernswert

place [pleɪs]   Ort, Stelle

✎ **Place and direction**

This is the place
where the acci-
dent happened.
∞ take place   stattfinden
☛ take a <u>seat</u>   <u>Platz</u> nehmen

plan [plæn]   Plan; planen
   What are your
   plans for the
   future?
∞ street plan   Straßenplan
   She is planning
   to go to America.

plane [pleɪn] ≈ aero-   Flugzeug
plane, airplane
✎ Transport

plant [plɑ:nt]   Pflanze; pflanzen
   Plants need light.
   We have planted
   an apple tree in
   our garden.

plaster ['plɑ:stə]   (Verbands-)Pflaster
✎ Danger and acci-
dents

plastic ['plæstɪk]   Plastik
   a plastic cup   eine Plastiktasse

plate [pleɪt]   Teller
✎ Laying the table

platform ['plætfɔ:m]   Bahnsteig
   The train to
   Manchester
   leaves from
   platform 6.

play [pleɪ]   spielen; Theater-
     stück
   play football   Fußball spielen
   play the guitar   Gitarre spielen
   play cards   Karten spielen
☛ play s.o.   <u>gegen</u> jdn. spielen
   Becker is playing   Becker spielt
   McEnroe.   gegen McEnroe.
➪ (tennis) player   (Tennis)spieler(in)
∞ playing fields   Sportplatz
∞ playground   Spielplatz
   do/perform a play   ein Stück
     aufführen

please [pli:z]   bitte
   Can I have some
   tea, please?
☛ Could you hand   Könntest du mir
   me the sugar,   bitte den Zucker
   please? – <u>Here</u>   reichen? – <u>Bitte-</u>
   <u>you are.</u>   <u>schön.</u>
➪ pleased   erfreut, zufrieden
   She was very   Sie freute sich
   pleased with the   sehr über das
   present.   Geschenk.
∞ Pleased to meet   Erfreut, Sie ken-
   you!   nenzulernen.

plenty (of) [ˈplentɪ]
≈ a lot/lots (of)
  There's plenty to
  eat and drink in
  the fridge.
  We've got plenty
  of time.

viel, eine Menge,
reichlich

pliers [ˈplaɪəz]
✎ Tools
☛ a pair of pliers

Zange

      eine Zange

plug [plʌg] ✎ Elec-
tricity in the household

Stecker

plum [plʌm] ✎ Fruit

Pflaume

plumber [ˈplʌmə]
✎ Jobs

Installateur(in),
Klempner(in)

3 pm [piːˈem] → am
✎ Expressions of time
  It's 7 pm.

3 Uhr nachmittags

    Es ist 7 Uhr
    abends.

  at 11 pm

    um 11 Uhr nachts

pocket [ˈpɒkɪt]
✎ Clothes
  He put his hands
  in his pockets.

Tasche (in Klei-
dungsstücken)

∞ pocket knife
∞ pocket money

Taschenmesser
Taschengeld

poem [ˈpəʊɪm]
⇨ poetry

Gedicht
Dichtung,
Gedichte

⇨ poet [ˈpəʊɪt]

Dichter(in)

point

Punkt; zeigen,
deuten

  I won the game
  with 55 points.

Ich gewann das
Spiel mit 55
Punkten.

∞ meeting point
☛ 4.5 cm (four
  point five
  centimetres)
☛ Der Punkt am
  Ende eines
  Satzes heiß *full
  stop*.

Treffpunkt
4,5 cm (vier
Komma fünf
Zentimeter)

poison [ˈpɔɪzn]
⇨ poisonous
[ˈpɔɪzənəs]

Gift
giftig

Poland [ˈpəʊlənd]
✎ Countries
⇨ Polish

Polen

polnisch;
Polnisch

⇨ Pole
∞ the Poles/the
  Polish

Pole, Polin
die Polen

police [pəˈliːs]
☛ Das Verb steht
  nach *police* in
  der Mehrzahl:
  The police <u>have</u>
  caught the
  thieves.

Polizei

Die Polizei <u>hat</u>
die Diebe gefaßt.

∞ police car
∞ policeman,
  policewoman
∞ police officer
  ✎ Jobs
∞ police station
  (*BE*), police
  department (*AE*)

Polizeiauto
Polizist,
Polizistin
Polizeibeamter/
-beamtin
Polizeiwache

politics [ˈpɒlɪtɪks]
⇨ politician
  [ˈpɒlɪtɪʃn]

Politik
Politiker(in)

pollution [pəˈluːʃn]

∞ water pollution

(Umwelt-)ver-
schmutzung
Wasserver-
schmutzung

⇨ pollute [pəˈluːt]
  Don't swim in
  that river. It is
  polluted.

verschmutzen

pond [pɒnd]

Teich

pool [puːl]
∞ swimming pool

(Schwimm-)Becken
Schwimmbad

poor [puːl] ⇔ rich
  His parents are
  too poor to buy
  him a bike.
  You've missed
  the bus? Poor
  thing!

arm

… Du Ärmste!

pop (music) [pɒp]
∞ a pop concert
∞ a pop group

Pop(musik)
ein Popkonzert
eine Popgruppe

popular [ˈpɒpjʊlə]

  a popular film
  star
  a popular sport

beliebt, weitver-
breitet

pork [pɔːk] ✎ Food
∞ pork chop

Schweinefleisch
Schweinekotelett

Portugal [ˈpɔːtjʊgəl]
✎ Countries
⇨ Portuguese
  [ˈpɔːtjʊgiːz]

Portugal

portugiesisch;
Portugiesisch;
Portugiese,
Portugiesin

∞ the Portuguese

die Portugiesen

possible ['pɒsɪbl] möglich
⇔ impossible
Is it possible to
get to the airport
in 20 minutes?
Come as soon as Komm so bald
possible. wie möglich.

post [pəʊst] → mail Post; (Brief) einwerfen, abschicken
I'll send you the
parcel by post. ... mit der Post ...
∞ post office Postamt
∞ postbox Briefkasten
∞ postman, Briefträger,
postwoman Briefträgerin
✎ Jobs
∞ postcard Postkarte
Can you post this Kannst du diesen
letter for me? Brief für mich
einwerfen?

poster [pəʊstə] *Poster*, Plakat

potato [pə'teɪtəʊ], Kartoffel, Kartoffeln
potatoes
✎ Vegetables

pot [pɒt] Topf; Kanne
∞ flowerpot Blumentopf
∞ teapot Teekanne
a pot of tea eine Kanne Tee

pound [paʊnd] Pfund (Gewichts-
und Geldeinheit)
Two pounds
(2 lb) of pears,
please.
How much is it?
– Two pounds
(£2).
∞ a pound note eine Pfundnote

powder ['paʊdə] Puder; Pulver
∞ baking powder Backpulver
∞ washing powder Waschpulver

power ['paʊə] Macht, Kraft,
Energie
The Church had
a lot of power in
the past.
∞ power station Kraftwerk
∞ (electric) power Strom
∞ power cut Stromausfall
⇨ powerful stark, kräftig
a powerful engine ein starker Motor

practical ['præktɪkl] praktisch
Tea bags are very
practical.

practice ['præktɪs] Training, Übung
I can't type very
well yet. I need
more practice.
∞ football practice Fußballtraining
⇨ practise ['præktɪs] üben, trainieren
You'll never learn
to ride a motor-
bike if you don't
practise.

pray [preɪ] beten
⇨ prayer [preə] Gebet

prefer [prɪ'fɜ] vorziehen, lieber
≈ like better mögen
Would you like
meat or fish? –
I'd prefer meat.

prepare [prɪ'peə] zubereiten; (sich)
vorbereiten
prepare a meal
prepare a trip
prepare for an sich auf eine Prü-
exam fung vorbereiten

prescription (ärztliches) Rezept
[prɪ'skrɪpʃn]
☞ recipe ['resɪpɪ] Kochrezept

present ['preznt] Geschenk
a birthday present

president Präsident(in)
['prezɪdənt]

press [pres] drücken
press a button

| Press to start |

pretty ['prɪtɪ] hübsch
⇔ ugly
a pretty girl

price [praɪs] (Kauf-)Preis
I bought this
poster at the ... zum Preis von
price of £2. £2 ...
☞ win a prize einen Preis
[praɪz] gewinnen

prince [prɪns] Prinz
Prince Charles is
the Prince of
Wales.
⇨ princess Prinzessin

prison ['prɪzn] Gefängnis
be in prison im Gefängnis
sitzen
⇨ prisoner Gefangene(r)

private ['praɪvət]   privat, Privat-
⇔ public
   a private car   ein Privatwagen

prize [praɪz]   Preis (den man
→ price   gewinnt)
   He won the first
   prize.

probably ['prɒbəblɪ]   wahrscheinlich
   You probably
   know that song.

problem ['prɒbləm]   Problem
   That's no
   problem.

produce [prə'djuːs]   produzieren, her-
≈ make   stellen
   This factory
   produces shoes.
⇨ producer   Hersteller(in),
     Produzent(in);
     Regisseur(in)
⇨ product   Produkt, Erzeug-
   ['prɒdʌkt]   nis
⇨ production   Produktion,
   [prə'dʌkʃn]   Herstellung

programme   Programm;
['prəʊgræm]   Sendung
∞ a theatre   ein Theater-
   programme   programm
∞ a radio   eine Radio-
   programme   sendung

progress ['prəʊgres]   Fortschritt(e)
   make (good)   (gute) Fort-
   progress   schritte machen
∞ be in progress   gerade geschehen,
     im Gange sein
   You can't go in.   … Es findet gera-
   There's a meeting   de eine Sitzung
   in progress.   statt.

project ['prɒdʒekt]   Projekt, Vorhaben

promise ['prɒmɪs]   (etw.) versprechen;
     (das) Versprechen

   She has prom-
   ised to come.
   If you make a
   promise, you
   must keep it.

proper ['prɒpə],   richtig, wie es sich
properly   gehört
   That's not a   Das ist kein rich-
   proper dog. It   tiger Hund. Er
   can't even bark   kann noch nicht
   properly!   einmal richtig
     bellen!

proud [praʊd]   stolz
   She's very proud   Sie ist sehr stolz
   <u>of</u> her new   <u>auf</u> ihr neues
   moped.   Moped.

pub [pʌb] ✎ In town   Wirtschaft, Kneipe,
     Pub

public ⇔ private   öffentlich; Öffent-
     lichkeit
   a public building   … ein öffentli-
     ches Gebäude
   The park is open   … der Öffentlich-
   to the public.   keit zugänglich.
⇨ publish   veröffentlichen

pudding ['pʊdɪŋ]   Pudding; Nach-
✎ Food   speise

pull [pʊl] ⇔ push   ziehen
   They tried to pull
   the car out of the
   river with a
   tractor.

pullover ['pʊləʊvə]   Pullover
✎ Clothes

pump [pʌmp]   Pumpe; pumpen
∞ pump up a type   einen Reifen
     aufpumpen

pupil ['pjuːpl]   Schüler(in)
   the pupils of the
   local comprehen-
   sive

purse [pɜːs]   Geldbeutel *(BE)*;
     Handtasche *(AE)*

push [pʊʃ] ⇔ pull   schieben, stoßen
   Can you help us
   to push the car?
   He pushed the
   door open.
∞ push s.th. over   etw. umstoßen

put [pʊt], **put, put**   stellen, setzen,
     legen
   Put the plates on
   the table, please.
Son: Dad, where
are the Baha-
mas?
Father: Ask your
mother. She al-
ways puts every-
thing away.

∞ put on (a jacket)   (eine Jacke) an-
     ziehen
∞ put on (make-up)   (Makeup) auf-
     tragen

∞ put (the potatoes) on	(die Kartoffeln) aufsetzen
∞ put up an umbrella	einen Schirm aufspannen
∞ put up (a lamp)	(eine Lampe) anbringen
∞ put (a house) up for sale	(ein Haus) zum Verkauf anbieten
∞ put out (the light)	(das Licht) ausmachen
∞ put s.o. through (on the phone)	jdn (am Telefon) durchstellen

puzzle ['pʌzl] Rätsel
∞ crossword puzzle Kreuzworträtsel
☛ jigsaw (puzzle) *Puzzle*(spiel)
['dʒɪgsɔ:]

pyjamas [pə'dʒɑ:- Schlafanzug
məz] ✎ Clothes
☛ a pair of pyjamas ein Schlafanzug

Q [kju:] is for

quality ['kwɒlɪtɪ] Qualität; Eigenschaft
This material is Dieses Material
(of) good quality. ist von guter
 Qualität.
Everybody has Jeder hat gute
good and bad und schlechte
qualities. Eigenschaften.
⇨ qualify sich qualifizieren,
 die nötige Befähigung erwerben
He is not quali- Er ist nicht für
fied for this job. diese Arbeit
 geeignet.
⇨ qualification Qualifikation,
 Befähigung

quarter ['kwɔ:tə] Viertel
a quarter of an eine Viertel-
hour stunde
quarter to/past Viertel vor/nach
three ✎ Express- drei
ions of time

queen [kwi:n] Königin
→ king
Queen Elizabeth
II (= the Second)
of England

question ['kwestʃn] Frage
∞ ask (s.o.) a (jdm.) eine Frage
question stellen

quick [kwɪk] schnell, rasch
⇔ slow
a quick worker

a quick look
Be quick!
We have to Wir müssen uns
decide quickly. schnell entschließen.

quiet ['kwaɪət] still, ruhig, leise
Be quiet, please.
a quiet life
talk in a quiet mit leiser Stimme
voice sprechen

quite [kwaɪt] ganz, ziemlich
You're quite right. Du hast ganz
 Recht.
He plays quite Er spielt ganz gut.
well.
He's quite a good Er ist ein ganz
player. guter Spieler.
I got quite a Ich bekam einen
shock when I ziemlichen
heard it. Schock …

R [ɑ:] is for

rabbit ['ræbɪt] Kaninchen
✎ Animals

race [reɪs] Rennen; rasen;
 Rasse
∞ a car race ein Autorennen
We watched the Wir beobachteten,
cars racing by. wie die Autos
 vorbeirasten.
∞ a racing car ein Rennwagen
∞ a racing driver ein(e) Renn-
 fahrer(in)
people of differ- Menschen unter-
ent races schiedlicher
 Rasse

racket ['rækɪt] (Tennis-, Federball-)
 Schläger
∞ tennis racket

radar ['reɪdɑ:] Radar(gerät)

radio ['reɪdɪəʊ] Radio; Funk
✎ Entertainment
electronics
listen to the radio Radio hören
hear s.th. on the etw. im Radio
radio hören
The policemen Die Polizisten
are talking to unterhalten sich
each other by über Funk.
radio.
∞ a radio-con- ein funkgesteuer-
trolled car ter Wagen
∞ a radio telephone ein Funktelefon

railway ['reɪlweɪ]   Eisenbahn
(BE) ≈ **railroad**
['reɪlrəʊd] *(AE)*
∞ (railway) station   Bahnhof

rain [reɪn]   regnen; Regen
✎ The weather
  It's raining.   Es regnet.
  It looks like rain.   Es sieht nach
      Regen aus.
∞ raincoat   Regenmantel
  ✎ Clothes
➪ rainy   regnerisch

rare [reə]; **rarely**   selten
['reəlɪ] ≈ seldom
  a rare flower
  I rarely see him.

rather ['rɑːðə]   ziemlich; lieber
  It's rather cold in   … ziemlich
  here.   kalt …
  I'd rather stay   Ich würde lieber
  here.   hierbleiben.

reach [riːtʃ]   erreichen
  He started at 8
  am and reached
  Exeter 3 pm.

read [riːd], **read**   lesen
[red], **read** [red]
  Have you read
  this article?
➪ reader ['riːdə]   Leser(in)

ready ['redɪ]   fertig
  Is breakfast
  ready?

real [rɪəl], **really**   richtig; wirklich
['rɪəlɪ]
  That was a real   … eine wirkliche
  surprise.   Überraschung.
  I was really   … wirklich
  surprised.   überrascht.
  Did that really   Ist das wirklich
  happen?   passiert?

reason ['riːzn]   Grund, Begründung
  There's no reason   Es gibt keinen
  to worry.   Grund, sich Sor-
      gen zu machen.
  Can you give   Kannst du Grün-
  reasons for your   de für deine Ent-
  decision?   scheidung an-
      geben?

receive [rɪˈsiːv]   erhalten, empfangen
  Did you receive   Hast du meine
  my message?   Nachricht er-
      halten?

➪ receiver   Empfänger(in);
      (Radio-)Emp-
      fänger;
      (Telefon-)Hörer
➪ reception   Empfang

recipe ['resɪpɪ]   (Koch-)Rezept
→ prescription

record ['rekɔːd]   Rekord; Schallplatte
∞ the world record
∞ a long-playing
  record (an LP)
➪ record [rɪˈkɔːd]   (auf Band) auf-
      nehmen
➪ recorder [rɪˈkɔːdə]   Recorder, Auf-
  ✎ Entertainment   zeichnungsgerät
  electronics
∞ cassette recorder   Kassettenrecorder

red [red] ✎ Colours   rot

regular ['regjʊlə]   regelmäßig
⇔ irregular
∞ regular verbs   regelmäßige
      Verben

relative ['relətɪv]   Verwandte(r)

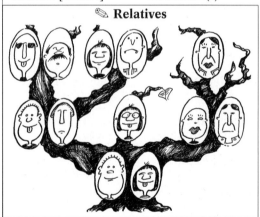

✎ **Relatives**

  She's a close/   Sie ist eine enge/
  near/distant   nahe/entfernte
  relative.   Verwandte.
➪ be related (to   (mit jdm.) ver-
  s.o.)   wandt sein

religion [rɪˈlɪdʒn]   Religion
➪ religious [rɪˈlɪdʒəs]   religiös,
      Religions-
∞ religious educa-   Religion(sunter-
  tion (R.E. [ɑːˈriː])   richt)

remain [rɪˈmeɪn]   bleiben; übrig-
      bleiben
  She remained   Sie blieb im Auto
  sitting in the car.   sitzen.

remember [rɪˈmembə]	sich erinnern
remember s.o./s.th.	sich an jdn./etw. erinnern
I can't remember the name of the town.	
☞ remind s.o. (of s.th.)	jdn. (an etw.) erinnern
This song reminds me of my holiday in Italy.	
Please remind me to post that letter.	
remote control [rɪˈməʊt kənˈtrəʊl] ✎ Entertainment electronics	Fernbedienung, Fernsteuerung
remove [rɪˈmuːv]	entfernen, wegschaffen
Please remove your things from my desk.	
rent [rent]	mieten; Miete
rent a car	einen Wagen mieten
How much is the rent for this flat?	Wie teuer ist die Miete für diese Wohnung?
repair [rɪˈpeə]	reparieren; Reparatur
Can you repair this watch?	
How much will the repairs be?	
∞ repair kit	Flickzeug, Reparaturausrüstung
repeat [rɪˈpiːt]	wiederholen
Could you repeat the last sentence, please?	
report [rɪˈpɔːt]	berichten, (sich) melden; Bericht
∞ report on s.th.	über etw. berichten
They are reporting on the tennis championships on TV.	
∞ report s.th. (to s.o.)	etw. (bei jdm.) melden
Has anybody reported the accident to the police yet?	
∞ report to s.o.	sich bei jdm. melden
Please report to the headmaster this afternoon.	
write a report	einen Bericht schreiben
∞ school report	Schulzeugnis
➪ reporter ✎ Jobs	Reporter(in)
rescue [ˈreskjuː] ≈ save	retten; Rettung
The drowning girl was rescued by a fisherman.	
∞ a rescue team	eine Rettungsmannschaft
rest [rest]	Rest; Pause, Rast; rasten, ruhen
I've just spent the rest of my pocket-money.	
Let's stop here for a rest.	
Let's rest under that tree for a while.	
restaurant [ˈrestrɒnt] ✎ In town	Restaurant
return [rɪˈtɜːn] ≈ come/go back	zurückkehren
After living in the USA for ten years she returned to England.	
rice [raɪs] ✎ Food	Reis
rich [rɪtʃ] ⇔ poor	reich
a rich family	
ride [raɪd], **rode** [rəʊd], **ridden** [ˈrɪdn]	reiten; fahren; Ritt; Fahrt
ride a horse	ein Pferd reiten
go riding	reiten gehen
ride a bike	radfahren
ride a motorcycle	Motorrad fahren
ride in a car/on a bus/in a train	in einem Auto/ Bus/Zug (mit-) fahren
∞ go for a ride	reiten gehen; eine Fahrt machen
go for a bike ride	mit dem Rad spazierenfahren
∞ give s.o. a ride (in a car)	jdn. (im Auto) mitnehmen

right [raɪt] ⇔ left

1. rechte(r/s), nach rechts

She wore a ring on her right hand.

Turn right. ... an der rechten Hand. Biegen Sie nach rechts ein.

∞ on the right — rechts
✎ Place and direction
The café is on the right when you cross the bridge.
Drive along Park Street and you'll see the hospital on your right. ... rechts von Ihnen.

⇔ wrong
Is this the right size? — ... die richtige Größe?
That's right. — Das stimmt./Das ist richtig.

2. richtig

∞ be right — recht haben
You're quite right. — Du hast ganz recht.
∞ alright/all right — in Ordnung, gut
→ all

3. direkt, genau, unmittelbar

There's the church, right in front of you.
right at the beginning — gleich am Anfang
I'll be right back. — Ich bin gleich zurück.

4. Recht

fight for one's rights — um seine Rechte kämpfen
have a/the right to do s.th. — das Recht haben, etw. zu tun

ring [rɪŋ], **rang** [ræŋ], **rang** — läuten; anrufen; Anruf; Ring
The telephone is ringing.
Peter rang about an hour ago. — ... hat ... angerufen.
∞ give s.o. a ring — jdn. anrufen
a gold ring — ein goldener Ring

ripe [raɪp] — reif
a field of ripe corn

river ['rɪvə] — Fluß
∞ the (River) Thames — die Themse

∞ the Mississippi (River) — der Mississippi

road [rəʊd] — (Land-)Straße
☛ street — Straße (innerhalb einer Ortschaft)
∞ down the road — die Straße herunter/hinunter
∞ up the road — die Straße herauf/hinauf
∞ road worker — Straßenarbeiter(in)
✎ Jobs

roast [rəʊst] — Braten; braten; gebraten
roast beef ✎ Food — Rinderbraten

robot ['rəʊbɒt] — Roboter

rock [rɒk] — Felsen, Stein; Rock(musik)
⇨ rocky — felsig
∞ the Rocky Mountains — (Gebirge in Nordamerika)
∞ a rock concert — ein Rockkonzert
∞ Rock 'n Roll (Rock and Roll)

rocket ['rɒkɪt] — Rakete
✎ Transport

roll [rəʊl] — rollen; Rolle; Brötchen
The ball rolled under the car.
a roll of toilet paper ✎ In the bathroom — eine Rolle Toilettenpapier
∞ a cheese/ham/sausage roll ✎ Food — eine Käse-/Schinken/Wurstbrötchen
⇨ roller — Rolle, Walze
∞ roller-skates — Rollschuhe
∞ roller-skating ✎ Sports and games — Rollschuhlaufen

roof [ru:f] — Dach
✎ House and flat

room [ru:m] — Zimmer; Platz
✎ House and flat
∞ bedroom — Schlafzimmer
There isn't enough room for my clothes in the wardrobe. — Im Schrank ist nicht genügend Platz für meine Kleider.

rough [rʌf] — rauh, uneben
⇔ smooth
rough hands
a rough road

round [raʊnd]
✎ Place and direction
a round table
They were sitting
round the table.

The car dis-
appeared round
the corner.
∞ look round
∞ show s.o. round
∞ turn round
∞ the other way
round
play a round (of
cards, golf, etc.)

rubber ['rʌbə]
rubber boots
(india) rubber
✎ My school bag

rugby [rʌgbɪ]
✎ Sports and games

rule [ru:l]
Can you explain
the rules of this
game?

ruler ['ru:lə]
✎ My school bag

run [rʌn], **ran** [ræn],
run [rʌn]
The dog has run
away.
This car runs on
solar cells.
Who runs this
business?
a 1,000 m run
⇨ runner

Russia ['rʌʃə]
✎ Countries
⇨ Russian

rund; um, herum;
Runde
ein runder Tisch
Sie saßen um
den Tisch
(herum).
Der Wagen ver-
schwand um die
Ecke.
sich umschauen
jdn. herumführen
(sich) umdrehen
anders herum

eine Runde
(Karten, Golf
usw.) spielen

Gummi
Gummistiefel
Radiergummi

Rugby

Regel, Spielregel

Lineal

laufen, rennen;
führen, leiten; Lauf
Der Hund ist
weggelaufen.
… läuft mit Hilfe
von Solarzellen.
Wer leitet dieses
Geschäft?
ein 1000-m-Lauf
Läufer(in)

Rußland

russisch; Rus-
sisch; Russe,
Russin

S [ɛs] is for

sack [sæk]

sad [sæd] ⇔ happy

safe [seɪf]

Be careful! This
ladder is not safe.

Sack

traurig

sicher, ungefährlich;
Safe, Panzerschrank

You should leave
your money in
the hotel safe.
⇨ safety
∞ safety belt
⇨ save [seɪv]

sail [seɪl]
⇨ sailing ✎ Sports
and games
go sailing
∞ sailing boat
⇨ sailor ✎ Jobs
a white sail

salad ['sæləd]
✎ Food
∞ salad dressing
∞ fruit salad
∞ ham salad

☛ lettuce

sale [seɪl]

∞ | **For sale** |

salt [sɔ:lt] ✎ Food

the **same** [seɪm]

Pam goes to the
same school as
her brother.
These rooms all
look the same.

sand [sænd]

sandwich
['sændwɪtʃ] ✎ Food

satellite ['sætəlaɪt]
∞ satellite dish
✎ Entertainment
electronics

Saturday ['sætədɪ]
✎ Days of the week

sauce [sɔ:s] ✎ Food
∞ saucepan
['sɔ:spæn]

saucer ['sɔ:sə]
✎ Laying the table

sausage ['sɒsɪdʒ]
✎ Food
Do you like
sausage?

Sicherheit
Sicherheitsgurt
retten; sparen

segeln; Segel
Segeln

Segeln gehen
Segelboot
Seemann
ein weißes Segel

Salat(gericht)

Salatsoße
Obstsalat
Salat mit
Schinken
Kopfsalat
(Pflanze)

Verkauf; Schlußver-
kauf, Ausverkauf

zu verkaufen

Salz

der-/die-/dasselbe,
gleich
Pam geht zur
selben Schule
wie Ihr Bruder.
… sehen alle
gleich aus.

Sand

Sandwich

Satellit
Satellitenanten-
ne/-schüssel

Samstag, Sonnabend

Soße
Kochtopf (mit
Stiel)

Untertasse

Wurst, Würstchen

Magst du Wurst?

There are two sausages left.	Es sind zwei Würstchen übrig.
save [seɪv]	retten; sparen
save s.o.'s life	jdm. das Leben retten
save money	Geld sparen
⇨ **safe** [seɪf]	sicher
⇨ **savings**	Ersparnisse
∞ savings account	Sparkonto
saw [sɔ:] ✎ Tools	Säge; sägen
say [seɪ], **said** [sed], **said**	sagen
☛Beachte die Aussprache von *says*: [sez]	
The clock says nine.	Die Uhr zeigt neun.
What does the sign say?	Was steht auf dem Schild?
be **scared (of)** [skeəd] ≈ be afraid (of)	Angst haben (vor)
scarf [skɑ:f] ✎ Clothes	Schal
scene [si:n]	Szene
the first scene of a play	
school [sku:l] ✎ In town, ✎ School subjects	Schule
at school	in der Schule
go to school	in die Schule gehen
∞ school bag	Schultasche

✎ My school bag

∞ school class	Schulklasse
∞ school report	Schulzeugnis
∞ primary school ['praɪmərɪ]	Grundschule
∞ secondary school ['sekəndrɪ]	weiterführende Schule

∞ comprehensive (school) [kɒmprɪ'hensɪv]	Gesamtschule
science ['saɪəns]	Wissenschaft; Naturwissenschaft
∞ domestic science ✎ School subjects	Hauswirtschafts- lehre
∞ science fiction	*Science-fiction*
scissors ['sɪʒəz] ✎ Tools	Schere
☛Where are the scissors?	Wo ist die Schere?
☛a pair of scissors	eine Schere
Scotland ['skɒtlənd] ✎ Countries	Schottland
⇨ Scottish	schottisch
⇨ Scot; Scotsman/ Scotswoman	Schotte, Schottin
∞ the Scots/the Scottish	die Schotten
screen [skri:n] ✎ Entertainment electronics	Bildschirm; (Kino-) Leinwand
screw [skru:]	Schraube; schrauben
∞ screwdriver ✎ Tools	Schraubenzieher
sea [si:]	Meer, (die!) See
∞ the North Sea	die Nordsee
∞ at the seaside	am Meer
∞ a seaside resort [rɪ'zɔ:t]	Badeort (am Meer), Seebad
season ['si:zn] ✎ Months and seasons	Jahreszeit
search [sɜ:tʃ]	(durch)suchen; Suche
They searched the whole forest. The search was given up after two days.	
seat [si:t]	Sitz, Sitzplatz
∞ front/back seat	Vorder-/Rücksitz
The cinema has 500 seats.	
∞ seat belt	Sitzgurt
second ['seknd]	zweite(r/s); Sekunde
the second of April (2nd April)	
∞ second-hand	gebraucht
a second-hand car	ein Gebraucht- wagen
one minute ten seconds	eine Minute zehn Sekunden

secret ['si:krɪt]　geheim; Geheimnis
a secret wish　ein geheimer
Wunsch

Can you keep a　Kannst du ein
secret?　Geheimnis be-
wahren.

secretary ['sekrətrɪ]　Sekretär(in)
✎ Jobs

see [si:], **saw** [sɔ:],　sehen
seen [si:n]
I've never seen
him here before.
∞ go/come and see　jdn. besuchen
s.o.　(gehen/kommen)
∞ See you later.　Bis später.
∞ I see.　Ach so.

seem [si:m]　scheinen
You seem to be　Du scheinst ent-
disappointed.　täuscht zu sein.

seldom ['seldəm]　selten
≈ rarely; ⇔ often
They seldom　Sie haben selten
have visitors.　Besuch.

self- [self]　Selbst-

| **Self-service** | Selbstbedienung |

⇨ -self, -selves (als
Endung):
myself　ourselves　ich selbst, mir, mich
yourself　yourselves　usw.
himself　themselves
herself
itself
I made that cake　Ich habe diesen
myself.　Kuchen selbst
gemacht.

Have you hurt　Hast du dich
yourself?　verletzt?
Help yourselves.　Bedient euch.

sell [sel], **sold**　verkaufen
[səʊld], **sold** ⇔ buy
He sold his old
car for £500.

send [send], **sent**　schicken
[sent], **sent**
I'll send you a
postcard.

sense [sens]　Sinn
∞ That doesn't　Das ergibt keinen
make sense.　Sinn.

sentence ['sentəns]　Satz
Can you read this
sentence?

September　September
[sep'tembə]
✎ Months and seasons
in September　im September

sergeant ['sɑ:dʒənt]　Polizeimeister;
Feldwebel

series ['sɪəri:z]　Serie(n) (Einzahl
und Mehrzahl)
a popular TV　ein beliebte Fern-
series　sehserie
There are many　Es gibt viele Un-
comedy series on　terhaltungsserien
TV.　im Fernsehen.

serious ['sɪərɪəs]　ernst
a serious prob-
lem
Stop laughing
and be serious
for a moment.

serve [sɜ:v]　bedienen, versorgen; servieren
Can I help you?–
I'm being served,　... – Ich werde
thank you.　schon bedient ...
Lunch will be　Das Mittagessen
served in 10　wird in 10 Minu-
minutes.　ten serviert.
⇨ service ['sɜ:vɪs]　Bedienung,
Service, Kunden-
dienst; Gottes-
dienst
The food in this
restaurant is
good, but the
service is bad.
Our church has
two services each
Sunday.
⇨ servant ['sɜ:vənt]　Diener(in)

set [set], **set, set**　setzen, stellen
≈ put
Set the box down
on the floor,
please.
∞ set an alarm　einen Wecker
clock　stellen
∞ set s.o. free　jdn. freilassen
∞ set off ≈ leave,　aufbrechen, los-
start　fahren

settle ['setl]　sich ansiedeln, sich
niederlassen
⇨ settler　Siedler(in)
⇨ settlement　Siedlung
['sətlmənt]

89

sew [səʊ], **sewed** [səʊd], **sewn** [səʊn]   nähen

I've got to sew on this button.   Ich muß diesen Knopf annähen.

∞ sewing machine ✎ Electricity in the household   Nähmaschine

shake [ʃeɪk], **shook** [ʃʊk], **shaken** ['ʃeɪkn]   schütteln; zittern, beben

∞ shake one's head   den Kopf schütteln

∞ shake s.o.'s hand   jdm. die Hand schütteln

∞ shake hands   sich (= einander) die Hände schütteln

The earth shook when the bomb exploded.   Die Erde bebte, als die Bombe explodierte.

shall [ʃæl], **should** [ʃʊd]   sollen

Shall I come with you?   Soll ich mitkommen?
You should be more careful.   Du solltest vorsichtiger sein.
I shouldn't eat so much.   Ich sollte nicht so viel essen.

shampoo [ʃæm'pu:] ✎ In the bathroom   Schampon, Haarwaschmittel

sharp [ʃɑ:p]   scharf, spitz
a sharp knife
a sharp needle

shave [ʃeɪv]   (sich) rasieren
He washed and shaved, then he woke his wife.   Er wusch and rasierte sich, …

⇨ shaver ✎ In the bathroom   Rasierapparat

she [ʃi:]   sie (Einzahl)

sheep [ʃi:p] ✎ Animals   Schaf, Schafe
☛ one sheep – two sheep
⇨ shepherd ['ʃepəd] ✎ Jobs   Schäfer(in)

sheet [ʃi:t]   Blatt (Papier); Bettlaken

Can you lend me a sheet of paper, please?
We've got to put clean sheets on the beds.

☛ the leaves of a tree   die Blätter eines Baumes

shelf [ʃelf], **shelves** [ʃelvz] ✎ Furniture   Bord, (Regal-)Brett; Regalbretter; Regal
Put the books back on the shelves, please.   Stellt die Bücher bitte wieder ins Regal zurück.

shine [ʃaɪn], **shone** [ʃɒn], **shone**   scheinen, leuchten, glänzen
The sun is shining.
I've cleaned the bathroom. Look how everything is shining.

ship [ʃɪp] ✎ Transport   Schiff

shirt [ʃɜ:t] ✎ Clothes   Hemd
∞ T-shirt   *T-Shirt*

shock [ʃɒk]   Schock; schockieren
∞ get a shock   einen Schock bekommen
⇨ shocking   schockierend
⇨ shocked   schockiert

shoe [ʃu:] ✎ Clothes   Schuh
a pair of shoes   ein Paar Schuhe
gym shoes ['dʒɪm ʃu:z]   Turnschuhe

shoot [ʃu:t], **shot** [ʃɒt], **shot**   schießen, erschießen
The gangsters shot at the police car.   … schossen auf …
One of the criminals was shot during the fight.   … wurde … erschossen.

shop [ʃɒp] ✎ In town   Laden
∞ shop assistant ✎ Jobs   Verkäufer(in)
∞ shop window   Schaufenster
⇨ shopping   Einkauf(en)
∞ go shopping   einkaufen gehen
∞ do the shopping   den Einkauf erledigen
∞ shopping centre   Einkaufszentrum

short [ʃɔ:t] ⇔ long   kurz
a short visit
a short man ⇔ tall   ein kleiner Mann
∞ a short story   eine Kurzgeschichte

↪ shorts ✎ Clothes — *Shorts*, kurze Hose

↪ shorten — kürzen

should [ʃʊd]
→ shall

shoulder [ˈʃəʊldə] — Schulter
✎ The human body

shout [ʃaʊt] ≈ cry, call — rufen; Ruf
"Stop!" he shouted.
Suddenly we heard a shout for help.

show [ʃəʊ] — zeigen; *Show*, Schau, Vorstellung
Can you show me your passport?
∞ show s.o. round (a place) — jdn. (an einem Ort) herumführen
a TV show — eine Fernsehshow

shower [ʃaʊə] — (Regen-)Schauer; Dusche
✎ The weather
✎ In the bathroom
Tomorrow it will be cloudy with showers.
Have you got a room with a shower?

shut [ʃʌt], **shut, shut** ≈ close — schließen
Have you shut the windows?
∞ shut up — den Mund halten

sick [sɪk] → ill — krank
a sick child — eine krankes Kind
∞ I feel sick. — Mir ist übel.

side [saɪd] — Seite, Rand
on the other side of the river — auf der andere Seite des Flusses
at the side of the road — am Straßenrand

sights [saɪts] — Sehenswürdigkeiten
the sights of London
∞ go sightseeing — *Sightseeing*/auf Besichtigungstour gehen

sign [saɪn] — Zeichen; Schild
I'll give you a sign when you can start.

Can't you read?
The sign says "Keep out"!
∞ signpost — Wegweiser

silent [ˈsaɪlənt] ≈ quiet — still, stumm, schweigsam
Why is everybody so silent tonight? Has anything happened?
↪ silence — Stille, Ruhe

silly [ˈsɪlɪ] — dumm, albern
Don't be silly!

silver [ˈsɪlvə] — Silber

simple [ˈsɪmpl] — einfach
a simple question
a simple life

since [sɪns] — seit; da (ja)
I've been waiting since four o'clock. — Ich warte schon seit vier Uhr.
☛ Bei einer Zeitdauer (*hours, days, weeks* usw.) sagt man *for*:
I've been waiting for two hours. — Ich warte schon seit zwei Stunden.
I won't get up before ten tomorrow, since it's Sunday. — .., da es Sonntag ist.

sing [sɪŋ], **sang** [sæŋ], **sung** [sʌŋ] — singen
↪ song — Lied
Let's sing a song.
↪ singer — Sänger(in)

single [ˈsɪŋgl] — einzeln; *Single* (-schallplatte); unverheiratet; *Single* (= Junggeselle, Jungesellin)
∞ a single room — ein Einzelzimmer
Is she married? – No, she's single.

sink [sɪŋk], **sank** [sæŋk], **sunk** [sʌŋk] — (ver)sinken; Ausguß, Spülbecken
The ship sank to the bottom of the sea.
He put the dirty dishes in the sink.

sir [sɜ:] — mein Herr (Anrede)
Thank you, sir. — Danke.

sister ['sɪstə] Schwester
✎ Relatives

sit [sɪt], **sat** [sæt], **sat** sitzen
He was sitting in
his armchair.
∞ sit down sich setzen
∞ sit up sich aufsetzen,
sich aufrichten

site [saɪt] Stelle, Platz
∞ building site Baustelle
∞ camping site/ Zeltplatz
campsite

situation [sɪtjʊ'eɪʃn] Situation, Lage
We are in a diffi-
cult situation.

size [saɪz] Größe
This jackct isn't
my size. It's too
big.

skate [skeɪt] Schlittschuh; Rollschuh; Schlittschuh/
Rollschuh laufen
∞ (ice-)skating Schlittschuh-
✎ Sports and laufen
games
∞ (roller-)skating Rollschuhlaufen
∞ skateboard *Skateboard*,
Rollbrett

ski [ski:] Ski; Ski laufen
✎ Sports and games
∞ (go) skiing Skilaufen (gehen)

skin [skɪn] Haut
✎ The human body

skirt [skɜ:t] Rock
✎ Clothes

sky [skaɪ] Himmel
There are dark Es sind dunkle
clouds in the sky. Wolken am
Himmel.
∞ skyscraper Wolkenkratzer
∞ skyline *Skyline*,
Silhouette
the skyline of
New York with
its skyscrapers

slave [sleɪv] Sklave, Sklavin

sleep [sli:p], **slept** schlafen; Schlaf
[slept], **slept**
∞ sleeping bag Schlafsack
☛ bedroom Schlafzimmer
My sister often
talks in her sleep. ... im Schlaf.

∞ go to sleep einschlafen
↪ be asleep schlafen
→ asleep

slow [sləʊ] langsam
⇔ quick, fast
a slow movement

small [smɔ:l] ⇔ big, klein
large
a small car
This shirt is too
small for me.

smell [smel] riechen; Geruch
I could smell
something
burning.
These flowers
smell good.
There was a
smell of cooking
in the house.

smile [smaɪl] lächeln; Lächeln
She smiled at me. Sie lächelte mich
an.
He received us
with a friendly
smile.

smoke [sməʊk] rauchen; Rauch
My parents don't
smoke.
The air was full
of smoke from
the chimneys.

smooth [smu:ð] glatt
⇔ rough
a smooth skin

snack [snæk] Imbiß
∞ snack-bar Imbißstube
✎ In town

snail [sneɪl] Schnecke

snake [sneɪk] Schlange
✎ Animals

snow [snəʊ] schneien; Schnee
✎ The weather
Look, it's
snowing.
We had a lot of
snow last winter.
↪ snowy verschneit,
schneereich
a snowy hill
It's snowy here. Es schneit hier
viel.

so [səʊ] daher, also; so
  I was tired, so I
  went to bed early.
  Don't be so silly.
☛ Vor einem
  Hauptwort steht
  such:
  He's <u>such</u> an Er ist <u>so</u> ein Idiot!
  idiot!
  They're <u>such</u> nice Sie sind <u>so</u> nette
  people. Leute.
∞ so far → far bisher, bis jetzt
∞ and so on und so weiter
  I like swimming. Ich schwimme
  – So do I. → nor, gern. – Ich auch.
  neither

soap [səʊp] Seife
✎ In the bathroom

sock [sɒk] ✎ Clothes Socke
  a pair of socks ein Paar Socken

socket ['sɒkɪt] Steckdose
✎ Electricity in the
household

sofa ['səʊfə] Sofa
✎ Furniture

soft [sɒft] ⇔ hard weich, sanft
  a soft bed
  soft music

solar ['səʊlə] Solar-, Sonnen-
∞ solar cells Solarzellen
∞ solar power Sonnenenergie

soldier ['səʊldʒə] Soldat(in)

some [sʌm; səm] einige, ein paar,
→ any etwas, ein bißchen
☛ *Some* steht nur
  in bejahten
  Sätzen.
  There are some … ein paar
  people in the Leute …
  street.
  We need some … etwas Brot.
  bread.
∞ somebody, jemand
  someone
  There's someone
  at the door.
∞ something etwas
  I've brought you
  something to eat.
∞ somewhere irgendwo(hin)
  They live some-
  where in Wales.
  Let's go some- Gehen wir
  where else. anderswohin.

∞ somehow irgendwie
  We haven't got
  enough money,
  but we'll get to
  Rome somehow.
∞ sometimes manchmal
  ✎ Expressions of
  time
  I sometimes go to
  school by bike.

son [sʌn] ✎ Relatives Sohn

song [sɒŋ] Lied
⇨ sing, sang, sung singen

soon [su:n] bald
  It will soon be
  dark.
∞ sooner or later früher oder später
∞ as soon as sobald
  I'll ring you as Ich rufe dich an,
  soon as I arrive. sobald ich an-
    komme.

Sorry. ['sɒrɪ] (I'm Es tut mir leid.
sorry.)
  He was sorry he Es tat ihm leid,
  couldn't come. daß er nicht
    kommen konnte.

sort [sɔ:t] ≈ kind Art, Sorte
  all sorts of books alle Arten von
    Büchern

sound [saʊnd] klingen; Klang, Ton,
    Geräusch
  That sounds Das klingt gut.
  good.
  the sound of den Klang von
  church bells Kirchenglocken
  There were Vom Nachbar-
  strange sounds zimmer kamen
  from the next seltsame Ge-
  room. räusche.
∞ sound engineer Toningenieur(in)

soup [su:p] ✎ Food Suppe

south [saʊθ] Süden; südlich,
→ north Süd-; nach Süden
  in the south of im Süden
  France Frankreichs
∞ south of südlich von
  (London) (London)
∞ South Wales Südwales
∞ go south nach Süden
    gehen
⇨ southern südlich, Süd-
  → northern

souvenir [su:vəˈnɪə] Andenken

93

space [speɪs]
Platz, Raum; Weltraum

There's not enough space here for so many people.
Hier ist nicht genügend Platz für so viele Leute.

a journey through space
eine Reise durch den Weltraum

∞ space flight
Weltraumflug

∞ spaceship
Raumschiff

∞ space shuttle
Raumfähre

Spain [speɪn]
Spanien
✎ Countries

⇨ **Spanish** ['spænɪʃ]
spanisch; Spanisch

⇨ **Spaniard** ['spænjəd]
Spanier(in)

∞ the Spanish/ the Spaniards
die Spanier

spare [speə]
überzählig, übrig; Ersatz-

∞ spare time
Freizeit

∞ spare room
Gästezimmer

∞ spare parts
Ersatzteile

speak [spi:k], **spoke** [spəʊk], **spoken** [spəʊkn]
sprechen

Do you speak English?
(On the telephone:) Julia Miller speaking.
Hier Julia Miller.

∞ English-speaking countries
englischsprachige Länder

⇨ speaker
Sprecher(in), Redner(in)

∞ (loud)speaker
Lautsprecher

⇨ speech [spi:tʃ]
Rede

special ['speʃl]
besondere(r/s), speziell

⇔ ordinary, usual
Today is a special day: my birthday.
What's going on? – Nothing special.
Was ist hier los? – Nichts Besonderes.

⇨ specialist
Spezialist(in)

speech [spi:tʃ]
Rede
→ speak

speed [spi:d]
Geschwindigkeit

at a speed of 70 miles per hour
mit einer Geschwindigkeit von 70 Meilen pro Stunde

∞ speed limit
Geschwindigkeitsbegrenzung

spell [spel]
buchstabieren; (richtig) schreiben

Can you spell your name, please?

Teacher: How do you spell "Mississippi"?
Pupil: The river or the state?

⇨ spelling
Rechtschreibung

∞ a spelling mistake
ein Rechtschreibfehler

spend [spend], **spent** [spent], **spent**
(Geld) ausgeben; (Zeit) verbringen

We've spent over £100 on souvenirs already
Wir haben schon über £100 für Andenken ausgegeben.

We're going to spend our holidays in Greece this year.
Wir verbringen unsere Ferien dieses Jahr in Griechenland.

spider ['spaɪdə]
Spinne
✎ Animals

spoon [spu:]
Löffel
✎ Laying the table

∞ teaspoon
Teelöffel

sport [spɔ:t]
Sport, Sportart

✎ **Sports and games**

I'm not very good at sport.
What's your favourite sport?

∞ sports centre
Sportzentrum

∞ sportsman, sportswoman
Sportler, Sportlerin

spring [sprɪŋ]
Frühling
✎ Months and seasons

square [skweə]   Quadrat; Platz (in einer Stadt)

∞ Trafalgar Square

stairs [steəz]   Treppe
✎ House and flat
☛ Immer in der Mehrzahl:
These stairs are dangerous.   Diese Treppe ist gefährlich.
∞ upstairs   oben (im Haus); nach oben (die Treppe hoch)

The bathroom is upstairs.
Let's go upstairs.
∞ downstairs   (nach) unten

stall [stɔ:l]   (Verkaufs-/Markt-) Stand

stamp [stæmp]   Briefmarke

stand [stænd], **stood** [stʊd], **stood**   stehen
He was standing near the window.
∞ stand up   aufstehen
He stood up and offered the old lady his seat.
∞ cannot stand   nicht ausstehen können

My aunt can't stand dogs.

star [stɑ:]   Stern
∞ the Stars and Stripes   das Sternenbanner (National-flagge der USA)

∞ pop star   Popstar

start [stɑ:t] ≈ begin/ beginning   anfangen, starten; Anfang, Start
It suddenly started to rain.   Es fing plötzlich zu regnen.
The engine won't start.   Der Motor will nicht ausspringen.
She started the car and drove off.   Sie ließ den Wagen an ...
I've got to start for school.   Ich muß mich auf den Wcg zur Schule machen.
⇨ starter   Vorspeise
We missed the start of the match.   Wir verpaßten den Anfang des Spiels.

state [steɪt]   Staat
∞ the United States (of America)   die Vereinigten Staaten

station [ˈsteɪʃn]   Bahnhof; Station
✎ In town
∞ bus station   Busbahnhof
∞ petrol station (BE), gas station (AE)   Tankstelle
∞ power station   Kraftwerk
∞ radio station   Radiosender

stationer [ˈsteɪʃnə]   Schreibwaren-händler(in)
∞ at the stationer's   im Schreib-warenladen

statue [ˈstætju:]   Statue, Standbild
∞ the Statue of Liberty   die Freiheits-statue

stay [steɪ]   bleiben; (vorüber-gehend) wohnen; Aufenthalt

I can only stay for a few minutes.   Ich kann nur ein paar Minuten bleiben.

Tourist: Can you tell me where this raod goes to?
Police officer: It doesn't go anywhere. It stays where it is.

stay at a hotel   in einem Hotel übernachten

stay with s.o.   bei jdm. wohnen
Did you stay at a hotel? – No, I could stay with an aunt.
Did you enjoy your stay in London?   Hat dir der Auf-enthalt in London gefallen?

steak [steik] ✎ Food   *Steak*
He ordered steak and chips.

steal [sti:l], **stole** [stəʊl], **stolen** [ˈstəʊln]   stehlen
Someone has stolen my watch.

steam [sti:m]   Dampf
∞ steam engine   Dampfmaschine
⇨ steamer   Dampfer
✎ Transport

steer [stɪə]   steuern, lenken
∞ steering wheel   Lenkrad

step [step]
Schritt; treten
∞ take a step
einen Schritt machen

∞ step by step
Schritt für Schritt
There's broken glass on the floor. Don't step on it.

stereo ['steriəʊ]
Stereo; Stereo-anlage
✎ Entertainment electronics

stick [stɪk], **stuck** [stʌk], **stuck**
Stock; stecken, kleben
∞ walking stick
Spazierstock
She stuck her finger through the hole.
Sie steckte den Finger durch das Loch.
Please don't stick any posters to the walls.
Bitte keine Plakate an die Wände kleben.
∞ be stuck
feststecken, festsitzen
∞ get stuck
steckenbleiben
The car got stuck in the mud.
Der Wagen blieb im Schlamm stecken.

⇨ sticker
Aufkleber, *Sticker*

still [stɪl]
(immer) noch; still, bewegungslos
Do you still collect stamps?
∞ stand/sit/lie still
still stehen/ sitzen/daliegen

stitch [stɪtʃ]
Stich
It's not a serious injury. It just needs a few stitches.

stocking ['stɒkɪŋ]
Strumpf
✎ Clothes

stomach ['stʌmək]
Magen; Bauch
✎ The human body

stone [stəʊn]
Stein
throw stones at s.o.
Steine auf jdn. werfen
a stone bridge
eine Brücke aus Stein

stop [stɒp]
anhalten, aufhören; Haltestelle
He stopped his car and got out. The train doesn't stop before Liverpool.

Please stop shouting. We must get off at the next stop.
∞ bus stop
Bushaltestelle
✎ In town

storm [stɔːm]
Sturm
✎ The weather
∞ thunderstorm
Gewitter
⇨ stormy
stürmisch

story ['stɔːrɪ]
Geschichte
tell s.o. a story
jdm. eine Geschichte erzählen

stove [stəʊv]
Ofen, Herd
✎ Electricity in the household

straight [streɪt]
gerade; geradewegs, direkt
a straight line
eine gerade Linie
go straight on
geradeaus gehen/ fahren
We went straight home.
Wir gingen direkt nach Hause.

strange [streɪndʒ]
fremd, unbekannt; seltsam
I expected to meet some people I knew, but I only saw strange faces. What a strange idea!
⇨ stranger
Fremde(r)
I'm a stranger in this town.
Ich bin fremd in dieser Stadt.

strawberry ['strɔːbərɪ] ✎ Fruit
Erdbeere

street [striːt] → road
(Stadt-/Dorf-) Straße
✎ In town
They went shopping in Oxford Street.
∞ street map/street plan
Stadtplan

strict [strɪkt]
streng
Our maths teacher is very strict.

strong [strɒŋ]
stark, kräftig
⇔ weak
We need some strong men to push the bus off the road.

student ['stju:dənt]   Student(in); *AE auch:* Schüler(in)

⮕ study ['stʌdɪ]   studieren; lernen

stupid ['stju:pɪd]   dumm
⇔ clever
What a stupid question!

subject ['sʌbdʒekt]   Thema; (Unterichts-)Fach

Let's change the subject.
What is your favourite subject at school?

✎ **School subjects**

success [sək'ses]   Erfolg
The film was a great success.
⮕ successful   erfolgreich

such [sʌtʃ] → so   solch, so
Are you going to watch "Dracula"?
– No, I don't like such horror films.   … solche Horrorfilme.
We've never had such terrible weather as this year.   … so schreckliches Wetter …

suddenly ['sʌdnlɪ]   plötzlich
We were having tea when suddenly the light went out.

sugar ['ʃʊgə]   Zucker
✎ Food

suit [su:t] ✎ Clothes   Anzug
∞ suitcase ['su:tkeɪs]   Koffer

summer ['sʌmə]   Sommer
✎ Months and seasons

sun [sʌn]   Sonne
The sun is shining.

∞ sunglasses ['sʌnglɑːsɪz]   Sonnenbrille
∞ sunshine ['sʌnʃaɪn]   Sonnenschein
⮕ sunny   sonnig
✎ The weather

Sunday ['sʌndɪ]   Sonntag
✎ Days of the week

supermarket ['su:pəmɑːkɪt] ✎ In town   Supermarkt

supper ['sʌpə]   Abendessen
∞ have supper   zu abend essen

sure [ʃʊə] ≈ certain   sicher
I'm sure I'm right.   Ich bin mir sicher, daß ich recht habe.

surf [sɜ:f]   surfen
✎ Sports and games
∞ surfboard   Surfbrett
⮕ surfing   Surfen

surgery ['sɜ:dʒərɪ]   (Arzt-)Praxis
∞ surgery hours   Sprechstunden

surname ['sɜ:neɪm] *(BE)* ≈ family name *(AE)*   Nachname

surprise [se'praɪz]   Überraschung; überraschen

What a nice surprise!
Don't tell them I'm coming. I want to surprise them.
⮕ surprised   überrascht
⮕ surprising   überraschend

Sweden ['swi:dn]   Schweden
✎ Countries
⮕ Swedish ['swi:dɪʃ]   schwedisch; Schwedisch
⮕ Swede [swi:d]   Schwede, Schwedin
∞ the Swedes/the Swedish   die Schweden

sweet [swi:t]   süß; Bonbon; Nachtisch

That cake is too sweet.
She gave the children each a sweet.
We ordered soup, a main course and a sweet.

97

swim [swɪm], **swam** [swæm], **swum** [swʌm]   schwimmen
∞ go swimming   schwimmen gehen
⇨ swimming   Schwimmen
   ✎ Sports and games
∞ swimming pool   Schwimmbad
∞ swimming trunks   Badehose
∞ swimsuit ['swɪmsuːt]   Badeanzug
   ✎ Clothes
⇨ swimmer   Schwimmer(in)

switch [swɪtʃ]   Schalter; (um)schalten
   I can't find the electric light switch.
∞ switch on (the light)   (das Licht) anschalten
∞ switch off   abschalten

Switzerland ['swɪtsələnd]   die Schweiz
   ✎ Countries
⇨ Swiss   schweizerisch; Schweizer(in)
∞ the Swiss   die Schweizer

T [tiː] is for

table ['teɪbl]   Tisch
   ✎ Furniture
∞ tablecloth   Tischtuch
∞ table tennis   Tischtennis
∞ lay the table   den Tisch decken
   ✎ Laying the table

tablet ['tæblɪt] ≈ pill   Tablette
   Take two tablets after meals.

tailor ['teɪlə] ✎ Jobs   Herrenschneider(in)

take [teɪk], **took** [tʊk], **taken** ['teɪkn] → bring   nehmen; (weg-)bringen; dauern; (Zeit) brauchen; machen .
   Don't forget to take your umbrella with you.   Vergißt nicht, deinen Schirm mitzunehmen.
   Can you take this parcel to the post office, please?   Kannst du dieses Päckchen bitte zur Post bringen?
   How long does the journey to Glasgow take?   Wie lange dauert die Fahrt nach Glasgow?

∞ take photos   Fotos machen
∞ take a break   Pause machen
∞ take a step   einen Schritt machen
∞ take place   stattfinden
∞ take part in   teilnehmen an
∞ take a message   eine Botschaft entgegennehmen, etw. ausrichten
∞ take care of   sich kümmern um
∞ take s.o. for a walk   jdn. spazierenführen
∞ take off ⇔ land; put on   starten, abheben; abnehmen, ausziehen
   The plane is taking off.
   He took off his helmet.
   Take off your dirty boots, please.

talk [tɔːk] ≈ speak   reden, sprechen; Gespräch
   Let's talk <u>about</u> something else.   Reden wir <u>über</u> etwas anderes.
   Can I talk <u>to</u> Mrs Jones, please?   Kann ich bitte <u>mit</u> Frau Jones sprechen?
   We had a long talk with him.   Wir haben ein langes Gespräch mit ihm geführt.

tall [tɔːl] ⇔ short   groß, hoch
   a tall man
   a tall tree

tank [tæŋk]   Tank
   fill up the tank   den Tank auffüllen
∞ fish tank   Aquarium
⇨ tanker   Tanker
∞ oil tanker   Öltanker

tap [tæp]   (Wasser-)Hahn
   ✎ In the bathroom
   turn on/off the tap   den Hahn auf-/zudrehen

tape [teɪp]   (Ton)band; Klebestreifen
∞ video tape   Videoband
∞ tape recorder   Tonbandgerät
   ✎ Entertainment electronics

taste [teɪst]   schmecken; Geschmack
   The egg tastes funny.   Das Ei schmeckt komisch.

It tastes <u>of</u> fish. | Es schmeckt <u>nach</u> Fisch.

a bitter taste | ein bitterer Geschmack

taxi ['tæksi] | Taxi
✎ Transport
  call a taxi | ein Taxi rufen
∞ taxi driver ✎ Jobs | Taxifahrer(in)

tea [ti:] ✎ Drinks | Tee; Abendessen
∞ a cup of tea | eine Tasse Tee
∞ tea bag | Teebeutel
∞ teacup | Teetasse
∞ tea spoon | Teelöffel
  ✎ Laying the table
  have tea | Tee trinken; zu abend essen (in Nordengland und Schottland)

teach [ti:tʃ], **taught** [tɔ:t], **taught** | lehren, unterrichten
  He teaches English and Italian.
  My aunt taught me (how) to play chess. | Meine Tante brachte mir das Schachspielen bei.
↪ teacher ✎ Jobs | Lehrer(in)
∞ English teacher | Englischlehrer(in)
∞ form teacher | Klassenlehrer(in)

team [ti:m] | Mannschaft, *Team*
∞ a basketball team

tear [teə], **tore** [tɔ:], **torn** [tɔ:n] | (zer)reißen
  Someone has torn a page out of the book.
  This cotton isn't strong enough. It might tear. | … Er könnte reißen.

tear [tɪə] | Träne
  He had tears in his eyes. | Er hatte Tränen in den Augen.

technical ['teknɪkl] | technisch
∞ technical college | Technische Fachschule
↪ technician [tek'nɪʃn] ✎ Jobs | Techniker(in)
∞ lab technician | Labortechniker(in)
↪ technology [tek'nɒlədʒɪ] | Technologie
∞ high tech(nology) | Spitzentechnologie

telefax ['telɪfæks] ≈ fax | Telefax, Fernkopierer

telegram ['telɪgræm] | Telegramm, Fernschreiben

telegraph ['telɪgrɑ:f] | Telegraf, Fernschreiber

telephone ['telɪfəʊn] ≈ phone | Telefon; telefonieren
∞ telephone number | Telefonnummer
∞ telephone box | Telefonzelle
∞ telephone directory [dɪ'rektrɪ] | Telefonbuch
∞ telephone company | Telefongesellschaft
∞ radio telephone telephone <u>for</u> an ambulance | Funktelefon (telefonisch) einen Krankenwagen rufen

television ['telɪvɪʒn] ≈ TV ✎ Entertainment electronics | Fernsehen; Fernsehapparat
∞ watch television | fernsehen
∞ be on television | im Fernsehen kommen
∞ television programme | Fernsehsendung
∞ television (set) | Fernsehapparat

tell [tel], **told** [təʊld], **told** | erzählen, sagen
  Did you tell her the story? | Hast du ihr die Geschichte erzählt?
  I haven't told anybody about it yet. | Ich habe noch niemandem davon erzählt.
  Tell them to come. | Sag ihnen, sie sollen kommen.
∞ tell on s.o. | jdn. verpetzen
∞ tell the time | die Uhrzeit ablesen

temperature ['temprɪtʃə] ✎ The weather | Temperatur

tennis ['tenɪs] ✎ Sports and games | Tennis
∞ table tennis | Tischtennis
∞ tennis court [kɔ:t] | Tennisplatz
∞ tennis racket | Tennisschläger
∞ tennis player | Tennisspieler(in)

tent [tent] | Zelt
☛ camping | Zelten

terrible ['terɪbl] | schrecklich
  a terrible accident

99

test [test]

∞ pass a test

∞ driving test
I'm going to have
my eyes tested
tomorrow.

Test, Prüfung;
prüfen, untersuchen
eine Prüfung
bestehen
Fahrprüfung
Ich lasse morgen
meine Augen
untersuchen.

text [tekst]
∞ textbook
✎ My school bag

Text
Lehrbuch

than [ðæn; ðən]
older than me
more than 500
less than 10

als
älter als ich
mehr als 500
weniger als 10

thank [θæŋk]

I forgot to thank
him for his help.

danken, sich
bedanken
Ich vergaß, mich
bei ihm für seine
Hilfe zu bedan-
ken.

∞ Thank you.
Thank you very
much.
⇨ Thanks.
∞ Thanks a lot.
∞ No thanks.

Danke.
Vielen Dank.

Danke.
Vielen Dank.
Nein danke.

that [ðæt; ðət]
→ those
What's that?
You've lost it?
That's terrible.
∞ that's why

He's on holiday.
– Oh, that's why
he doesn't an-
swer the phone.

1. das (hinweisen-
des Fürwort)
Was ist das?
… Das ist
schrecklich.
deshalb, aus
diesem Grund

Who's that girl
over there?
∞ that day

I'll never forget
that day.
That day I got up
early.

2. der/die/das …
da, jene(r/s)
Wer ist das Mäd-
chen da drüben?
jener Tag; an
jenem Tag

a machine that
saves a lot of
time

3. der/die/das (in
Relativsätzen)
eine Maschine,
die viel Zeit spart

I know that she
likes you.

4. daß
Ich weiß, daß sie
dich mag.

the [ðə; ðɪ]
☛ Vor einem Mit-
laut spricht man
[ðə], vor einem
Selbstlaut [ðɪ]:
the teacher [ðə
'tiːtʃə]
the air [ðɪ 'eə]

der, die, das

theatre ['θɪətə]
✎ In town
go to the theatre
an evening at the
theatre

Theater

ins Theater gehen
ein Abend im
Theater

**their, them, them-
selves** → they

then [ðen]
First we had tea,
then we went for
a walk.
∞ now and then

dann; damals

ab und zu, dann
und wann

My uncle went to
Australia in 1970.
He was only 22
then.

there [ðeə; ðə]
Tom is over there,
behind the tree.
Put the books
there, on the
table.
There is nothing
to do at the
moment.
Are there any
problems?

da(hin), dort(hin); es
Tom ist dort
drüben, …
Leg die Bücher
dorthin, auf den
Tisch.
Es gibt im
Moment nichts
zu tun.
Gibt es
Probleme?

these [ðiːz] → this
How much are
these postcards?

∞ these days

diese (Mehrzahl)
Wieviel kosten
diese Post-
karten?
heutzutage

they [ðeɪ]
⇨ their [ðeə]
⇨ them [ðem, ðəm]
⇨ themselves
[ðəm'selvz]
Where are Martin
and Becky? –
They are riding
their bikes.
I can see them
from the window.
They are enjoying
themselves.

sie (Mehrzahl)
ihr
ihnen, sie
sich (selbst)

thick [θɪk] ⇔ thin — dick, dicht
  a thick book
  thick fog
☛ Bei Personen
  sagt man *fat*:
  a fat woman — eine dicke Frau

thief [θi:f], **thieves** [θi:vz] — Dieb(in), Diebe, Diebinnen

thin [θɪn] ⇔ thick, fat — dünn
  a thin book
  a thin girl

thing [θɪŋ] — Ding, Sache
  What's that strange thing in the garden? — Was ist das seltsame Ding im Garten?
  I need a few things from the supermarket. — Ich brauche ein paar Sachen vom Supermarkt.
  The only thing we can do is wait. — Das Einzige was wir tun können ist warten.
  Don't worry. Things will get better again. — Mach dir keine Sorgen. Es wird schon wieder besser.

↪ something, anything — etwas
↪ nothing ['nʌθɪŋ] — nichts
↪ everything — alles

think [θɪŋk], **thought** [θɔ:t], **thought** — (nach)denken; meinen, glauben
  Think before you answer. — Denk nach, bevor du antwortest.
∞ think s.th. over — etw. überdenken
∞ think of s.o./s.th. — an jdn./etw. denken
  She only thinks of herself. — Sie denkt nur an sich.
  Do you think we'll manage? — Glaubst du, daß wir es schaffen?
  What do you think of our plan? — Was hältst du von unserem Plan?

third [θɜ:d] — dritte(r/s); Drittel
  the third of April (3rd April)
  a third of the packet — ein Drittel der Packung

thirsty ['θɜ:stɪ] — durstig
  Are you thirsty? — Hast du Durst?

this [ðɪs] → these — dies, das (hier); diese(r/s)
  Who's this? — Wer ist das?

(On the phone:) This is Barbara. — Hier (spricht) Barbara.
This radio is better than that one. — Dieses Radio (hier) ist besser als das da.
∞ this time — diesmal
∞ this morning/ afternoon/ evening — heute morgen/ vormittag/nach- mittag/abend

those [ðəʊz] → that — die/diese (da/dort); jene (Mehrzahl)
  Can you get me those magazines over there? — Kannst du mir diese Zeitschrif- ten dort drüben holen?
  in those days/ years — in jenen Tagen/ Jahren

through [θru:] — durch
  go through a door — durch eine Tür gehen
∞ put s.o. through (on the phone) — jdn. durchstellen (am Telefon)

throw [θrəʊ], **threw** [θru:], **thrown** [θrəʊn] — werfen
  He threw the ball 70 metres. — Er warf den Ball 70 m weit.

thunder ['θʌndə] — Donner
∞ thunderstorm — Gewitter
  ✎ The weather

Thursday ['θɜ:zdɪ] — Donnerstag
  ✎ Days of the week

ticket ['tɪkɪt] — (Fahr-/Eintritts-) Karte
∞ bus ticket — Busfahrkarte
∞ plane ticket — Flugschein
∞ theatre ticket — Theaterkarte
∞ ticket collector — Schaffner(in)
  ✎ Jobs

tie [taɪ] ✎ Clothes — binden; Krawatte
  She tied her horse to a tree.
  He was wearing a shirt and a tie.

tiger ['taɪgə] — Tiger
  ✎ Animals

till [tɪl] ≈ until — bis
  ✎ Expressions of time
  We played cards till midnight.
  Wait till I come back.

time [taɪm]   Zeit; Mal

✎ **Expressions of time**

It's time to get up.
Can you tell me
the exact time,
please
∞ time of day   Tageszeit
∞ timetable   Fahrplan;
     Stundenplan
∞ in time   rechtzeitig
We arrived just in   … gerade noch
time to say good-   rechtzeitig …
bye to him.
∞ on time   pünktlich
The bus wasn't
on time so we
missed the train.
for the first/last   zum ersten/
time   letzten Mal
three times   dreimal
I've been here   Ich war schon
three times.   dreimal hier.

tin [tɪn] *(BE)*   Dose, Büchse
≈ can *(AE)*
a tin of beans   eine Dose Bohnen
∞ tin opener   Dosenöffner

tired ['taɪəd]   müde
He was so tired
that he fell asleep
at the table.

to [tʊ; tə]   1. in Richtungs-
✎ Place and direction   angaben:
Is this the way to   … zum Bahn-
the station?   hof?
I'm going to
London to-
morrow.   … nach London.
It's 2 km from   … von hier bis
here to the city   zur Stadtmitte.
centre.
go to bed   ins Bett gehen
go to school   in die Schule
     gehen

Have you ever   Warst du schon
been to Scotland?   einmal in
     Schottland?

✎ Expressions of time   2. in Zeitgaben:
from nine to ten   von neun bis
     zehn
It's ten to five.   Es ist zehn vor
     fünf.
It's two minutes   Es ist zwei (Mi-
to two.   nuten) vor zwei.
at quarter to   um Viertel vor
twelve   zwölf

     3. zur Angabe des
     Zwecks oder der
     Absicht (wozu?
     wofür?):
I'm looking for a   …, um den
knife to cut the   Kuchen zu
cake.   schneiden.
It's time to leave.   Es ist Zeit zu
     gehen.
Let's take some-   Nehmen wir
thing with us to   etwas zu essen
eat.   mit.

     4. bei Personen:
     wem? an wen?
Don't give it to   Gib es nicht ihm,
him, give it to me.   gib es mir.
Have you written   Hast du Oma
to Grandma yet?   schon ge-
     schrieben?
a letter to John   ein Brief an John

     5. nach bestimmten
     Verben und
     Eigenschafts-
     wörtern:
Try to be on time.   Versuche, pünkt-
     lich zu sein.
Tim wants to   Tim will Ita-
learn Italian.   lienisch lernen.
It's difficult to   Es ist schwierig
understand.   zu verstehen.

toast [təʊst] ✎ Food   *Toast*
⇨ toaster   *Toaster*
✎ Electricity in the
household

today [tə'deɪ]   heute
✎ Expressions of time
☛ this morning/   heute morgen/
evening   abend
tonight   heute nacht;
     heute abend

toe [təʊ]   Zehe
✎ The human body

102

together [tə'geðə]
They work
together.
zusammen
Sie arbeiten
zusammen.

toilet ['tɔɪlɪt]
✎ House and flat
Toilette

tomato [tə'mɑːtəʊ],
tomatoes [tə'mɑː-
təʊz] ✎ Vegetables
Tomate, Tomaten

tomorrow [tə'mɒrəʊ]
✎ Expressions of time
tomorrow morn-
ing
morgen

morgen früh;
morgen vormittag

tongue [tʌŋ]
✎ The human body
Zunge

tonight [tə'naɪt]
✎ Expressions of time
I think I'll go to
bed early tonight.
We're going to
the cinema
tonight.
☛ I didn't sleep
well last night.
heute nacht; heute
abend

... heute (= ver-
gangene) nacht ...

too [tuː]
I'm going to
make myself a
sandwich. Would
you like one, too?
☛ not ... either
→ either
I don't know her
either.
This jacket is too
small for you.
Does it hurt? –
No, it's not too
bad.
∞ too much
→ much
∞ too many
→ many
auch; (all)zu

…Möchtest du
auch eines?
auch nicht

Ich kenne sie
auch nicht.
Diese Jacke ist
dir zu klein.
Tut es weh? –
Nein, es ist nicht
allzu schlimm.
zuviel

zuviele

tool [tuːl]
Werkzeug

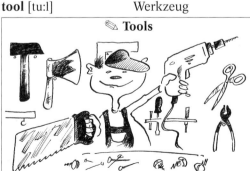

✎ **Tools**

tooth [tuːθ], **teeth**
[tiːθ]
✎ The human body
∞ toothpaste
∞ toothbrush
✎ In the bathroom
∞ brush one's teeth

∞ have (a) tooth-
ache
Zahn, Zähne

Zahnpasta
Zahnbürste

sich die Zähne
putzen
Zahnschmerzen
haben

top [tɒp] ⇔ bottom
at the top of a
mountain
at the top of a
page
Spitze, oberes Ende
auf dem Gipfel
eines Berges
oben auf einer
Seite

tortoise ['tɔːtəs]
✎ Animals
(Land-)Schildkröte

touch [tʌtʃ]
Don't touch the
plate, it's hot.
berühren

tour [tʊə]

go on a bike tour

a bus tour
a tour of the city
centre
Tour, Fahrt, Rund-
gang
eine Radtour
machen
eine Busfahrt
ein Rundgang
durch die
Innenstadt

⇨ tourist ['tʊərɪst]
Tourist(in)

towards [tə'wɔːdz]
✎ Place and direction
She was running
towards the sea.
in Richtung auf, auf
… zu

towel ['taʊəl]
✎ In the bathroom
Handtuch

tower ['taʊə]
✎ In town
∞ the Tower of
London
Turm

town [taʊn]
∞ in town
Stadt
in der Stadt

✎ **In town**

103

∞ go to town	in die Stadt gehen
∞ town hall	Rathaus
toy ['tɔɪ]	Spielzeug
∞ a toy car	ein Spielzeugauto
∞ a toyshop	ein Spielwaren-laden
tractor ['træktə] ✎ Transport	Traktor
traffic ['træfɪk] There's a lot of traffic today.	Verkehr Heute ist viel Verkehr.
∞ traffic lights ✎ In town	Verkehrsampel
☛The (traffic) lights <u>are</u> red.	Die Ampel <u>ist</u> rot.
∞ traffic jam	Verkehrsstau
train [treɪn] ✎ Transport	Zug; trainieren; ausbilden
∞ go by train	mit dem Zug fahren
∞ catch/miss the train	den Zug errei-chen/verpassen
∞ <u>on</u> the train	<u>im</u> Zug
train a team	eine Mannschaft trainieren
a trained nurse	eine ausgebildete Krankenschwester
⇨ trainer ≈ coach	*Trainer*(in)
⇨ training	*Training*; Ausbildung
∞ a training course	ein Ausbildungs-kurs
tram [træm] ✎ Transport	Straßenbahn
∞ tram driver ✎ Jobs	Straßenbahn-fahrer(in)
transistor [træn'sɪstə]	Transistor
∞ transistor radio ✎ Entertainment electronics	Transistorradio
transport ['trænspɔːt]	Transport, Beförde-rung

✎ **Transport**

∞ means of transport [miːnz]	Transportmittel
travel ['trævl] He wants to travel round the world for a year.	reisen
∞ travel agent → agent	Reisefachmann/-frau
⇨ traveller	Reisende(r)
∞ traveller's cheque	Reisecheck
tree [triː] He is sitting <u>in</u> the tree.	Baum Er sitzt <u>auf</u> dem Baum.
∞ apple tree	Apfelbaum
∞ Christmas tree	Weihnachtsbaum
trick [trɪk] do tricks	Trick, Kunststück Kunststücke vor-führen
trip [trɪp] a day trip to the seaside	Ausflug, Fahrt ein Tagesausflug ans Meer
go for/take a trip	eine Fahrt machen
trouble ['trʌbl]	Ärger, Schwierig-keiten, Probleme
∞ have trouble with s.th./s.o.	Ärger mit etw./ jdm. haben
∞ be in trouble	in Schwierig-keiten sein
∞ look for trouble	Streit suchen
I'd love to come, but the trouble is, I haven't got enough money.	…, aber das Problem ist, daß …
trousers ['traʊzəz] ✎ Clothes	Hose(n)
☛Immer Mehrzahl: Where <u>are</u> my trousers?	Wo <u>ist</u> mein Hose?
☛Vor *a* und Zahlwörtern steht *pair(s) of*:	
a pair of trousers two pairs of trousers	<u>eine</u> Hose <u>zwei</u> (Paar) Hosen
truck [trʌk] *(AE)* ≈ lorry *(BE)*	Lastwagen
∞ truck driver	Lastwagen-fahrer(in)
true [truː] ⇔ false a true story true gold	wahr, echt
⇨ truth [truːθ]	Wahrheit

trumpet ['trʌmpɪt]　　Trompete
✎ Musical instruments

try [traɪ]　　versuchen; Versuch
He tried to get　　Er versuchte
up, but he was　　aufzustehen, …
too weak.
∞ try hard　　sich viel Mühe
　　geben

If you don't try
harder, you won't
pass the test.
∞ try on (a jacket)　　(eine Jacke) an-
　　probieren
It's worth a try.　　Es ist einen
　　Versuch wert.

T-shirt ['tiːʃɜːt]　　*T-Shirt*
✎ Clothes

Tuesday ['tjuːzdɪ]　　Dienstag
✎ Days of the week

tunnel ['tʌnl]　　Tunnel
∞ the Channel　　der (Ärmel-)
Tunnel　　Kanaltunnel

Turkey ['tɜːkɪ]　　Türkei
✎ Countries
⇨ Turkish　　türkisch;
　　Türkisch
⇨ Turk　　Türke, Türkin
∞ the Turks/the　　die Türken
Turkish

turn [tɜːn]　　abbiegen, (sich)
　　drehen; Drehung
∞ turn right/left　　nach rechts/links
　　abbiegen
∞ turn round　　(sich) umdrehen
The man walking
in front of me
suddenly turned
round.
She turned her
chair round to
the window.
∞ turn (the radio)　　(das Radio) lei-
down/up　　ser/lauter stellen
∞ turn (the light)　　(das Licht) ein-/
on/off　　ausschalten
∞ turn to s.o.　　sich jdm. zuwen-
　　den
∞ turn s.th. into　　etw. in etw. ande-
s.th. else　　res umwandeln
They are going to
turn the old
factory into a
museum.
No left turn.　　Linksabbiegen
　　verboten.

∞ It's my/your turn.　　Ich bin/Du bist
　　an der Reihe.

TV ['tiː'viː] → tele-　　Fernsehen; Fern-
vision　　sehapparat

twice [twaɪs] ≈ two　　zweimal
times
twice a day/a　　zweimal am Tag/
week　　in der Woche

type [taɪp]　　Typ, Art; tippen,
　　maschineschreiben
a type of car　　ein Autotyp
⇨ typical (of)　　typisch (für)
['tɪpɪkl]
Have you typed　　Hast du den Brief
the letter yet?　　schon getippt?
⇨ typist ✎ Jobs　　Schreibkraft
⇨ typewriter　　Schreibmaschine

tyre ['taɪə]　　Reifen
∞ bike tyre　　Fahrradreifen

U [juː] is for

ugly ['ʌglɪ]　　häßlich
⇔ beautiful
an ugly building

UK ['juː'keɪ]　　Vereinigtes König-
✎ Countries　　reich
= United Kingdom
(of England, Wales,
Scotland and
Northern Ireland)

UFO ['juːfəʊ]　　*UFO*
= unidentified　　unbekanntes
flying object　　Flugobjekt
[ˌʌnaɪ'dentɪfaɪd]

umbrella [ʌm'brelə]　　Schirm

un- [ʌn]　　un-
unhappy　　unglücklich
[ʌn'hæpɪ]
unfriendly　　unfreundlich
[ʌn'frendlɪ]
unpopular　　unbeliebt
[ʌn'pɒpjʊlə]

uncle ['ʌŋkl]　　Onkel
✎ Relatives

under ['ʌndə]　　unter
⇔ on, over
✎ Place and direction
He lives under a
bridge.
She put her bag
under the bed.

∞ underground ['ʌndəgraʊnd] — unterirdisch, Untergrund
an underground lake — ein unterirdischer See
∞ the Underground (BE) ≈ subway (AE) — U-Bahn
∞ underline [ʌndə'laɪn] — unterstreichen

understand [ʌndə'stænd], **understood** [ʌndə'stʊd], **understood** — verstehen
I don't understand you.

uniform ['juːnɪfɔːm] — Uniform
✎ Clothes
A lot of English children wear school uniform.

unite [juː'naɪt] — (sich) vereinigen
∞ the United Kingdom → UK — das Vereinigte Königreich
∞ the United Nations (UN) — die Vereinten Nationen
∞ the United States of America (USA) — die Vereinigten Staaten von Amerika
⇨ unit ['juːnɪt] — Einheit
⇨ union ['juːnjən] — Union, Vereinigung

university [juːnɪ'vɜːsɪti] — Universität

until [ʌn'tɪl] ≈ **till** — bis
✎ Expressions of time
I'll stay until Sunday. — Ich bleibe bis Sonntag.
Wait until I call you. — Warte, bis ich dich rufe.
∞ not until — erst (an/um/zu), nicht vor
We won't be back until Monday. — Wir werden erst am Montag zurück sein.

up [ʌp] ⇔ down — hinauf, herauf; oben
✎ Place and direction
walk up a hill — einen Berg hinaufgehen
∞ up here/there — hier/dort oben; hier/dort hoch
It's cold up here. — Es ist kalt hier oben.
Don't go up there. — Geh nicht dort hinauf.
∞ get up — aufstehen

∞ fill up — auffüllen
∞ run/drive up to s.o. — auf jdn. zulaufen/zufahren
∞ clean up — aufräumen, putzen
∞ dry up — austrocknen
∞ upstairs → stairs — die Treppe hoch; oben (einen Stock höher)

us [ʌs] — uns
Can you help us?

use [juːz] — benutzen, anwenden
Can I use your calculator?
⇨ user [juːzə] — Benutzer(in)

use [juːs] — Gebrauch; Nutzen
This door is not for public use. — Diese Tür ist nicht für den öffentlichen Gebrauch bestimmt.
What's the use of a fast car in such heavy traffic? — Welchen Nutzen hat ...?
⇨ useful [juːsfʊl] ⇔ useless — nützlich
⇨ used [juːst] — gewohnt
∞ be used to s.th. — etw. gewohnt sein
I'm not used to getting up so early. — Ich bin es nicht gewohnt, so früh aufzustehen.
∞ get used to s.th. — sich an etw. gewöhnen
∞ used to [juːstə] — ... früher ...
He used to be a taxi driver, but now he works in a factory. — Er war früher Taxifahrer, ...
☛ Verwechsle nicht:
He is used to work**ing** hard. — Er ist es gewohnt, hart zu arbeiten.
He used to work hard. — Er arbeitete früher hart.

usual ['juːzʊəl], **usually** — üblich, gewöhnlich
We'll meet tomorrow at the usual time. — Wir teffen uns morgen zur üblichen Zeit.
∞ as usual — wie gewöhnlich
He was late as usual. — Er kam wie gewöhnlich zu spät.
I usually get up at seven. — Ich stehe gewöhnlich um sieben auf.

V [viː] is for

vacation [vəˈkeɪʃn]
(AE) ≈ holidays *(BE)*
Ferien, Urlaub

vacuum cleaner
[ˈvækjʊəm kliːnə]
✎ Electricity in the household
Staubsauger

valuable [ˈvæljʊəbl]
a valuable ring
wertvoll
↪ value [ˈvæljuː]
Wert

van [væn]
✎ Transport
Lieferwagen

vegetables
[ˈvedʒtəbl]
Gemüse

✎ **Vegetables**

a vegetable | ein Gemüse, eine Gemüseart

We eat a lot of vegetables. | Wir essen viel Gemüse.
Carrots are my favourite vegetable. | Karotten sind mein Lieblingsgemüse.

very [ˈverɪ]
That's very good.
She works very carefully.
sehr
∞ very much
He doesn't talk very much.
We miss you very much.
sehr viel; sehr
Er redet nicht sehr viel.
Wir vermissen dich sehr.

video [ˈvɪdɪəʊ]
✎ Entertainment electronics
Video
∞ video recorder | Videorecorder
∞ video cassette | Videokassette

view [vjuː]
a good view of the sea
Aussicht
eine schöne Aussicht aufs Meer

village [ˈvɪlɪdʒ]
Dorf

---

visit [ˈvɪzɪt]
Have you visited the museum yet?
besuchen; Besuch
Hast du schon das Museum besucht?
Are you here on a visit?
Bist du zu Besuch hier?
↪ visitor
Besucher(in)

voice [vɔɪs]
∞ (talk) in a loud voice
Stimme
laut (reden)

volleyball [ˈvɒlɪbɔːl]
✎ Sports and games
Volleyball

W [ˈdʌbljuː] is for

wait [weɪt]
∞ wait <u>for</u> s.o.
∞ waiting-room
warten
<u>auf</u> jdn. warten
Wartezimmer

waiter [ˈweɪtə],
waitress [ˈweɪtˈrɪs]
✎ Jobs
Waiter, the bill, please.
Kellner, Kellnerin
Herr Ober, zahlen bitte!

wake (up) [weɪk],
woke [wəʊk],
woken [ˈwəʊkn]
Please wake me at seven.
I woke up at six this morning.
wecken; aufwachen
↪ awake [əˈweɪk]
⇔ asleep
wach

Wales [weɪlz]
✎ Countries
Wales
↪ Welsh [welʃ]
walisisch; Walisisch
↪ Welshman, Welshwoman
∞ the Welsh
Walisisch
Waliser, Waliserin
die Waliser

walk [wɔːk]
We got off the bus and walked up the road.
He likes walking in the mountains.
(zu Fuß) gehen, wandern; Spaziergang
∞ go for a walk
einen Spaziergang machen

wall [wɔːl]
✎ House and flat
There were some pictures on the wall.
Wand; Mauer

There's a thick wall around the castle.

wallet ['wɒlɪt] — Brieftasche

want [wɒnt] — wollen, mögen
She didn't want to come with us. — Sie wollte nicht mitkommen.
They want me to stay. — Sie möchten, daß ich bleibe.

war [wɔ:] ⇔ peace — Krieg
∞ the Second World War — der Zweite Weltkrieg

wardrobe ['wɔ:drəʊb] — Kleiderschrank
✎ Furniture

warm [wɔ:m] ⇔ cold — warm
✎ The weather

wash [wɒʃ] — waschen
I've got to wash my hands. — Ich muß mir die Hände waschen
∞ wash the dishes — das Geschirr spülen
∞ wash up — spülen, abwaschen
∞ do the washing — die Wäsche waschen
∞ washing machine — Waschmaschine
✎ Electricity in the household
∞ wash basin ['wɒʃbeɪsn] — Waschbecken
✎ In the bathroom

waste [weɪst] — verschwenden; Abfall
She wastes all her money <u>on</u> sweets. — Sie verschwendet ihr ganzes Geld <u>für</u> Süßigkeiten.
∞ wastepaper — Papierabfall
∞ wastepaper basket — Papierkorb

watch [wɒtʃ] — (zu-/an-)schauen; beobachten; Armbanduhr
∞ watch TV — fernsehen
watch a TV programme — sich eine Fernsehsendung anschauen
watch s.o. carefully — jdn. genau beobachten
∞ watch out — aufpassen
My watch has stopped. — Meine Uhr ist stehengeblieben.

water ['wɔ:tə] — Wasser
∞ water pipe — Wasserrohr
∞ mineral water — Mineralwasser
✎ Drinks
∞ sea water — Meerwasser

wave [weɪv] — winken; Welle
She waved at us. — Sie winkte uns zu.
He waved his hands. — Er winkte mit den Händen.
There were big waves out on the lake. — Draußen auf dem See waren große Wellen.

way [weɪ] — Weg; Richtung; Art und Weise
I met her on my way to school. — … auf dem Weg zur Schule.
Is Pete coming? – Yes, he's on his way. — … Ja, er ist schon unterwegs.
∞ Vorfahrt achten!

∞ by the way — übrigens
Which way did he go? — In welche Richtung ging er?
∞ the other way round — andersherum, umgekehrt
She has a strange way of laughing. — Sie hat eine seltsame Art zu lachen.
You're doing it the wrong way. — Du machst es falsch. Mach es so.
Do it this way.

we [wi:] — wir

weak [wi:k] ⇔ strong — schwach
a weak heart

wear [weə], **wore** [wɔ:], **worn** [wɔ:n] — tragen (von Kleidung)
He's wearing a blue coat. — Er trägt einen blauen Mantel.
☛ He <u>was carrying</u> a suitcase. — Er <u>trug</u> einen Koffer.

weather ['weðə] — Wetter

✎ **The weather**

108

He goes out <u>in</u> good and bad weather. — Sie geht <u>bei</u> gutem und schlechtem Wetter aus.

∞ weather forecast ['fɔ:kɑ:st] — Wettervorhersage

Wednesday ['wenzdɪ] — Mittwoch
✎ Days of the week

week [wi:k] — Woche
✎ Days of the week
∞ weekday — Wochentag
∞ at the weekend — am Wochenende

weigh [weɪ] — wiegen
I've weighed my suitcase.
It weighs 15 kg.
➪ weight [weɪt] — Gewicht

welcome ['welkəm] — willkommen
Welcome to Wales. — Willkommen in Wales!
☛ Thanks a lot. – You're welcome. — Vielen Dank. – Bitteschön.

well [wel] — gut; gesund; na ja, also

☛ Steigerung: well, better, best → good
She paints well. — Sie malt gut.
She paints better than me. — Sie malt besser als ich.
∞ Well done! — Gut gemacht!
∞ well-known — bekannt, berühmt
≈ famous
get well — gesund werden
∞ Get well soon! — Gute Besserung!
Are you well? — Geht es dir gut?
Isn't that a good idea? – Well, I'm not sure. — … – Na ja, ich bin mir nicht sicher.

west → north — Westen; westlich, West-
✎ Place and direction
∞ west of — westlich von
∞ the West Indies — die Westindischen Inseln
➪ western — westlich, West-; *Western*
the western regions — die westlichen Gebiete
I'm watching a western.

wet [wet] ⇔ dry — naß, regnerisch
✎ The weather

| WET PAINT | — Vorsicht, frisch gestrichen!

what [wɒt] — was, was für (ein/eine), welche(r/s)
What's that? — Was ist das?
∞ What about …? — Wie wär's/ist es mit …?
→ about
What's the weather like? — Wie ist das Wetter?
What colour do you like best? — Welche Farbe magst du am liebsten?
What a strange idea! — Was für eine seltsame Idee!

wheel [wi:l] — Rad
∞ front/back wheel — Vorder-/Hinterrad
∞ steering wheel — Lenkrad

when [wen] — wann; wenn; als
✎ Expressions of time
When will you be back? — Wann bist du zurück?
I'll help you when I've finished breakfast. — Ich helfe dir, wenn ich mit dem Frühstück fertig bin.
When we arrived at the station, the train had already left. — Als wir am Bahnhof ankamen, war der Zug schon weg.

where [weə] — wo; wohin
Where's Tim? — Wo ist Tim?
Where are you going? — Wohin gehst du?
Where's he from? — Woher kommt er?

which [wɪtʃ] — welche(r/s); der, die, das
Which of the books did you like best? — Welches der Bücher hat dir am besten gefallen?
I need a knife which cuts very well. — … ein Messer, das sehr gut schneidet.
☛ Bei Personen sagt man *who*: a mechanic who knows his job

while [waɪl] — während; Weile
✎ Expressions of time
While Ann laid the table, Helen made a salad. — Während Ann den Tisch deckte, …
☛ Vor einem Hauptwort steht *during*:
<u>during</u> our holidays — <u>während</u> unserer Ferien

It took us a while to find the house.

Wir brauchten eine Weile, bis wir das Haus fanden.

∞ for a while

eine Weile, eine Zeitlang

Can you wait for a while?

Kannst du eine Weile warten?

whisper ['wɪspə]   flüstern

white [waɪt]   weiß
✎ Colours

who [hu:]   wer, wen, wem; der, die, das

Who's that?   Wer ist das?
Who did you call?   Wen hast du angerufen?

Who are you talking about?   Von wem redet ihr?
Do you know the girl who is sitting by the window?   ... das Mädchen, das am Fenster sitzt?
☛ Bei Sachen sagt man *which*:
a machine which doesn't work   eine Maschine, die nicht funktioniert

whole [həʊl]   ganz
What did you do the whole day?   Was hast du den ganzen Tag gemacht?

whose [hu:z]   wessen; dessen, deren
Whose dog is this?   Wem gehört dieser Hund?
Are you the girl whose father rang this morning?   Bist du das Mädchen, dessen Vater heute morgen angerufen hat?

why [waɪ]   warum
Why didn't you come to our party?
∞ that's why   deshalb
We were all in the garden, that's why we didn't hear the phone.

wide [waɪd]   breit, weit
⇔ narrow
a wide river
The door is wide open.

wife [waɪf]   Ehefrau
✎ Relatives

wild [waɪld]   wild
wild animals
∞ wildlife   die Tierwelt

will [wɪl], **would** [wʊd]   werden
Things will change soon.   Die Dinge werden sich bald ändern.
What would you like to do today?   Was würdest du heute gern tun?
☛ Kurzformen:
'll = will
won't = will not
'd = would
wouldn't = would not
I think I'll come, too.   Ich glaube, ich komme auch.
We won't be back until ten.   Wir werden erst um zehn zurück sein.
I'd rather stay at home.   Ich würde lieber zu Hause bleiben.
If you got up earlier, you wouldn't always be late for school.   Wenn du früher aufstehen würdest, würdest du nicht immer zu spät zur Schule kommen.

win [wɪn], **won** [wʌn], **won**   gewinnen
Who won the race?   Wer hat das Rennen gewonnen?
➪ winner   Gewinner(in)

wind [wɪnd]   Wind
✎ The weather
➪ windy   windig
∞ windscreen ['wɪndskri:n]   Windschutzscheibe

wind (up) [waɪnd], **wound** [waʊnd], **wound**   (Uhr) aufziehen

window ['wɪndəʊ]   Fenster
✎ House and flat
∞ shop window   Schaufenster
   ✎ In town

wine [waɪn]   Wein
✎ Drinks

wing [wɪŋ]   Flügel; Tragfläche
the wings of a bird
the wings of a plane

winter ['wɪntə]   Winter
✎ Months and seasons

wipe [waɪp]   (ab)wischen
   She wiped the
   table with a wet
   cloth.
⇨ windscreen   Scheibenwischer
   wiper

wire ['waɪə]   Draht

wish [wɪʃ]   wünschen; Wunsch
   We wish you   Wir wünschen
   luck.   dir viel Glück.
   I wish you were   Ich wünschte, du
   here.   wärest hier.
   Best wishes for   Die besten Wün-
   the New Year!   sche zum neuen
     Jahr!

with [wɪð]   mit; bei
⇔ without
   a book with a red   ein Buch mit ei-
   cover   nem roten Ein-
     band
   Have you got the   Hast du die Fahr-
   tickets with you?   karten dabei?
   I'm staying with   Ich wohne zur
   friends at the   Zeit bei Freunden.
   moment.
∞ within [wɪˈðɪn]   innerhalb (von)
   She phoned six
   times within an
   hour.

without [wɪˈðaʊt]   ohne
⇔ with
   We won't go
   without you.
   He left without   Er ging, ohne
   saying goodbye.   sich zu verab-
     schieden.

woman ['wʊmən],   Frau, Frauen
women ['wɪmɪn]
✎ People
∞ a business woman   eine Geschäftsfrau
∞ an Englishwoman   eine Engländerin

wonder ['wʌndə]   sich fragen; Wunder
   I wonder why   Ich frage mich,
   she didn't answer   warum sie mei-
   my letter.   nen Brief nicht
     beantwortet hat.
   No wonder   Kein Wunder,
   you're fat if you   daß du dick bist,
   eat so much.   ...
∞ wonderful   wunderbar

wood [wʊd]   Holz; Wald
   Put some more
   wood on the fire,
   please.

∞ woodwork   Holzarbeiten,
   ✎ School subjects   Tischlern

wool [wuːl]   Wolle

word [wɜːd]   Wort

Mother: I don't
want to hear
those bad words
again, Jim.
Jim: But Mum,
Shakespeare uses
them quite a lot.
Mother: Then
don't play with
him again.

work [wɜːk]   arbeiten; funktio-
     nieren; Arbeit
   He works in a
   tool factory.
   Does this
   machine work?
   When do you get
   home from
   work?
∞ at work   bei der Arbeit
∞ go to work   zur Arbeit gehen
∞ out of work   arbeitslos
∞ workday   Arbeitstag
∞ workshop   Werkstatt
⇨ worker ✎ Jobs   Arbeiter(in)
∞ road worker   Straßenarbei-
     ter(in)
∞ office worker   Büroangestell-
     te(r)

world [wɜːld] ≈ earth   Welt
   I'd like to travel   ... um die Welt ...
   around the world
   one day.
   He's one of the   Er ist einer der
   richest people <u>in</u>   reichsten Leute
   the world.   <u>auf</u> der Welt.
∞ a world language   eine Weltsprache
∞ worldwide   weltweit

worry ['wʌrɪ]   sich Sorgen ma-
     chen; Kummer
   Don't worry
   about your
   budgies. I'll look
   after them.
   You don't look
   happy. Do you
   have any
   worries?
⇨ worried   besorgt, beun-
     ruhigt

worse [wɜːs] → bad

schlechter, schlimmer

My headache is getting worse and worse.

Mein Kopfweh wird immer schlimmer.

(the) worst [wɜːst] → bad

schlechteste(r), schlimmste(r), am schlechtesten, am schlimmsten

Maths is my worst subject.

Mathe ist mein schlechtestes Fach.

The whole band played badly, but the guitarist played the worst.

… spielte am schlechtesten.

worth [wɜːθ]
The house is worth a million.
Do you think we have a chance of winning? – It's worth a try.

wert
Das Haus ist eine Million wert.

… – Es ist einen Versuch wert.

would [wʊd] → will

wound [wuːnd]
≈ injure; injury
He was badly wounded in the fight.
The wound on his arm hurt a lot.

verwunden; Wunde

Er wurde bei dem Kampf schwer verwundet.
Die Wunde an seinem Arm schmerzte sehr.

write [wraɪt], **wrote** [rəʊt], **written** ['rɪtn]
She's writing a letter.
∞ write s.th. down

schreiben

etw. aufschreiben

wrong [rɒŋ] ≈ false;
⇔ right, correct
the wrong answer
∞ What's wrong?

falsch

Was ist los (=nicht in Ordnung)?

X [eks] **is for**

Xmas ['eksməs]
≈ Christmas ['krɪsməs]

(umgangssprachlich für:) Weihnachten

X-ray ['eksreɪ]

Röntgenaufnahme; röntgen

∞ take an X-ray of s.th. ≈ x-ray s.th.

etw. röntgen

Doctor: I've x-rayed you and I've found an alarm-clock in your stomach. Haven't you got any problems with it?
Patient: No, the only problem is winding it up every morning.

Y [waɪ] **is for**

yard [jɑːd]

Yard (Längenmaß); Hof; *AE auch:* Garten

One yard is about 91 cm.
I met her in the school yard today.
∞ front yard (*AE*)
≈ front garden (*BE*)

… auf dem Schulhof …
Vorgarten

yawn [jɔːn]

gähnen

year [jɪə]
✎ Expressions of time
∞ Happy New Year!

Jahr

Gutes neues Jahr!

yellow ['jeləʊ]
✎ Colours

gelb

yes [jes] ⇔ no
Would you like some more cake? – Yes, please.

ja

yesterday ['jestədeɪ]
✎ Expressions of time
∞ the day before yesterday

gestern

vorgestern

yet [jet]
They haven't arrived yet.

Have you bought the tickets yet?

noch; schon
Sie sind noch nicht angekommen.

Hast du die Karten schon gekauft?

you [juː]

du; ihr; Sie

young [jʌŋ] ⇔ old
a young girl
⇨ youth [juːθ]
∞ youth hostel

jung

Jugend
Jugendherberge

Z [zed] is for

zebra [ˈzebrə]
✎ Animals
∞ zebra crossing
  ✎ In town

Zebra

Zebrastreifen

zero [ˈzɪərəʊ]
12 degrees below zero
☞ Bei Telefonnummern sagt man *o* [əʊ], bei Mannschaftsspielen *nil* [nɪl], beim Tennis *love* [lʌv]:

Null, null
12 Grad unter Null

My number is seven-o-three-four-one.
The football match ended two-nil.
Steffi Graf is leading fifteen-love.

... sieben-null-drei-vier-eins.

... zwei zu null.

... fünfzehn zu null.

Reißverschluß

zip (fastener) [ˈzɪp-fɑːsnə] *(BE)*/**zipper** [ˈzɪpə] *(AE)*

zoo [zuː]
∞ zoo-keeper
  ✎ Jobs

Zoo
Tierpfleger(in), Zoowärter(in)

II. Deutsch-englische Wortliste

Immer wenn du einen englischen Brief, eine Postkarte oder eine kleine Erzählung abfassen sollst, wirst du das eine oder andere Wort nachschlagen müssen. In der folgenden Wortliste findest du alles, was in der englisch-deutschen Liste enthalten ist, noch einmal kurz und bündig deutsch-englisch geordnet. Wenn es Verwechslungen geben könnte, steht eine zusätzliche Erklärung in Klammern:

> **Geist** *(Gespenst)* ghost
> ~ *(Verstand)* mind

Auch die drei Formen der unregelmäßigen Verben sowie schwierige Mehrzahlformen werden mit angegeben:

> **abfahren** leave/left/left   **Blatt/Blätter** *(Baum)*
>   leaf/leaves

Das Zeichen „~", das auch in großen Wörterbüchern verwendet wird, heißt Tilde und ersetzt das deutsche oder englische Stichwort:

> **Apfel** apple
> **~baum** ~ tree   (für: **Apfelbaum** apple tree)

Wenn das Stichwort groß, das „Tildewort" aber klein geschrieben wird, oder umgekehrt, findest du den großen oder kleinen Anfangsbuchstaben vor der Tilde:

> **Erfolg** success
> **e~reich** ~ful   (für: **erfolgreich** successful)

Gelegentlich findest du auch eine Doppeltilde. Sie steht für das Stichwort und das unmittelbar vorangehende „Tildewort":

> **Meister** *(im Sport)*
> champion
> **~schaft** ~ship   (für: **Meisterschaft** championship
> **~~skämpfe** ~~s   **Meisterschaftskämpfe** championships)

Wie in der englisch-deutschen Wortliste werden die folgenden Abkürzungen verwendet:

s.o.	someone
s.th.	something
etw.	etwas
jdm.	jemandem
jdn.	jemanden

Ein Tip zum Schluß: Wenn du einmal unsicher bist, ob du das englische Wort richtig anwendest, schlage es in der englisch-deutschen Wort nach, denn dort findest du ausführliche Hinweise und Beispiele.

A

ab *(weg)* off
  ab und zu now and then
abbiegen: nach rechts/links ~ turn right/left
Abend evening; night
  ~essen dinner; supper; tea
  Guten ~. Good evening.
  am ~/abends in the evening
  heute a~ this evening; tonight
  Heiliger ~ Christmas Eve
Abenteuer adventure
aber but
abfahren leave/left/left
Abfahrt departure
Abfall litter; waste
  ~eimer litter bin
abfertigen *(Gepäck)* check in
  Abfertigung check-in
abfliegen leave/left/left; take off (take/took/taken)
Abflug departure
abgeben *(einreichen)* hand in
Abgeordneter des britischen Unterhauses Member of Parliament (MP)
abheben *(Flugzeug)* take off (take/took/taken)
abholen: jdn. ~ *(mitnehmen)* pick s.o. up
  jdn. vom Bahnhof ~ meet s.o. at the station (meet/met/met)
abkühlen cool
ablesen: die Urzeit ~ tell the time (tell/told/told)
abnehmen *(Hut)* take off (take/took/taken)
abreißen *(Gebäude)* knock down
abschalten *(Licht)* switch off (the light)
abschicken *(Brief)* post (a letter)
abschließen *(mit Schlüssel)* lock
Abschluß end; finish
abschreiben copy

absetzen *(Hut)* take off (take/took/taken)
Abteilung department
abwaschen wash up
abwischen wipe
Ach so. I see.
achten/achtgeben (auf) mind; look out (for)
  Achtung, Stufe! Mind the step!
Ackerboden/~land farmland
Adresse address
Affe monkey
Agent(in) agent
Agentur agency
Ahnung: keine ~ no idea
aktiv active
  das A~ the ~ voice
Alarm alarm
albern silly
alle all
  ~s anything; everything
  Alles Gute. All the best.
allein alone; on one's own
allgemein general
  im ~en in ~
allzu too
als as; than; when
  als ob as if
also *(na ja)* well
  ~ *(deshalb)* so
alt old
  ~modisch old-fashioned
Alter age
Amerika America
  ~ner(in)/a~nisch American
Ampel *(Verkehrs~)* (traffic) lights
amtlich official
an: ~ der Ecke at the corner
  am Fenster at/by the window
  an der Küste on the coast
  am Morgen/Nachmittag/Abend in the morning/afternoon/evening
  am Sonntag on Sunday
  am Telefon on the (tele)phone
  am Wochenende at the weekend
anbauen grow/grew/grown

anbieten offer
  etw. zum Verkauf ~ put s.th. up for sale (put/put/put)
anbringen *(befestigen)* fix; put up (a lamp)
andauern continue; go on (go/went/gone); last
Andenken souvenir
andere(r/s) other
  andere others
  ein ~(r/s) another
  etwas ~s something else
  andererseits on the ~ hand
ändern/sich ~/Änderung change
anders different
  ~herum the other way round
  jemand ~ someone else
  ~wo(hin) somewhere else
Anfall attack
  Herz~ heart ~
Anfang beginning; start
  a~en begin/began/begun; start
  Anfänger(in) beginner; learner
Anführer(in) leader
angeben *(beim Zoll)* declare
Angebot offer
Angelegenheit matter
angreifen/Angriff attack
Angst fear
  ~ einjagen frighten
  ~ haben (vor) be/feel frightened (of) (feel/felt/felt); be afraid/scared (of)
  ~schrei cry of fear
anhalten stop
Anhalter: per ~ fahren hitchhike
Anhänger(in) *(Fan)* fan
ankommen arrive
Ankunft arrival
anlocken attract
Annonce ad/advert/advertisement; notice
Anorak anorak
Anordnung *(Gestaltung)* layout
Anpfiff *(Spiel)* kick-off
anprobieren try on
anrufen call; (tele-) phone; ring/rang/rung

  jdn. ~ give s.o. a ring (give/gave/given)
  Anruf (phone) call; ring
  Anrufer(in) caller
anschalten *(Licht)* switch on (the light)
anschauen look at
anschließen: sich jdm. ~ join s.o.
Anschrift address
ansiedeln: sich ~ settle
anstatt instead of
Anstellung employment; job
Anstoß *(Spiel)* kick-off
antreiben drive/drove/driven
Antwort/antworten answer
anwenden use
Anzeige *(Annonce)* ad/advert/advertisement; notice
anziehen *(anlocken)* attract
  ~d attractive
  ~ *(Kleidung)* put on (put/put/put)
  sich ~ dress
Anzug suit
anzünden light/lit/lit
Apfel apple
  ~baum ~ tree
  ~saft ~ juice
Apotheker(in) chemist
  in der Apotheke at the ~'s
April April
Aquarium fish tank
Arbeit job; work
  bei der ~ at work
  zur ~ gehen go to work (go/went/gone)
  arbeiten work
  ~er(in) worker
  ~geber(in) employer
  ~nehmer(in) employee
  a~slos out of work
  ~slosigkeit unemployment
  ~stag workday
Architekt(in) architect
Ärger trouble
ärgerlich *(zornig)* angry
Arm arm
  ~banduhr watch
arm poor
Ärmelkanal (the) Channel
  ~tunnel ~ Tunnel
Art kind; sort; type
  ~ und Weise way

Artikel article
Arznei medicine
Arzt/Ärztin doctor
Assistent(in) assistant
assistieren assist
Ast branch
Atlantischer Ozean Atlantic Ocean
Atomkraft atomic energy
Attraktion attraction
  attraktiv attractive
auch also; too; as well
  ich ~ so do/am/can/ ... I
  ~ nicht not ... either; neither; nor
auf on
  ~ dem Baum in the tree
  ~ dem Bild in the picture
  ~ Englisch in English
  ~ dem Lande in the country
  ~ dem Sportplatz at the playing fields
  ~ der Straße in the street
  ~ der Welt in the world
  ~ ... zu towards
aufbrechen *(sich auf den Weg machen)* set off (set/set/set); start
Aufenthalt stay
aufessen finish up
auffahren auf crash into; hit/hit/hit
aufführen *(ein Stück)* do/perform (a play) (do/did/done)
  Aufführung performance
auffüllen fill up
Aufgabe job
aufgeben *(aufhören)* give up (give/gave/ given)
aufgeregt excited
aufhängen hang up (hang/hung/hung)
aufheben *(vom Boden)* pick up
aufhören stop; finish
Aufkleber sticker
auflegen: Make-up ~ put on make-up (put/ put/put)
  den Hörer ~ hang up (hang/hung/hung)
aufmachen open

aufnehmen *(auf Band)* record
aufpassen take care (of) (take/took/taken); watch out
Aufprall crash
  aufprallen auf etw. hit s.th. (hit/hit/hit); crash (into s.th.)
aufpumpen pump up
aufräumen clean up
aufregend exciting
aufrichten: sich ~ sit up (sit/sat/sat)
aufsetzen: die Kartoffeln ~ put the potatoes on (put/ put/put)
  sich ~ sit up (sit/sat/ sat)
aufspannen *(Schirm)* put up (an umbrella) (put/put/put)
aufstehen get up (get/ got/got); stand up (stand/stood/stood)
  ~ *(aus dem Bett)* get up
auftauchen *(erscheinen)* appear
auftragen *(Makeup)* put on (make-up) (put/put/put)
auftreten *(vor Publikum)* perform
  Auftritt ~ance
aufwachen wake (up) (wake/woke/woken)
aufwachsen grow up (grow/grew/grown)
aufzeichnen *(auf Band)* record
  Aufzeichnungsgerät recorder
aufziehen *(Uhr)* wind (up) (wind/wound/ wound)
Aufzug lift
Auge eye
Augenblick moment
  Einen ~, bitte. Just a ~, please.
  im ~ at the ~
August August
aus: ~ dem Haus heraus/hinaus out of the house
  ~ London from London
  ~ Papier made of paper
ausbessern mend; repair
ausbilden train

Ausbildung ~ing; education
  ~skurs training course
ausborgen: sich ~ borrow
Ausdruck expression
Ausflug trip
ausfüllen *(Formular)* fill in (a form)
Ausgang *(Tür)* exit
  ~ *(Ende)* ending
ausgeben *(Geld)* spend/spent/spent
ausgehen *(Feuer)* go out (go/went/gone)
Ausguß sink
auskommen: mit jdm. ~ get along with s.o. (get/got/got)
Auskunft information
Ausland: im/ins ~ abroad
  Ausländer(in) foreigner
  ausländisch foreign
ausleihen: sich etw. von jdm. ~ borrow s.th. from s.o.
  jdm. etw. ~ lend s.th. to s.o. (lend/lent/ lent)
ausliefern deliver
ausmachen *(Licht)* put out (the light) (put/ put/put)
  Es macht mir nichts aus. I don't mind.
Ausnahme: mit ~ von except
ausnutzen make use of (make/made/made)
ausputzen clean out
Ausrede excuse
ausrichten: etw. *(eine Botschaft)* **~** take a message (take/took/ taken)
Ausrüstung equipment; kit
ausschalten *(Licht)* switch/turn off (the light)
aussehen look
außer except
außerdem besides
außerhalb von outside
äußerst most
Aussicht (auf) view (of)
ausstehen: nicht ~ können cannot stand
aussteigen get off (a bus) (get/got/got)

Australien Australia
  Australier(in)/australisch Australian
  australisches Hinterland outback
austrinken finish up
austrocknen dry up
Ausverkauf sale
auswandern emigrate
  Auswanderer/Auswanderin emigrant
auswendig by heart
ausziehen *(Kleidung)* take off (take/took/ taken)
Auszubildende(r) apprentice
Auto car
  ~ fahren *(selbst)* drive/drove/driven
  mit dem ~ fahren go by ~ (go/went/gone)
  ~bahn *(BE)* motorway; *(AE)* highway
  ~rennen ~ race
  ~waschanlage ~ wash
  ~werkstatt garage
Automat machine
Axt axe

B

Baby baby
  ~sitter ~-sitter
  b~sitten ~-sit
backen bake
  Backofen oven
  Backpulver baking powder
Bäcker baker
Bad/~ewanne bath
  ein ~ nehmen take a ~ (take/took/taken)
  ~eanzug bathing suit; swimsuit
  ~ehose swimming trunks
  ~eort *(am Meer)* seaside resort
  ~ezimmer bathroom
Bahn *(Eisen~)* railway
  ~hof (~) station
  ~linie ~ line
  ~steig platform
bald soon
Balkon balcony
Ball ball
Banane banana
Band *(Kapelle)* band
  (Schnür-)~ tie
  (Ton-)~ tape

Bande gang
Bank *(Sitz~)* bench
~ *(Geldinstitut)* bank
~konto ~ account
~note ~note
Bar bar
Bär bear
Eis~ polar ~
bar: ~ bezahlen pay in cash (pay/paid/paid)
Bargeld cash
Bart beard
Baseball baseball
Basketball basketball
~mannschaft ~ team
Batterie battery
Bauch belly; stomach
bauen build/built/built; construct
Bau construction
Baustelle building/ construction site
Bauer/Bäuerin farmer
~nhaus farmhouse
~nhof farm
Baum tree
Baumwolle cotton
~feld ~ field
~hemd ~ shirt
Beamter/Beamtin officer
beantragen apply for
beantworten answer
beben shake/shook/ skaken
Becken *(Schwimm~)* pool
bedanken: sich bei jdm. ~ thank s.o.
bedauern *(bemitleiden)* pity
~swert pitiful
bedecken cover
bedeuten mean/meant/ meant
bedeutend important
bedienen: jdn. ~ serve s.o.
sich ~ help oneself
einen Computer ~ operate a computer
Bedienung *(Service)* service
beeilen: sich ~ hurry
beenden complete; finish; end
Befähigung qualification
befehlen/Befehl order
befestigen fasten; fix
Beförderung *(Transport)* transport
befragen interview

befreien free
befürchten fear; be afraid of
Beginn beginning; start
beginnen begin/ began/begun; start
begraben bury
Begründung reason
behaglich comfortable
behalten keep/kept/ kept
Behälter container
bei: ~ jdm. sein be with s.o.
~ der Arbeit at work
~ Tag/Nacht by day/ night
~ schlechtem Wetter in bad weather
beim Bäcker at the baker's
beibringen *(lehren)* teach/taught/taught
beide both
die ~n Brüder the two brothers
Beifallrufe cheers
Beil axe
Bein leg
beinahe almost; nearly
Beispiel example
zum ~ (z. B.) for ~ (e. g.)
beißen bite/bit/bitten
beitreten *(einem Club)* join (a club)
bekämpfen fight/ fought/fought
bekannt famous; well-known
bekommen get/got/got; receive
beleuchten light/lit/lit
Belgien Belgium
Belgier(in)/belgisch Belgian
beliebt popular
bellen bark
bemerken *(wahrneh-men)* notice
Bemerkung comment
bemitleiden pity
benachrichtigen inform
benehmen: sich ~ act; behave
benutzen use
Benutzer(in) user
Benzin *(BE)* petrol; *(AE)* gas
beobachten watch; look at
bequem *(behaglich)* comfortable
bereits already

Berg moutain
~mann miner
~steigen (~) climbing
~steiger(in) (~) climber
~werk mine
berichten/Bericht (über) report (on)
Beruf job
b~liche Laufbahn career
~sberater(in) careers officer
~sberatung(sstelle) careers office
berühmt famous; well-known
berühren touch
beschädigen damage
beschäftigen employ
beschäftigt busy
Bescheinigung certificate
beschließen decide
beschreiben describe
Beschreibung description
beschweren: sich ~ complain
besetzt *(Telefonleitung)* busy
Besichtigung: auf ~stour gehen go sightseeing (go/went/ gone)
besitzen have (got) (have/had/had); own
Besitzer(in) owner
besondere(r/s) special
besorgt worried
besser better
beste(r/s)/am besten best
bestehen *(Prüfung)* pass (an exam)
bestellen/Bestellung order
eine Bestellung entgegennehmen take an ~ (take/took/ taken)
Besuch/besuchen visit
zu ~ sein be on a ~
~ haben have company (have/had/had)
~er(in) visitor
jdn. besuchen (gehen/kommen) go/come and see s.o. (go/went/gone; come/came/come)
beten pray
betrunken sein be drunk

Bett bed
~laken sheet
betteln beg
Bettler(in) beggar
beunruhigt worried
Beutel bag
bevor before
bewachen guard
bewaffnet armed
bewegen/sich ~ move
Bewegung movement
b~slos still
bewerben: sich ~ um apply for
bewölkt cloudy
bezahlen pay/paid/paid
Bibliothek library
Biene bee
Bier beer
Bild picture
~erbuch ~ book
Bildschirm screen
~arbeiter(in) computer operator
billig cheap
binden tie
Biologie biology
Birne pear
Glüh~ bulb
bis until; till
~ (spätestens) by
~her/~ jetzt so far
bißchen: ein ~ a bit (of); a little; some
bitte please
B~schön. *(nach „Danke")* You're welcome.
Hier, ~~. Here you are.
bitten ask; beg
bitter bitter
Blase *(Gas~)* bubble
blasen blow/blew/ blown
Blatt/Blätter *(Baum)* leaf/leaves
~ *(Papier)* sheet
blau blue
bleiben keep/kept/ kept; remain; stay
Bleistift pencil
Blick look
Blitz/blitzen flash
Block block
~schrift ~ letters
Wohn~ ~ of flats
blond fair
Blume flower
~ntopf ~ pot
Blumenkohl cauli-flower
Bluse blouse
Blut blood

blutig bloody
Boden *(unteres Ende)* bottom
  (Erd-)~ ground
  (Fuß-)~ floor
Bohne bean
bohren/Bohrer drill
  Bohrmaschine drilling machine
Bonbon *(BE)* sweet; *(AE)* candy
Boot boat
  ~fahren ~ing
Bord *(Schiff)* board
  (Regal-)~(e) shelf/shelves
borgen: sich etw. von jdm. ~ borrow s.th. from s.o.
  jdm. etw. ~ lend s.th. to s.o. (lend/lent/lent)
böse auf angry at
Botschaft message
  eine ~ entgegennehmen take a ~ (take/took/taken)
Boxen boxing
  Boxer boxer
Brand fire
  in ~ sein bew on fire
braten fry; roast
  (der) B~/ge~ roast
  Bratkartoffeln fried potatoes
  Bratpfanne frying pan
  Rinder~ roast beef
brauchen need
  (Zeit) ~ take (time) (take/took/taken)
  nicht (zu tun) ~ needn't (do)
braun brown
brechen break/broke/broken
breit broad; wide
Bremse/bremsen brake
brennen burn/burnt/burnt; be on fire
  Brennholz firewood
Brett board
  Schwarzes ~ noticeboard
Brief letter
  ~freund(in) pen-friend
  ~kasten letterbox; post-box
  ~marke stamp
  ~tasche wallet
  ~träger(in) postman/postwoman
  ~umschlag envelope

Brille glasses
bringen: *(her~)* bring/brought/brought *(weg~)* take/took/taken
Brite/Britin Briton
  die Briten the British
  britisch British
  die Britischen Inseln the British Isles
Brot bread
Brötchen roll
Brücke bridge
Bruder brother
Brust(korb) chest
Buch/buchen book
  ~handlung ~shop
  Bücherei library
Büchse *(BE)* tin; *(AE)* can
Buchstabe letter
  buchstabieren spell
bügeln/Bügeleisen iron
Bulle bull
Bundesrepublik (Deutschland) Federal Republic (of Germany)
Burg castle
Büro office
  ~angestellte(r) ~ worker; clerk
Bürste/bürsten brush
Bus bus
  mit dem ~ fahren go by ~ (go/went/gone)
  ~bahnhof ~ station
  ~fahrer(in) ~ driver
  ~fahrkarte ~ ticket
  ~haltestelle ~ stop
  Reise~ coach
  ~reise coach tour
Butter butter

C

Café café; coffeeshop
Cafeteria cafeteria
Cent cent
Chance chance
Charterflug charter flight
China China
  Chinese/Chinesin/chinesisch/C~ Chinese
  Chinesenviertel Chinatown
Chips *(Kartoffel~)* *(BE)* crisps; *(AE)* chips
Chor *(Gesangs~)* choir

Christ(in)/christlich Christian
Christus Christ
Clown clown
Club club
Comicheft comic
Computer computer
Couch couch; sofa
Cousin/~e cousin
Creme cream

D

da/dahin there
  da (ja) *(weil)* since
Dach roof
  ~boden attic
daher *(deshalb)* so; that's why; therefore
damals then
Dame lady
  meine ~ madam
  ~nschneider(in) dressmaker
Dampf steam
  ~er ~er
  ~maschine ~ engine
danach after that
Däne/Dänin Dane
  die Dänen the ~s/the Danish
  Dänemark Denmark
  dänisch/D~ Danish
danken thank
  Danke. Thank you./Thanks.
  Vielen Dank. Thank you very much./Thanks a lot.
  Nein Danke. No thanks.
dann then
  ~ und wann now and ~
das the
  ~ (hier) this
  ~ (da/dort) that
dasein exist
daß that
Datum date
Dauerlauf jogging
  ~ machen jog
dauern last; take/took/taken
Decke cover
  (Woll-/Bett-)~ blanket
  (Zimmer-)~ ceiling
  Deckel cover
decken: den Tisch ~ lay the table (lay/laid/laid)

dein(e) your
  deine(r/s) yours
denken think/thought/thought
  an jdn./etw. ~ ~ of s.o./s.th.
der/die/das the; that; which; who
  ~ (hier) this
  ~ (da/dort) that
  ~selbe the same
deren whose
deshalb so; that's why; therefore
Designer(in) designer
dessen whose
Detektiv detective
deuten point
deutsch/D~/D~e(r) German
  D~land Germany
Dezember December
Dialog dialogue
dich you; yourself
dicht *(Nebel)* thick
Dichter(in) poet
  Dichtung poetry
dick thick
  ~ (Personen) fat
die the; who; which; that
  ~ (hier) this; these;
  ~ (da/dort) that; those
Dieb(e)/Diebin(nen) thief/thieves
Diele hall
Diener(in) servant
Dienstag Tuesday
dies(e/r) this; that;
  diese *(Mehrzahl)* these/those
diesmal this time
Diktat dictation
diktieren dictate
Ding thing
dir you; yourself
direkt direct
  ~(Sendung) live
  ~ (unmittelbar) right; straight
Direktor(in) director
Disko(thek) disco
Doktor doctor
  Herr/Frau Dr. Smith Dr (Doctor) Smith
Dollar dollar
Dom cathedral
Donner thunder
Donnerstag Thursday
doof dumb
doppelt double
  Doppeldeckerbus double-decker
Dorf village

dort/~hin there
  ~ oben/~ hoch up there
Dose *(BE)* tin; *(AE)* can
  ~nöffner ~ opener
Drachen *(Papier~)* kite
  ~fliegen hang-gliding
Draht wire
draußen outside; outdoors
drehen/sich ~/Drehung turn
drinnen inside; indoors
dritte(r/s)/Drittel third
Drogen drugs
drücken press; push
Dschungel jungle
du you
Dudelsack bagpipe
dumm stupid; dumb
  ~(albern) silly;
  Dummkopf fool
dunkel/D~heit dark
  ~blau ~ blue
  ~rot ~ red
dünn thin
Dunst mist
durch through
  jdn. (am Telefon) ~stellen put s.o. ~ (put/put/put)
  (quer) ~ across
durchsuchen search
dürfen may; be allowed to
  nicht ~ musn't
durstig thirsty
  Durst haben be ~
Dusche shower

E

ebenfalls too; as well; also
echt true
Ecke corner
Edelstein jewel
egal: Das ist ~ It doesn't matter.
  Es ist mir ~. I don't care.
Ehe marriage
  ~frau wife
  ~mann husband
ehe before
ehrlich honest
Ei egg
Eiche oak
eigene(r/s) own
Eigenschaft quality
eigentlich actually
Eile/eilen hurry

Eimer bucket
ein(e) a/an; one
  einer/eines one
  eines Tages one day
einander one another; each other
Einbahnstraße one-way street
Einband cover
einbeziehen include
Einbrecher(in) burglar
einfach easy; simple
  ~(nur) just
Eingang entrance; entry
Einheimische local people
Einheit unit
einige some; any; a few
Einkauf shopping
  den ~ erledigen do the ~ (do/did/done)
  ~sliste ~ list
  ~szentrum ~ centre
  einkaufen gehen go ~ (go/went/gone)
einmal once
einreichen hand in
eins one
einsam lonely
einsammeln collect
einschalten *(Licht)* switch/turn on (the light)
einschlafen go to sleep (go/went/gone); fall asleep (fall/fell/fallen)
einschließen *(enthalten)* include
einsteigen get on (a bus) (get/got/got)
eintreten enter; go/come in(go/went/gone; come/came/come)
Eintritt entrance; entry
  ~sgebühr entrance fee
  ~skarte ticket
einwandern immigrate
einwerfen *(Brief)* post (a letter)
Einwohner(in) *(Staat)* citizen
Einzel.../einzeln single
  ~kind only child
  ~zimmer single room
einzige(r/s) only
Eis ice
  ~hockey ~ hockey
  ~krem ~-cream
  ~laufen ~ skating
Eisen iron

~bahn *(BE)* railway; *(AE)* railroad
  ~bergwerk iron mine
Elefant elephant
Elektriker(in) eletrician
elektrisch electric
Elektrizität electricity
Elektronik electronics
  elektronisch electronic
Ellbogen elbow
Eltern parents
empfangen receive
  Empfänger(in) receiver
  Empfang reception
Ende end; ending; finish
  oberes ~ top
  unteres ~ bottom
enden/be~ end; finish
endlich at last; finally
Endspiel final
Energie energy; power
eng narrow
Engel angel
England England
  Engländer(in) Englishman/-woman
  die Engländer the English
english/E~ English
  E~lehrer(in) ~ teacher
  ~sprachige Länder ~-speaking countries
  E~stunde ~ lesson
Enkel... grand...
  ~kind grandchild
  ~sohn ~son
  ~tocher ~daughter
entdecken discover
Ente duck
entfernen take off (take/took/taken); remove
Entfernung distance
entfliehen escape
entführen kidnap
enthalten contain
entlang along
entschließen: sich ~ decide; make up one's mind (make/made/made)
Entschluß decision
entschuldigen/Entschuldigung excuse
Entsetzen horror
entsetzlich horrific
enttäuschen disappoint
  enttäuscht disappointed
entweder ... oder either ... or

entweichen escape
entwerfen design
entwickeln/sich ~ develop
  Entwicklung ~ment
  ~sland ~ing country
Entwurf design
er he
  ~ *(betont)* him
Erbse pea
Erdbeere strawberry
  Erdbeermarmelade ~ jam
Erde earth
Erdgeschoß ground floor
Erdkugel globe
Erdkunde geography
Erdteil continent
Ereignis event
Erfahrung experience
erfinden invent
  Erfinder(in) inventor
  Erfindung invention
Erfolg success
  e~reich ~ful
erfreut glad; happy; pleased
erhalten *(bekommen)* get/got/got; receive
erhängen hang/hanged/hanged
erhitzen heat
erinnern: sich an etw. ~ remember s.th.
  jdn an etw. ~ remind s.o. of s.th.
erkälten: sich ~ catch a cold (catch/caught/caught)
  Erkältung cold
  erkältet sein have a cold (have/had/had)
erklären explain
erlauben allow; let/let/let
ernähren feed/fed/fed
erraten guess
  ernst serious
erreichen reach
  einen Zug ~ catch a train (catch/caught/caught)
Ersatz... spare
  ~teile ~ parts
erscheinen appear
erschießen shoot/shot/shot
erschrecken: jnd. ~ frighten s.o.
  erschrocken frightened
Ersparnisse savings

erst *(noch nicht mehr als)* only
~ *(nicht vor)* not until
~ *(zuerst)* first
erste(r/s)/als ~ first
Erste Hilfe ~ aid
ersticken choke
ertragen bear/bore/borne
erwachsen/E~e(r) adult; grown-up
erwähnen mention
erwarten expect
erwürgen choke
erzählen tell/told/told
Erzeugnis product
Erziehung education
es it
Esel donkey
Essen food
~ *(Mahlzeit)* meal
~ **auf Rädern** meals on wheels
essen eat/ate/eaten; have/had/had
Eßzimmer dining-room
Etui case
etwas something; anything; some; any
~ **anderes** something else
~ **Geld** some/any money
euch you; yourselves
euer/eure your
eure(r/s) yours
Europa Europe
europäisch/Euro-päer(in) European
die Europäische Union the European Union
das europäische Festland the Continent
festlandeuropäisch continental
Euroscheck Eurocheque
ewig for ever
Examen exam(ination)
existieren exist
Experte/Expertin expert
explodieren explode
Explosion explosion
extra extra

F

Fabrik factory
~**arbeiter(in)** ~ worker
Fach *(Unterrichts~)* subject
Fachmann expert
Faden cotton
fähig sein, etw. zu tun be able to do s.th.
Fahne flag
Fähre ferry
fahren *(allgemein)* go/went/gone
(selbst Auto) ~ drive/drove/driven
in einem Auto/Bus (mit)~ ride in a car/on a bus (ride/rode/ridden)
Motorrad ~ ride a motorcycle
rad~ ride a bike
Fahrer(in) driver
Fahrgast passenger
Fahrkarte ticket
~**nautomat** ~ machine
Fahrplan timetable
Fahrpreis fare
Fahrprüfung driving test
Fahrrad bicycle; bike
~**reifen** ~ tyre
~**tour** ~ tour
Fahrschüler(in) learner driver
Fahrt tour; trip; ride
eine ~ machen go for a ride (go/went/gone)
fair fair
fallen fall/fell/fallen; drop
~ **lassen** drop
fällen *(Baum)* chop down; cut down (cut/cut/cut)
falls if
falsch false; wrong
falten fold
Familie family
~**nname** *(BE)* surname; *(AE)* family name/second name
Fan fan
fangen catch/caught/caught
fantastisch fantastic
Farbe colour;
~ *(zum Streichen)* paint

Farm farm
fast almost; nearly
faszinieren fascinate
Faszination fascination
faul lazy
Fax (tele)fax
Februar February
Federmäppchen pencil case
Fehler mistake
Feier party
fein fine
Feld field
Feldwebel sergeant
Fell fur
Felsen rock
felsig rocky
Fenster window
Ferien *(BE)* holidays; *(AE)* vacation
fern far (away)
Fern...: ~**bedienung** remote control
~**kopierer** (tele)fax
~**schreiben** telegram
~**schreiber** telegraph
Fernsehen television; TV
im ~ on ~
f~ watch ~
Fernseher/Fernseh-apparat ~ (set)
Fernsehsendung ~ programme
Ferne: in der ~ in the distance
fertig ready
~**bringen** manage
fesseln *(faszinieren)* fascinate
Fest party; festival
~**spiele** festival
fest firm
~**machen** fasten; fix
~**sitzen/~stecken** be stuck
fett/Fett fat
feucht damp
Feuer/feuern fire
~**melder** ~ alarm
~**wehr** ~ brigade
~~**mann** ~man
~**zeug** lighter
Fieber fever
Filiale branch
Film *(BE)* film; *(AE)* movie
Finale final
finden find/found/found
Finger finger
~**nagel** ~nail
Firma company; firm

Fisch/~e/fischen fish
~**er** fisherman
~**erboot** fishing boat
~**ernetz** fishing net
fischen gehen go fishing (go/went/gone)
fit fit
Fitneß fitness
~**training** ~ training
flach flat
Flagge flag
Flamme flame
in ~n stehen be in ~s
Flasche bottle
Fleisch meat
~**pastete mit Nieren** steak and kidney pie
Fleischer butcher
flicken mend; repair
Flickzeug repair kit
Fliege fly
fliegen fly/flew/flown; go by plane (go/went/gone)
~**de Untertasse** flying saucer
Floh flea
~**markt** ~ market
Flucht escape
Flug flight
~**gast** passenger
~**gesellschaft** airline
~**hafen** aiport
~**schein** plane ticket
~**zeug** aeroplane; (air)plane
Flügel wing
Flur *(Haus~)* hall
Fluß river
flüstern whisper
folgen *(nachgehen)* follow
Fön hair dryer
Form form
in ~ sein be fit
Formular form
Forst forest
Förster(in) ~er; *(AE)* ~ ranger
fort away
Fortschritt(e) progress
fortsetzen continue
Fortsetzung auf Seite ... continued on page ...
Fortsetzung folgt to be continued
Foto photo
ein ~ machen take a ~ (take/took/taken)
~**apparat** camera
~**graf(in)** photographer

120

~kopie/f~~ren ~copy

~~rgerät ~copier

Frage question

eine ~ stellen ask a ~

fragen ask

sich ~ wonder

Frankreich France

französisch/F~ French

Franzose ~man

Französin ~woman

Frau/~en woman/ women

Frau Smith Mrs Smith

Ehefrau wife

Fräulein *(Anrede)* Miss

frei free

jdn. ~lassen set s.o. free (set/set/set)

im Freien (sein) (be) outdoors

F~bad outdoor swimming pool

F~heit freedom; liberty

F~~sstatue Statue of Liberty

F~zeit free time; spare time

Freitag Friday

fremd foreign; strange

F~sprache foreign language

F~e(r) foreigner; stranger

F~enführer(in) guide

fressen eat/ate/eaten

Freude joy

freuen: sich auf etw. ~ look forward to (doing) s.th.

sich über etw. ~ be pleased with s.th.

Freund(in) friend

Freund *(eines Mädchens)* boy~

Freundin girl~

freundlich friendly; kind

auf ~e Weise in a friendly way

Friede peace

friedlich ~ful

Friedhof cemetery; graveyard

frieren/ge~ freeze/ froze/frozen

frisch fresh

~ gestrichen wet paint

Friseur(in) hair dresser; hair stylist

Frisur hairdo; hairstyle

froh glad; happy; pleased

Fröhlichliche Weih-nachten! Merry Christmas.

Frosch frog

Frost frost

frostig frosty

früh early

früher: Er war ~ ... He used to be ...

~ oder später sooner or later

Frühling spring

Frühstück breakfast

kleines ~ continental ~

f~en have ~ (have/ had/had)

fühlen/sich ~ feel/felt/felt

sich wohl ~ be com-fortable

führen lead/led/led

~ *(Geschäft)* manage; run/ran/run

ein Tagebuch ~ keep a diary (keep/kept/kept)

~d leading

(An)führer(in) leader

Fremdenführer(in) guide

Führerschein driving licence

füllen fill

Füllung ~ing

Füller/Füllfederhalter pen

Fundbüro lost property office

Funk radio

f~gesteuerter Wagen ~-controlled car

~telefon ~ telephone

funktionieren work

für for

~ immer ~ ever

Furcht fear

fürchten/sich ~/be~ be afraid (of s.th.); feel frightened (feel/felt/felt); fear (s.th.)

Fürsorge care

Fuß/Füße foot/feet

zu ~ gehen go on ~ (go/went/gone); walk

~weg ~path

Fußball football

~feld ~ field

~mannschaft ~ team

~trainer ~ coach

~training ~ practice

Fußboden floor

Fußgänger(in) pedestrian

~überweg ~ crossing

~zone ~ area

Fußweg (foot)path

Futter *(zum Fressen)* food

füttern feed/fed/fed

G

Gabe gift; present

Gabel fork

gähnen yawn

Gallone gallon

Gang *(Flur)* corridor

im ~ sein be in progress

Gangster gangster

Gans/Gänse goose/ geese

ganz all; whole; quite

Garage garage

Garantie/garantieren guarantee

Garten garden; *(AE)* yard

~arbeit ~ing

~geräte ~ing tools

Gärtner(in) ~er

Gas gas

~herd ~stove

Gast guest

Gästehaus ~house

Gästezimmer spare room

Gebäude building

geben give/gave/given; hand

Gebet prayer

Gebiet area

Gebirge mountains

geboren born

Gebrauch use

gebraucht second-hand; used

G~wagen ~ car

Gebühr fee

Geburt birth

~sdatum date of ~

~sort place of ~

~stag ~day

Alles Gute zum ~~. Happy ~~.

~urkunde ~ certificate

Gedicht poem

~e poems; poetry

Gedränge jam

Geduld patience

geduldig patient

geeignet fit

Gefangene(r) prisoner

Gefängnis prison

gefrieren freeze/froze/frozen

Gefrierschrank/ -truhe freezer

Gefühl feeling

gegen against

Gegend area

Gegenteil opposite

gegenüber opposite; across the street

geheim/Geheimnis secret

gehen go/went/gone

in die Stadt ~ ~ to town

zu Fuß ~ go on foot; walk

gehören: jdm. ~ belong to s.o.

zu etw. ~ be part of s.th.

gehörlos deaf

Geist *(Gespenst)* ghost

~ *(Verstand)* mind

Gelände ground

gelangen (nach/zu) get (to) (get/got/got)

gelb yellow

Geld money

~beutel purse

~schein *(BE)* (bank)note; *(AE)* bill

~strafe fine

Gelegenheit *(Chance)* chance

Gemälde painting

Gemeindesaal church hall

Gemeinschaft community

Gemüse vegetables

ein ~ a vegetable

genau exact(ly); just; right

General general

generell general

genießen enjoy

genug/genügend enough

Geographie geography

Gepäck *(BE)* luggage; *(AE)* baggage

gerade straight

~ *(soeben)* just

~ geschehen be in progress

~wegs straight

Geräusch noise; sound

g~voll noisy

gerecht fair
gern: etw. ~ tun like/enjoy/love doing s.th.
Geruch smell
Gesamtschule comprehensive (school)
Geschäft business
~sführer(in) manager
~smann businessman
~sfrau businesswoman
~sstelle agency
geschäftig busy
geschehen go on (go/went/gone); happen
gerade ~ be in progress
gescheit clever
Geschenk present; gift
Geschichte *(Fach)* history
~ *(Erzählung)* story
geschieden divorced
Geschirr dishes
~ **spülen** wash the ~; wash up
~spülmaschine dishwasher
geschlossen closed
Geschmack taste
~screme ~ cream
Gespenst ghost
Gespräch conversation; talk
Gestalt form
Gestaltung layout
gestern yesterday
~ **abend** last night
gesund healthy
~ **werden** get well (get/got/got)
G~heit health
Getränk drink
Getreide cereal; *(BE)* corn
~produkt cereal
Gewalt force
Gewerbe industry
Gewicht weight
gewinnen win/won/won
Gewinner(in) winner

gewiß certain; sure
Gewitter thunderstorm
gewöhnen: sich ~ an get used to (get/got/got)
gewöhnlich normal; ordinary; usual
~ *(normalerweise)* usually
gewohnt: etw. ~ sein be used to s.th.
Gift poison
giftig ~ous
Gipfel: auf dem ~ at the top
Giraffe giraffe
Gitarre guitar
~ **spielen** play the ~
Gitarrist(in) guitarist
glänzen shine/shone/shone
Glas glass
ein ~ Milch a ~ of milk
glatt smooth
glauben believe
~ *(meinen)* think/thought/thought
gleich *(nicht unterschiedlich)* equal; the same
~ **am Anfang** right at the beginning
gleiten glide
Globus globe
Glocke bell
Glück happiness; luck
~ **haben** be lucky
jdm viel ~ wünschen wish s.o. good luck
zum ~ luckily
~wunsch/~wünsche congratulations
glücklich happy
Glühbirne bulb
Gold gold
golden golden; gold
Golf *(Spiel)* golf
~platz ~ course
Gott God
zu ~ beten pray to God
~ **sei Dank!** Thank God!
~esdienst service
Grab grave
Grad degree
30 ~ Celsius 30 ~s centigrade
Gramm gram
Grammatik grammar
Grapefruit grapefruit
Gras grass
gratis free

Gratuliere! Congratulations!
grau grey
Grauen horror
Grenze border
Grieche/Griechin/griechsisch/G~ Greek
Griechenland Greece
Grill/grillen grill
gregrillte Würstchen ~ed sausages
Grimassen schneiden make faces (make/made/made)
groß big; large; tall
~artig fantastic; great
G~buchstabe capital letter
G~britannien Great Britain
G~eltern grandparents
G~mutter grandmother
G~vater grandfather
G~stadt city
Größe size
grün green
Grund *(Boden)* ground
~ *(Argument)* argument
~ *(Begründung)* reason
Grund.../grundlegend basic
~wortschatz ~ vocabulary
~schule primary school
Gruppe group; gang
Gruß/grüßen: Viele Grüße. Best wishes.
Grüße ihn von mir. Give him my love.
Gummi rubber; gum
Kau~ chewing gum
Radier~ (india) rubber
Gurke cucumber
Gurt/Gürtel belt
gut good; well; fine; nice; all right/alright
~ **gemacht** well done
~ **in Mathe** good at maths
Alles Gute. Best wishes.
Gute Besserung! Get well soon!
Guten Morgen/Abend. Good morning/evening.

Guten Tag. Hello; Hi.
~aussehend good-looking
Güte: Du liebe ~! Goodness!; Oh dear!
Gymnasium grammar school
Gymnastik gym(nastics)

H

Haar/~e hair
~bürste ~brush
~trockner ~ dryer
~waschmittel shampoo
haben have (got) (have/had/had)
hacken chop
Hafen *(See~)* harbour
~anlagen docks
~arbeiter(in) docker
Hahn *(Wasser~)* tap
Hähnchen chicken
halb half
eine ~e Stunde ~ an hour
~ **zehn** ~ past ten
H~finale semi-final
H~mond ~ moon
Hälfte/~n half/halves
Halle hall
~nbad indoor swimming pool
hallo hello; hi
Hals neck
~kette ~lace
halten *(fest~/ab~)* hold/held/held
~ *(lassen)* keep/kept/kept
jdn die Daumen ~ keep one's fingers crossed for s.o.
~ *(an~)* stop
Haltestelle stop
Hamburger hamburger
Hammer hammer
Hamster hamster
Hand hand
~ball ~ball
~bremse ~brake
~schuh glove
~tasche *(BE)* ~bag; *(AE)* purse
~tuch towel
Hände hoch! Hands up!
Hände weg! Hands off!

handeln (*etw. tun*) act
Handelszentrum commercial centre
Handlung action
hängen hang/hung/hung
hart hard
hassen hate
häßlich ugly
Hau ab! Get lost!
Haupt.../hauptsächlich main
  ~bahnhof central station
  ~stadt capital
  ~verkehrsstraße (*AE*) highway
Haus house
  ~arbeit ~work
  ~aufgaben homework
  ~frau ~wife
  ~halt ~hold
  ~mannskost home cooking
  ~tier pet
  ~tür front door
  ~wirt(in) landlord/landlady
  ~wirtschaftslehre domestic science
  im ~ (bleiben) (stay) indoors
  nach Hause home
  zu Hause at home
Haut skin
heben/hoch~ lift
Heft (*Schul~*) exercise-book
Heiliger Abend Christmas Eve
Heim/heim home
  Wohnheim hostel
Heimatstadt home town
Heirat marriage
heiraten marry; get married (get/got/got)
heiß hot
  Heißluftballon hot air balloon
Heizgerät/-körper heater
Heizung heating
  Zentral~ central ~
helfen help; assist; give s.o. a hand (give/gave/given)
hell bright; light
  ~blau light blue
  ~grün ~ green
Helm helmet
Hemd shirt
Henne hen

herauf up
heraus out; outside
  ~finden find out (find/found/found)
Herbst autumn
Herd cooker; stove
herein in
  ~kommen come in (come/came/come); enter
Herr gentleman
  Herr Miller Mr Miller
  mein ~ (*Anrede*) sir
  ~enschneider(in) tailor
herstellen produce
  Hersteller(in) producer
  Herstellung production
herüber over
herum (a)round
  jdn (an einem Ort) ~führen show s.o. round (a place) (show/showed/shown)
herunter down
  die Treppe ~ ~stairs
Herz heart
Herzlichen Glückwunsch! Congratulations!
heute today
  ~ abend this evening; tonight
  ~ morgen/~ vormittag this morning
  ~ nachmittag this afternoon
  ~ (*= kommende*) **Nacht** tonight
  ~ (*= vergangene*) **Nacht** last night
heutzutage these days
Hi-Fi high fidelity; hi-fi
Hieb blow
hier/~her here
  ~ draußen out ~
  ~ drinnen in ~
  ~ in der Nähe near ~
  ~ oben/~ hoch up ~
  Hier (spricht) ... This is ... (speaking).
Hilfe help; aid
  Erste ~ first aid
Himmel sky
hinauf up
hinaus out; outside
  ~gehen go out (go/went/gone)

hinein in
  ~gehen go in; enter
hinlegen: sich ~ lie down (lie/lay/lain)
hinter behind
Hinter... back
  ~grund ~ground
  ~rad ~ wheel
  ~tür ~ door
hinüber over
hinunter down
  die Treppe ~ ~stairs
Hitze heat
Hobby hobby
hoch high; tall
Hockey hockey
Hof yard
hoffen/Hoffnung hope
holen fetch; get/got/got
Holz wood
  ~arbeiten ~work
Honig honey
hören hear/heard/heard
  auf jdn. ~ listen to s.o.
  Radio ~ listen to the radio
Horoskop horoscope
Horror horror
  ~geschichte ~ story
Hose(n) trousers
Hotel hotel
hübsch pretty
Hubschrauber helicopter
Hügel hill
Huhn chicken; hen
Humor humour
Hund dog
Hunger hunger
  ~ haben be hungry
hungrig hungry
hüpfen jump
Hut hat
Hütte hut

I

ich I
  ~ (*betont*) me
ideal/Ideal ideal
Idee idea
ihm him
ihn him
Ihnen you
ihnen them
ihr her; you
  ihr(e) her; their
  ihre(r/s) hers; theirs
Ihr(e) your
  Ihre(r/s) yours

Imbiß snack
  ~stube café; cafeteria; snackbar
immer always
  für ~ for ever
  ~ mehr more and more
  ~ wieder again and again
in in; inside
  in (hinein) into
  im Bus on the bus
  im Fernsehen on television
  im Radio on the radio
  in der Nacht at night
  in der/die Schule at/to school
  in der/die Stadt in/to town
Inder(in)/indisch Indian
Indianer(in)/indianisch Indian
Indien India
Industrie industry
Information(en) information
informieren inform
Ingenieur(in) engineer
innen inside; indoors
  I~stadt city centre
innerhalb (von) within
Insel (*allgemein*) island
  ~ (*in Eigennamen*) (the) Isle (of ...)
Inserat ad/advert/advertisement
Installateur(in) plumber
installieren install
Instrument instrument
intelligent intelligent; bright
  Intelligenz intelligence
Interesse/interessieren interest
  interessant ~ing
  interessiert ~ed
international international
Interview/i~en interview
irgend: ~ etwas anything; something
  ~ jemand anybody/anyone; somebody/someone
  ~wie somehow
  ~wo(hin) anywhere; somewhere
ironisch ironical

Italien Italy
  italienisch/I~/
  Italiener(in) Italian

J

ja yes
Jacke jacket
  Strick~ cardigan
jagen chase; hunt; go
  hunting (go/went/
  gone)
Jäger(in) hunter
Jahr year
  Ein gutes neues ~!
  Happy New Y~!
  ~eszeit season
  ~hundert century
  ~markt (fun) fair
Januar January
Jazz jazz
je *(pro)* per
Jeans jeans
jede(r/s) each; every
  jeder(mann)
  everyone; everybody
  jeder beliebige any;
  anyone/-body
jedenfalls anyway
jemals ever
jemand someone/some-
  body; anyone/-body
  ~ anders ~ else
jene(r/s) that
  jene *(Mehrzahl)*
  those
  ~r Tag/an ~m Tag
  that day
jetzt now
Job job
joggen jog
  Jogging jogging
Joystick joystick
Jugend youth
  ~club ~ club
  ~herberge ~ hostel
Juli July
jung young
Junge boy
Junggeselle/-gesellin
  single
Juni June
Juwel jewel
  ~ier(in) ~ler

K

Kaffee coffee
  ~stube ~ shop
Käfig cage

Kahn boat
Kalb/Kälber calf/calves
Kalender calendar
kalt/Kälte cold
  mir ist ~ I feel ~
  (feel/felt/felt)
Kamel camel
Kamera camera
  ~mann ~man
Kamin chimney
Kamm/kämmen comb
Kampf/(be)kämpfen
  fight/fought/fought
Känguruh kangaroo
Kaninchen rabbit
Kanister can
Kanne pot
Kapelle *(Musik~)* band
Kapitän captain
Kappe cap
Karate karate
Karotte carrot
Karte card
  Eintritts~/Fahr~
  ticket
  Land~ map
Kartoffel(n) potato(es)
  ~chips *(BE)* crisps;
  (AE) chips
Kartonpapier
  cardboard
Käse cheese
  ~brötchen ~ roll
Kasse *(in Geschäften)*
  cash-desk
Kassette cassette
  ~nrecorder
  ~ recorder
Katalog catalogue
Kathedrale cathedral
Katze cat
kaufen buy/bought/
  bought
Kaufhaus department
  store
Kaugummi chewing
  gum
kaum hardly
kein(e) no; not ... any
  keine(r/s) none
  keiner (= *niemand*)
  no one/nobody
  ~e(r/s) von beiden
  neither (of the two)
Keks biscuit
Keller cellar
Kellner waiter
  ~in waitress
kennen know/knew/
  known
  jdn ~lernen meet
  s.o. (meet/met/met);
  get to know s.o. (get/
  got/got)

Kenntnis(se)
  knowledge
Kerl fellow; guy
Kerze candle
Ketchup ketchup
Kette chain
Kfz-Mechaniker(in)
  car mechanic
kicken kick
Kilometer kilometre
Kind/~er child/
  children; kid(s)
  ~ergarten
  kindergarten
  ~ergärtner(in)
  kindergarten teacher
Kino cinema
Kirche church
  ~nlied hymn
Kirsche cherry
Kissen cushion
  Kopf~ pillow
Kiste box
klagen (über) complain
  (about)
Klang sound
klar clear
Klasse *(Schul~)* class;
  form
  ~nkamerad(in)
  classmate
  ~nlehrer(in) form
  teacher
  ~nzimmer classroom
Klavier piano
kleben stick/stuck/
  stuck
  Klebestreifen tape
Kleid dress
  ~er/~ung clothes
  ~erbügel coat hanger
  ~erbürste clothes
  brush
  ~erschrank
  wardrobe
klein little; small
  ~ (Körpergröße) short
  K~buchstabe small
  letter
  K~geld change
  K~lastwagen
  pick-up (truck)
Klempner(in) plumber
klettern climb
Klima climate
Klingel bell
  klingeln ring (the
  bell) (ring/rang/rung)
klingen sound
klopfen/Klopfen knock
Klotz block
klug clever
Kneipe pub
Knie knee

Knochen bone
Knopf button
Knoten knot
  einen ~ machen/
  lösen tie/untie a ~
Koch/Köchin cook
  ~buch ~book/
  cookery book
  ~club cookery club
  ~rezept recipe
  ~topf *(mit Stil)*
  saucepan
kochen *(Essen)* cook;
  do the ~ing (do/did/
  done)
  ~ (bei 100° C) boil
  Tee/Kaffee ~ make
  tea/coffee (make/
  made/made)
Kocher cooker
Koffer suitcase
  ~raum boot
Kohl cabbage
Kohle coal
  ~bergwerk ~ mine
Kollege/Kollegin:
  Studien~ fellow
  student
komisch funny
kommen come/came/
  come
  Komm schon! Come
  on!
  (hin)~ *(gelangen)*
  get (to) (get/got/got)
Kommentar comment
Kondition *(gute*
  körperliche ~)
  fitness
König king
  ~in queen
  ~reich kingdom
  das Vereinigte ~~
  the United Kingdom
  (U. K.)
können *(fähig sein)*
  can/could; be able to;
  know how to (know/
  knew/known)
  (vielleicht) ~ may/
  might
Konserven canned food
konstruieren construct
  Konstruktion ~ion
Kontinent continent
Konto account
Kontrolle control
  unter ~ halten keep
  under ~ (keep/kept/
  kept)
  kontrollieren contol;
  check
  Kontrolliste
  checklist

Konzert concert
  ~saal ~ hall
Kopf head
  ~hörer ~phone
  ~kissen pillow
  ~salat lettuce
Kopie/kopieren copy
Korb basket
  ~ball ~ ball
Korn corn
  ~feld ~field
Körper body
  k~lich physical
korrekt correct
Korridor corridor
korrigieren correct
kosten/Kosten cost/
  cost/cost
  ~los free
Kotelett chop
krachen/K~n crash
Kraft energy; force;
  power
  ~werk power station
kräftig powerful; strong
krank ill; sick
  ~ werden fall ill
  (fall/fell/fallen)
Kranken...: ~haus
  hospital
  ~schwester nurse
  ~versicherung
  health insurance
  ~wagen ambulance
Krawatte tie
Kreuz/kreuzen cross
  das Rote ~ the Red
  Cross
  ~worträtsel ~word
  (puzzle)
Krieg war
Kriminal...: ~beamter/
  ~beamtin detective
  ~geschichte ~ story
kriminell criminal
Krokodil crocodile
Krone crown
  die Kronjuwelen the
  Crown Jewels
Küche kitchen
Kuchen cake
Kugelschreiber biro
Kuh cow
kühl/kühlen cool
  K~schrank fridge
Küken chicken
Kummer worry
kümmern: sich ~ um
  look after; mind; take
  care of (take/took/
  taken)
Kunde/Kundin
  customer
  ~ndienst service

Kunst art
  ~stück trick
Künstler(in) artist
kurz short
  ~e Hose shorts
  K~geschichte ~ story
  kürzen shorten
küssen/sich ~/Kuß kiss
Küste coast

L

Labortechniker(in) lab
  technician
lächeln/Lächeln smile
lachen (über) laugh (at)
Laden shop
  ~tisch counter
Lage *(Situation)*
  situation
  in der ~ sein, zu ...
  be able to ...
Lager *(Zelt~)* camp
  ~feuer ~fire
Lamm lamb
Lampe lamp
Land country; land
  ~karte map
  ~schaft countryside
  ~straße road;
  (BE) highway
  ~wirt(in) farmer
landen land
lang/lange long
  3 Tage ~ for 3 days
  L~spielplatte
  long-playing record
langsam slow
langweilig boring
Lärm noise
  l~end noisy
lassen *(zu~)* let/let/let
  ~ *(veran~)* make/
  made/made
  ~ *(übrig~/zurück~)*
  leave/left/left
Lastwagen *(BE)* lorry;
  (AE) truck
  ~fahrer(in) ~ driver
laufen/Lauf run/ran/
  run
  Läufer(in) runner
  (berufliche)
  Laufbahn career
laut loud
  ~ *(geräuschvoll)*
  noisy
  etw. ~ vorlesen read
  s.th. aloud (read/
  read/read)
  ~ reden talk in a
  loud voice

~er stellen turn up
L~sprecher
  loudspeaker
läuten ring/rang/rung
leasen lease; rent
Leben life/lives
  am ~ alive
  ~smittel food
  ~~händler(in) grocer
  ~sversicherung ~
  insurance
leben live; be alive
  ~d live; living
  ~dig alive; lively
  lebhaft lively
Leder leather
  ~jacke ~ jacket
leer/~en empty
legen lay/laid/laid; put/
  put/put
  sich hin~ lie down
  (lie/lay/lain)
Lehrbuch textbook
Lehre apprenticeship
lehren teach/taught/
  taught
Lehrer(in) teacher
Lehrling apprentice
leicht *(einfach)* easy
  ~ *(Gewicht)* light
leid: es tut mir ~ (I'm)
  sorry
leiden: nicht ~ können
  can't stand
leider ... I'm afraid ...
leihen: jdm etw. ~ lend
  s.th. to s.o. (lend/
  lent/lent)
  sich etw. von jdm. ~
  borrow s.th. from s.o.
Leinwand *(Kino~)*
  screen
leise quiet
  ~r stellen turn down
leiten lead/led/led
  ~ *(Geschäft)*
  manage; run/ran/run
Leiter *(zum Besteigen)*
  ladder
Leiter(in) director
Leitung *(Rohr)* pipe
  Rohr~ pipeline
  Telefon~ telephone
  line
Lektion lesson
lenken steer
  Lenkrad ~ing wheel
lernen learn; study
  L~de(r) learner
lesen read/read/read
  Leser(in) reader
letzte(r/s) final; last
  die ~n Jahre the last
  few years

leuchten shine/shone/
  shone
Leute people
Licht light
liebe(r) dear
  Liebe Grüße an ...
  Give my love to ...
  etw. lieber mögen
  like s.th. better; prefer
  s.th.
  Ich würde lieber ...
  I'd rather ...; I'd
  prefer to ...
  du solltest lieber ...
  you'd better
Liebe/lieben love
  ~sgeschichte ~ story
Lieblings... favourite
Lied song
  Weihnachts~
  Christmas carol
liefern deliver
liegen lie/lay/lain
Lift lift
Limonade lemonade
Lineal ruler
Linie line
  eine ~ ziehen draw a
  ~ (draw/drew/
  drawn)
linke(r/s)/~e Seite left
  links (von) on the ~
  (of)
  nach ~ abbiegen
  turn ~
Lippe lip
  ~nstift ~stick
Liste list
Liter litre
Loch hole
Löffel spoon
Lokal bar
lokal local
  L~zeitung
  ~ newspaper
los: Was ist ~? What's
  the matter?; What's
  wrong?
losfahren leave/left/
  left; set off (set/set/
  set); start
Löwe lion
Luft air
  ~ballon balloon
  Heiß~ballon hot air
  balloon
  ~kissenboot
  hovercraft
  ~post airmail
lügen/Lüge lie/lied/
  lied
lustig funny

M

machen do/did/done; make/made/made; have/had/had; take/took/taken
  Macht es dir etwas aus ...? Do you mind ...?
Macht power
Mädchen girl
Magen stomach
Mahlzeit meal
Mai May
Mais *(AE)* corn
Mal: zum ersten ~ for the first ~
  dreimal three times
malen/an~ paint
  Maler(in) ~er
  Malerpinsel paintbrush
Mama Mum
manchmal sometimes
Mann/Männer man/men
  Ehemann husband
Mannequin model
Mannschaft team
Mantel coat
Mappe case
Markt market
  ~platz ~ place
Marmelade jam
  Orangen~ marmalade
März March
Maschine machine; engine
  ~nschaden breakdown
  m~schreiben type
Material material
Mathematik mathematics
  Mathe maths
Matsch mud
  matschig muddy
Mauer wall
Maus/Mäuse mouse/mice
Mechaniker(in) mechanic
Medikamente drugs
Medizin medicine
Meer sea
  am ~ at the ~side
  ~schweinchen guinea pig
  ~wasser ~ water
Mehl flour
mehr more
Meile mile

meilenweit for miles and miles
mein(e) my
  meine(r/s) mine
meinen *(sagen wollen)* mean/meant/meant
  ~ *(denken)* think/thought/thought
meist: das ~e/die ~en/am ~en most
Meister *(im Sport)* champion
  ~schaft ~ship
  ~~skämpfe ~~s
melden: etw. (bei jdm.)
  ~ report s.th. (to s.o.)
  sich bei jdm. ~ report to s.o.
Menge: Menschen~ crowd (of people)
  eine ~ *(viel)* a lot (of); lots (of); plenty (of)
Mensch: der ~ man
  ~en men, people
  ~~menge crowd (of people)
  menschlich human
Messe *(Handels~)* fair
Messer knife/knives
Metall metal
Meter metre
Metzger butcher
mexikanisch/Mexikaner(in) Mexican
  Mexiko Mexico
mich me; myself
Miete rent
mieten lease; rent
Mikro... micro...
  ~phon ~phone
  ~skop ~scope
  ~wellenherd ~wave (oven)
Milch milk
  ~mann ~man
Million million
  ~är(in) millionaire
mindestens at least
Mine *(Bergwerk)* mine
Mineralwasser mineral water
Minigolf crazy golf; mini-golf
Minute minute
mir me; myself
mischen mix
Mischung mixture
mit with
  ~ 16 at (the age of) 16
  ~ *(einer Geschwindigkeit von)* ... at (a speed of) ...

  ~ dem Auto/Bus by car/bus
  M~kommen come along (come/came/come)
  jdn. im Auto ~nehmen give s.o. a ride/lift (give/gave/given)
Mitglied member
Mitleid pity
Mitschüler(in) *(AE)* fellow student
Mittagessen dinner; lunch
  zu Mittag essen have ~ (have/had/had)
Mitte/Mittel.../mittlere(r/s) middle
Mitteilung message; notice
Mittelalter (the) Middle Ages
Mittelpunkt centre
Mitternacht midnight
Mittwoch Wednesday
Mixer mixer
Möbel furniture
Mode fashion
  die neueste ~ the latest ~
  ~zeichner(in) ~ designer
Modell model
  ~eisenbahn ~ railway
modern modern
  ~isieren modernize
modisch fashionable
mögen like; want
  lieber ~ like better; prefer
möglich possible
Mohrrübe carrot
Moment moment
Monat month
Mond moon
  ~licht ~light
Monster monster
Montag Monday
Mopen moped
Morgen morning
  morgens in the ~
  um 8 Uhr morgens at 8 am
morgen tomorrow
  ~ früh/~ vormittag ~ morning
Motor engine; motor
  ~boot motor-boat
  ~rad motor-bike; motorcycle
müde tired
Mühe: sich viel ~geben try hard

Mund mouth
  den ~ halten shut up (shut/shut/shut)
Münze coin
Museum museum
Musical musical
Musik music
  ~er(in) musician
  m~alisch musical
  ~instrument musical instrument
Müsli muesli
müssen have (got) to (have/had/had); must
  nicht ~ needn't
Mutter mother
Mutti Mum
Mütze cap

N

na ja well
nach after
  zehn ~ zehn ten past ten
  ~ Hause gehen go home (go/went/gone)
  ~ London gehen go to London
  weggehen ~ Australien leave for Australia (leave/left/left)
  jdm. ~laufen run after s.o. (run/ran/run)
  ~ meiner Uhr ist es ... by my watch it's ...
Nachbar(in) neighbour
  ~schaft ~hood
nachdenken think/thought/thought
nachlässig careless
Nachmittag afternoon
  nachmittags in the ~
  um drei Uhr nachmittags at three pm;
Nachname *(BE)* surname; *(AE)* family name/second name
Nachricht(en) news
  ~ *(Botschaft)* message
  ~enagentur news agency
nachschlagen *(Wort)* look up (a word)
nachsehen have a look (have/had/had)

Nachspeise dessert; pudding; sweet
nächste(r/s)/als ~ next
  die ~n Wochen the ~ few weeks
Nacht night
  in der ~/nachts at ~
Nachteil disadvantage
Nachtisch dessert; pudding; sweet
Nadel needle
Nagel/nageln nail
  Fingern~ finger~
nahe/in der/die Nähe (von) near
  hier in der Nähe ~ here
nähen sew/sewed/sewn
  Nähmaschine sewing machine
Nahrung(smittel) food
Name name
  Vor~ *(BE)* Christian ~; *(AE)* first ~
  Nach~ *(BE)* sur~; *(AE)* family ~/ second ~
Narr fool
Nase nose
naß wet
Nation nation
  die Vereinten ~en the United Nations
national national
  N~flagge ~ flag
  N~hymne ~ anthem
  N~ität nationality
  N~park national park
Natur nature
  ~wissenschaft science
  Natur.../natürlich natural
natürlich natural
  ~ *(selbstverständlich)* naturally; of course
Nebel fog; mist
  neblig foggy
neben beside; next to
  ~an next door
nehmen take/took/ taken
nein no
Nerv nerve
  nervös nervous
nett nice
Netz net
  ~ball ~ball
neu new
  die neuesten Nachrichten the latest news

auf dem neuesten Stand up-to-date
Neuigkeit(en) news
Neujahr the New Year
  ~stag New Year's Day
neulich the other day
nicht not
  ~ mehr not ... any more
  N~raucher(in) non-smoker
nichts nothing
nie/noch ~ never
nieder down
  sich ~lassen settle
niedrig low
niemand nobody; no one; not ... anybody/anyone
nirgends/nirgendwo(hin) nowhere; not ... anywhere
noch (immer) still; yet
  ~ ein(e) another
  ~ einige/~ etwas some more
  ~ einmal again; once more
  ~ nicht not yet
  ~ nie never
  ~ größer even bigger
Norden/nach ~ north
  Nord.../nördlich north; northern
  ~pol the North Pole
  (nach) Nordosten/ Nordost... north-east
normal normal; ordinary
Norwegen Norway
  Norweger(in)/ norwegisch/N~ Norwegian
Not.../Notfall emergency
  ~ausgang ~ exit
  ~ruf ~ call
Note *(Zensur)* mark
  (Bank-/Musik-)~ note
nötig necessary
Notiz note; notice
  ~buch notice book
  ~brett notice board
notwendig necessary
November November
Null love; nil; o; zero
Nummer number
nur just; only
Nuß nut
Nutzen use
  nützlich ~ful

nutzlos ~less
nutzen: etw. (aus)~ make use of s.th. (make/made/made)

O

ob if
oben at the top (of)
  ~ *(im Haus)* upstairs
  dort ~ up there
Ober: Herr ~! Waiter!
oberhalb von above
oberste(r/s) top
Obst fruit
  ~- und Gemüse-händler(in) greengrocer
  (gedeckter) ~kuchen fruit pie
  ~salat fruit salad
obwohl although
Ochse/~n ox/oxen
oder or
Ofen stove
  Back~ oven
offen open
öffentlich/Ö~keit public
offiziell official
Offizier officer
öffnen/sich ~ open
  Öffnungszeiten ~ing hours
oft often
ohne without
  ~ Unterbrechung non-stop
Ohnmachtsanfall blackout
Ohr ear
Öl oil
  ~gesellschaft ~ company
  ~tanker ~ tanker
  ölig oily
Olympische Spiele Olympic Games
Onkel uncle
Operation operation
  (jdn.) operieren operate (on s.o.)
Orange/o~(farben) orange
  ~nmarmelade marmalade
  ~nsaft ~ juice
Ordner *(Akten~)* folder
Ordnung order
  in ~ okay/OK; all right/alright

Organisation organization; association
organisieren organize
Ort place
  örtlich/Orts... local
  Ortsansässige local people
Osten/nach ~ east
  Ost.../östlich east; eastern
Ostern Easter
Österreich Austria
  ~er(in)/ö~isch Austrian
Overall overall
Ozean ocean

P

Paar pair
  ein ~ Socken a ~ of socks
  ein paar a few; some
Pacht/pachten lease; rent
Päckchen packet
packen pack
Packung packet
Paket parcel
Palast palace
Pampelmuse grapefruit
Panne *(Motor)* breakdown
Panzerschrank safe
Papa dad
Papagei parrot
Papier paper
  ~abfall waste~
  ~korb ~~ basket
Pappe cardboard
  Pappkarton ~ box
Paprika(schote) pepper
Paradies paradise
Park/parken park
  ~platz car ~
Parlament parliament
Partner(in) partner
Party party
Paß passport
  ~kontrolle ~ control
Passagier passenger
passen/~d fit
passieren happen
Pastete pie
Patient(in) patient
Pause break; rest
  ~ machen take a break (take/took/ taken)
Pech bad luck
  ~ haben be unlucky

Pelz fur
  ~mantel ~ coat
Penny/Pence penny/
  pence
Pension *(Gästehaus)*
  guesthouse
perfekt perfect
Person person
  ~alcomputer ~al
  computer
persönlich personal
Pfad path
Pfanne pan
Pfannkuchen pancake
Pfeffer pepper
Pfeife *(Tabaks~)* pipe
Pferd horse
Pfirsich peach
Pflanze/pflanzen plant
Pflaster*(Verbands~)*
  plaster
Pflaume plum
Pflicht duty
pflücken pick
Pfund pound
  ~note ~ note
Phantasie imagination
Physik physics
  physikalisch
  physical
Picknick/picknicken
  picnic
Pille pill; tablet
Pilot(in) pilot
Pilz mushroom
pink pink
Pinsel (paint)brush
Plakat poster
Plan/planen plan
Plastik plastic
platt flat
Platz *(Raum)* room;
  space
  ~ *(Stelle)* place; site
  ~ *(in Stadt)* square
  ~ nehmen take a
  seat (take/took/
  taken)
  Fußball~ football
  field/ground
  Spiel~ playground
  Sport~ playing
  field(s)
Platzwunde cut
plötzlich suddenly
Polen Poland
  die ~ the Poles/the
  Polish
  Pole/Polin Pole
  polnisch/P~ Polish
Politik politics
  ~er(in) politician
Polizei police
  ~auto ~ car

~beamter/~beamtin
  ~ officer
  ~meister sergeant
  ~wache *(BE)* ~ station; *(AE)* ~ depart-
  ment
Polizist(in) policeman/
  policewoman
Pommes frites
  (BE) chips;
  (AE) French fries
Pop(musik) pop
  (music)
  ~gruppe ~ group
  ~konzert ~ concert
  ~star ~ star
Portugal Portugal
  Portugiese/-sin/
  portugiesisch/P~
  Portuguese
  die Portugiesen the
  Portuguese
Post mail; post
  ~amt post office
  ~karte ~card
Poster poster
praktisch practical
Präsident(in) president
Praxis *(Arzt~)* surgery
Preis *(Kauf~)* price
  ~ *(Gewinn)* prize
Prinz prince
  ~essin princess
privat/Privat... private
pro per
Problem problem
  ~e ~s; trouble
Produkt product
  ~ion ~ion
Produzent(in) producer
produzieren produce
Programm programme
Projekt project
Prospekt leaflet
Prost! Cheers!
Prozent per cent
prüfen check; test
Prüfung exam(ination);
  test
  eine ~ ablegen take
  a(n) ~ (take/took/
  taken)
  eine ~ bestehen pass
  a(n) ~
Pub pub
Pudding pudding
Puder powder
Pullover pullover
Pulver powder
Pumpe/pumpen pump
Punkt point
  ~ *(am Satzende)* full
  stop
pünktlich on time

putzen clean
  ein Zimmer clean
  (up)/do a room (do/
  did/done)
  sich die Zähne ~
  brush one's teeth
Puzzle(spiel) jigsaw
  (puzzle)

Q

Quadrat square
Qualifikation
  qualification
  sich qualifizieren
  qualify
Qualität quality
quer über/~ durch
  across

R

Rad *(am Auto)* wheel
  Fahrrad bicycle; bike
  radfahren cycle; go
  by bike (go/went/
  gone); ride a bike
  (ride/rode/ridden)
  ~fahrer(in) cyclist
Radar(gerät) radar
Radiergummi (india)
  rubber
Radio radio
  ~ hören listen to
  the ~
  ~sender ~ station
  ~sendung
  ~ programme
  ~wecker clock ~
Rakete rocket
Rand side
rasch quick; fast
rasen race
rasieren/sich ~ shave
  Rasierapparat
  shaver
Rasse race
Rast/rasten rest
Rat(schlag) advice
  ein ~ some ~; a piece
  of ~
raten/er~ guess
Rathaus town hall
Rätsel puzzle
Rauch/rauchen smoke
rauh rough
Raum room; space
  ~fähre space shuttle
  ~pfleger(in) cleaner
  ~schiff spaceship

räumen/ab~/aus~ clear
Rauschgift drugs
Rechnung bill
Recht right
  r~ haben be ~
  ~sanwalt/~sanwältin
  lawyer
  ~schreibung spelling
  ~schreibfehler
  spelling mistake
  r~zeitig in time
rechte(r/s)/rechte Seite
  right
  rechts (von) on the ~
  (of)
  nach rechts abbiegen
  turn ~
Recorder recorder
Rede speech
  reden talk; speak/
  spoke/spoken
  Redner(in) speaker
Regal/~bretter shelves
  Regelbrett shelf
Regel rule
  regelmäßig regular
  regeln: den Verkehr ~
  control the traffic
Regen/regnen rain
  ~mantel ~coat
  regnerisch rainy; wet
Regierung government
Regisseur(in) producer
reich rich
reichen *(geben)* hand
  Mir reicht es! I've
  had enough!
reif ripe
Reifen tyre
Reihe: jd. ist an der ~
  it's s.o.'s turn
  ~nfolge order
reinigen clean
  Reinigung *(chemi-*
  sche ~) dry-cleaning
Reis rice
Reise journey
  ein ~ machen go on
  a ~ (go/went/gone)
  ~büro travel agency
  ~bus coach
  ~fachfrau/~~mann
  travel agent
  ~führer *(Buch)*
  guide
  ~paß passport
  ~scheck traveller's
  cheque
  reisen travel
  Reisende(r) traveller
reißen tear/tore/torn
Reißverschluß *(BE)* zip
  (fastener); *(AE)*
  zipper

reiten ride/rode/ridden
Rekord record
Rektor headmaster
Religion religion
  ~s.../religiös religious
  ~sunterricht religious education (R.E.)
Rennen race
  Rennwagen racing car
  Rennfahrer(in) racing driver
rennen run/ran/run
Reparatur repair
  ~ausrüstung ~ kit
reparieren fix; repair
Reporter(in) reporter
Rest rest
Restaurant restaurant
retten rescue; save
Rettung rescue
  ~smannschaft ~team
Rezept: ärztliches ~ prescription
  Koch~ recipe
richtig correct; real(ly); right; proper(ly)
Richtung direction; way
  Himmels~ direction
  in ~ auf towards
riechen smell
Riese/riesig giant
Rinder cattle
  ~braten roast beef
  Rindfleisch beef
Ring ring
Ritt ride
Roboter robot
Rock skirt
Rock(musik) rock
  ~konzert ~ concert
Rohr pipe
  ~leitung ~line
Rollbrett skateboard
Rolle/rollen roll
  es spielt keine Rolle it doesn't matter
Rollschuh/~ laufen (roller-)skate
  ~laufen (roller-) skating
röntgen/R~aufnahme x-ray
rosa pink
rot red
Rücken/Rückseite back
  Rücksitz ~ seat
Ruf/rufen call; shout; cry
Rugby rugby
Ruhe *(Stille)* silence

jdn in ~ lassen leave s.o. alone (leave/left/ left)
ruhen rest
ruhig peaceful; quiet
Rührgerät mixer
  Rührschüssel mixing bowl
rund/Runde round
  R~gang tour
Russe/Russin/russisch/ R~ Russian
  Rußland Russia

S

Saal hall
Sache thing
  ~ *(Angelegenheit)* matter
Sack bag; sack
Safe safe
Saft juice
Säge/sägen saw
sagen say/said/said; tell/told/told
Sahne cream
Salat(gericht) salad
  Kopf~ lettuce
  ~soße salad dressing
  ~ mit Schinken ham salad
Salz salt
sammeln collect
  Sammlung collection
Samstag Saturday
Sand sand
Sandwich sandwich
sanft soft
Sänger(in) singer
Sanitäter ambulance man
Satellit satellite
  ~enantenne/-schüssel ~ dish
satt: etw. ~ haben be fed up with s.th.
Satz sentence
sauber clean
  ~machen ~ up
Schach chess
Schachtel box
  eine ~ Zigaretten a packet of cigarettes
schade: es ist ~, daß ... it's a pity (that) ...
Schaden damage
Schaf(e) sheep
  Schäfer(in) shepard
  Schäferhund sheepdog

schaffen: etw. ~ manage s.th.
  es ~ make it (make/ made/made)
Schaffner(in) ticket collector
Schal scarf
Schale *(Schüssel)* bowl
Schallplatte disc; record
schalten/um~ switch
  an~/ab~ switch/turn on/off
Schalter *(Bank/Post)* counter
  ~ *(elektrisch)* switch
  ~beamter/~beamtin clerk
Schampon shampoo
scharf *(Messer)* sharp
schätzen *(vermuten)* guess
Schau show
  ~fenster shop window
  ~spieler actor
  ~~in actress
schauen/nach~ look; have a ~ (have/had/ had)
  jdn. an~ look at s.o.
  (bei etw.) zu~ watch (s.th.)
  sich um~ look round
Schauer *(Regen~)* shower
Scheck cheque
  ~karte ~ card
Scheibe *(runde ~)* disc
  ~nwischer windscreen wiper
scheiden: sich ~ lassen get a divorce (get/ got/got)
  geschieden divorced
  Scheidung divorce
scheinen *(den Anschein haben)* seem
  ~ *(leuchten)* shine/ shone/shone
Scheinwerfer headlight
Schere scissors
  eine ~ a pair of ~
schicken send/sent/ sent
schieben push
schießen shoot/shot/ shot; fire
Schiff boat; ship
Schild sign
Schildkröte *(Land~)* tortoise
Schinken ham
  ~brötchen ~ roll

Schirm umbrella
Schlaf sleep
  ~anzug pyjamas
  ein ~~ a pair of pyjamas
  ~sack sleeping bag
  ~zimmer bedroom
schlafen be asleep; sleep/slept/slept
Schlag blow; knock
schlagen hit/hit/hit
Schlager hit
Schläger *(Tennis~)* racket
Schlagzeile headline
Schlagzeug percussion
  ~er(in) drummer; percussionist
Schlamm mud
  schlammig muddy
Schlange snake
schlau clever
Schlauch *(Wasser~)* hose
schlecht/~er/am ~esten bad/worse/worst
schließen close; shut/ shut/shut
  ab~/zu~ lock
schließlich at last; finally
schlimm/~er/am ~sten bad/worse/worst
Schlittschuh/~ laufen (ice-)skate
  ~laufen (ice-)skating
Schloß *(Gebäude)* castle
  ~ *(zum abschließen)* lock
Schluß end; finish
  ~verkauf sale
Schlüssel key
schmal narrow
schmecken taste
Schmerz(en) ache; pain
schmerzen hurt/hurt/ hurt
Schmetterling butterfly
Schmuck jewel(le)ry
  ~stück jewel
schmutzig dirty
Schnecke snail
Schnee snow
  s~reich snowy
schneiden cut/cut/cut
Schneider(in):
  Damen~dressmaker
  Herren~ tailor
schneien snow
schnell fast; quick
Schnellhefter folder
Schnellzug fast train
Schnitt cut

Schock/schockieren shock
  einen ~ bekommen get a ~ (get/got/got)
  schockierend ~ing
  schockiert ~ed
Schokolade chocolate
  eine Tafel ~ a bar of ~
schon already
  ~ *(in Fragen)* yet
  ~ einmal *(in Fragen)* ever
  S~ gut! Forget it!
schön beautiful; fine; nice
  S~heit beauty
Schornstein chimney
  ~feger(in) ~ sweep
Schotte/Schottin Scot; Scotman/-woman
  die Schotten the Scots/the Scottish
  schottisch Scottish
  Schottland Scotland
Schrank cupboard
  Kleider~ wardrobe
Schraube/schrauben screw
  ~nzieher ~driver
schrecklich awful; horrible; terrible
Schrei cry; shout
Schreib...: ~kraft typist
  ~maschine typewriter
  ~tisch desk
  ~warenhändler(in) stationer
  im ~warenladen at the stationer's
schreiben write/wrote/written
  etw. auf~ ~ s.th. down
  ~ *(Rechtschreibung)* spell
schreien cry; shout
Schritt step
  ~ für ~ ~ by ~
  einen ~ machen take a ~ (take/took/taken)
Schuh shoe
Schul.../Schule school
  ~abgänger(in) ~ leaver
  ~hof ~ yard
  ~klasse ~ class
  ~leiter headmaster
  ~tasche ~ bag
  ~zeugnis ~ report
  Gesamt~ comprehensive (~)

weiterführende ~ secondary ~
Schüler(in) *(BE)* pupil; *(AE)* student
Schulter shoulder
Schüssel bowl
Schußwaffe gun
schütteln shake/shook/shaken
  jdm die Hand ~ ~ s.o.'s hand
  sich *(einander)* **die Hände ~** ~ hands
  den Kopf ~ ~ one's head
schwach weak
schwarz/Schwarze(r) black
  Schwarzes Brett noticeboard
Schweden Sweden
  Schwede/Schwedin Swede
  die Schweden the ~s/the Swedish
  schwedisch/S~ Swedish
schweigsam silent
Schwein pig
  ~efleisch pork
  ~~pastete pork pie
  ~ekotelett pork chop
Schweiz Switzerland
  ~er(in)/s~erisch Swiss
  die ~er the Swiss
schwer *(schwierig)* difficult; hard
  ~ *(Gewicht)* heavy
Schwester sister
schwierig difficult; hard
  S~keiten trouble
  in S~~ sein be in trouble
schwimmen swim/swam/swum
  S~ swimming
  Schwimmbad swimming pool
  Schwimmbecken (swimming) pool
  Schwimmer(in) swimmer
See *(der ~)* lake
  ~ *(die ~)* sea
  ~bad seaside resort
  ~mann sailor
Segel/segeln sail
  ~boot ~ing boat
  ~fliegen gliding
  ~flugzeug glider
sehen see/saw/seen
Sehenswürdigkeiten sights

sehr very (much); most
Seife soap
  ~nblase ~ bubble
sein be/was – were/been
sein(e) his; its
  seine(r/s) his
seit *(Zeitspanne)* for
  ~ *(Zeitpunkt)* since
Seite *(Buch)* page
  ~ *(rechte/linke ~)* side
Sekretär(in) secretary
Sekunde second
selbe: der~/die~/das~ the same
Selbst... self-...
  ~bedienung self-service
  ~~srestaurant cafeteria
selbst: du ~ you ... yourself
  er ~ he ... himself
  ich ~ I ... myself
  ihr ~ you ... yourselves
  Sie ~ you ... yourself/yourselves
  sie ~ she ... herself; they ... themselves
  wir ~ we ... ourselves
selbständig on one's own
selten rare; rarely; seldom
seltsam funny; strange
senden *(Rundfunk/ Fernsehen)* broadcast
  Sendung broadcast; programme
  (Radio)sender (radio) station
September September
Serie(n) series
Service service
Sessel armchair
setzen put/put/put; set/set/set
  sich ~ sit down (sit/sat/sat)
  sich auf~ sit up
Shorts shorts
Show show
sich herself; himself; itself; themselves; yourself; yourselves
sicher *(gewiß)* certain; sure
  ~ *(ungefährlich)* safe
  S~heit safety
  S~~sgurt safety belt
Sie you

sie she; her; they; them
sieden boil
Siedler(in) settler
Siedlung settlement
Silber silver
Silhouette *(einer Stadt)* skyline
Silvester New Year's Eve
singen sing/sang/sung
Single single
sinken sink/sank/sunk
Sinn sense
  ~ für Humor a ~ of humour
  einen ~ ergeben make ~ (make/made/made)
Situation situation
Sitz/~platz seat
  ~gurt seat-belt
sitzen sit/sat/sat
Ski/~ laufen ski
  ~laufen skiing
Sklave/Sklavin slave
so like this; so; such
  (genau) so (...wie) (just) as (... as)
sobald as soon as
Socke sock
soeben just
Sofa sofa; couch
sofort at once
sogar even
Sohn son
Solar... solar
  ~energie ~ energy/power
  ~zellen ~ cells
solch such
Soldat(in) soldier
sollen shall/should
Sommer summer
sondern but
Sonnabend Saturday
Sonne sun
  ~nbrille ~ glasses
  ~nschein ~shine
  ~nenkraft solar energy/power
  ~nzellen solar cells
  sonnig sunny
Sonntag Sunday
sonst else
  ~ noch etwas? anything ~?
Sorge care; worry
  sich ~n machen worry
sorgfältig careful
Sorte kind; sort
Soße sauce
  Salat~ (salad) dressing

sowieso anyway
Spanien Spain
  Spanier(in) Spaniard
  die Spanier the Spaniards/the Spanish
  spanisch/S~ Spanish
spannend exciting
sparen save
Sparkonto savings account
Spaß *(Vergnügen)* fun
  ~ *(Witz)* joke
  ~ *(=Witze)* **machen** joke
  ~ haben an etw. enjoy s.th.
  es macht ~ it's fun
  Viel ~! Enjoy yourselves.
spät late
  zu ~ kommen be ~
  Bis später! See you later!
Spazierfahrt ride
  eine ~ machen go for a ~ (go/went/gone)
Spaziergang walk
  spazierengehen go for a ~ (go/went/gone)
  jnd. spazierenführen take s.o. for a ~ (take/took/taken)
  Spazierstock walking stick
Speicher *(Dachboden)* attic
Speiseeis ice-cream
Speisekarte menu
Spezialist(in) specialist
speziell special
Spiegel mirror
  ~eier fried eggs
Spiel game
  ~ *(Fußball, Tennis usw.)* game
  ein ~ machen play a game
  ~platz playground
  ~regel rule
  ~warenladen toy shop
  ~zeug toy
  ~~auto toy car
spielen play; act
Spinne spider
spitz *(Nadel)* sharp
Spitze top
  ~ntechnologie high tech(nology)

Sport/~art sport
  ~club ~s club
  ~ler(in) ~sman/~swoman
  ~platz playing fields
  ~sendung sports programme
  ~unterricht physical education
  ~zentrum sports centre
Sprache language
sprechen speak/spoke/spoken; talk
Sprecher(in) speaker
Sprechstunden *(beim Arzt)* surgery hours
springen *(hüpfen)* jump
spülen *(Geschirr)* wash up; wash the dishes
  Spülbecken sink
  Spülmaschine dishwasher
spüren feel/felt/felt
Staat state
  ~sangehörigkeit nationality
  ~sbürger(in) citizen
Stadt town
  Groß~ city
  ~mitte city centre
  ~plan street map; street plan
Stand *(Markt~/Verkaufs~)* stall
  auf dem neuesten ~ up-to-date
  ~bild statue
ständig: etw. ~tun keep (on) doing s.th. (keep/kept/kept)
Stange bar
Star *(Person)* star
stark powerful; strong; heavy
Stärke force
Start start
starten start
  ~ *(Flugzeug)* take off (take/took/taken)
Station station
statt instead of
  ~ dessen instead
stattfinden take place (take/took/taken)
Statue statue
Staub dust
  staubig dusty
  ~sauger vacuum cleaner
Steak steak
Steckdose socket
stecken stick/stuck/stuck

fest~ be stuck
  ~bleiben get stuck (get/got/got)
Stecker plug
Stecknadel pin
stehen stand/stood/stood
  ~bleiben stop
  ~~ *(versagen)* break down (break/broke/broken)
stehlen steal/stole/stolen
steigen/be~ climb
  einen Drachen ~ lassen fly a kite (fly/flew/flown)
Stein stone; rock
Stelle *(Beruf)* job
  ~ *(Ort)* place; site
stellen put/put/put; set/set/set
  einen Wecker ~ set an alarm clock
  (das Radio) leiser/lauter ~ turn (the radio) down/up
stellvertretender Geschäftsführer assistant manager
sterben die
  ~d/im S~ dying
Stereo/~anlage stereo
Stern star
  das ~enbanner the Stars and Stripes
steuern *(Fahrzeug lenken)* steer
  ~ *(Ablauf regeln)* control
  Steuerrad steering weel
  Steuerung control
Stich *(Nähen)* stitch
Stiefel boot
Stier bull
Stift *(Nadel)* pin
still quiet; silent; still
  ~ daliegen lie still (lie/lay/lain)
  ~ sitzen sit still (sit/sat/sat)
  ~ stehen stand still (stand/stood/stood)
Stille silence
Stimme voice
Stirn forehead
Stock stick
  Stock(werk) floor
Stoff cloth; material
stolz sein auf be proud of
stören disturb
Stoß knock

stoßen (gegen) push; knock (at)
Strafe *(Geld~)* fine
Strand beach
Straße *(Land~)* road
  ~ *(Orts~)* street
  ~narbeiter(in) road worker
  ~nbahn tram
  ~~fahrer(in) tram driver
  ~nplan street map/plan
  ~nseite side of the road/street
  die ~ her-/hinunter down the road/street
  die ~ her-/hinauf up the road/street
streichen *(anmalen)* paint
Streichholz match
Streit: ~ haben have an argument (have/had/had)
  ~kräfte armed forces
  ~ suchen look for trouble
streiten argue
streng strict
stricken knit
  Strickjacke cardigan
  Stricknadel knitting needle
Strom electricity; (electric) power
  ~ausfall power cut; blackout
Strumpf stocking
Stück piece
  Theater~ play
Student(in) student
studieren study
Stuhl chair
stumm dumb
  ~ *(schweigsam)* silent
  taub~ deaf and dumb
Stunde hour
  Unterrichts~ lesson, **~nplan** timetable
Sturm storm
  stürmisch stormy
Suche/(durch)suchen search
  etw./jdn. suchen look for s.th./s.o.
Süden/nach ~ south
  Süd.../südlich south; southern
  Südwesten/nach ~/ Südwest... south-west

Supermarkt supermarket
Suppe soup
surfen surf
  Surfen surfing
  Surfbrett surfboard
süß sweet
  Süßigkeiten *(BE)* sweets; *(AE)* candy
Szene scene

T

Tablette pill; tablet
Tafel *(für Anzeigen)* board
  ~ Schokolade bar of chocolate
Tag day
  ~ für ~ ~ by ~
  ~ und Nacht ~ and night/night and ~
  ~ebuch diary
  ein ~~ führen keep a diary (keep/kept/kept)
  eines ~es one ~
  bei ~eslicht by ~light
  ~eszeit time of ~
  ~eszeitung daily paper
  tagsüber by ~
täglich daily
Tank tank
  ~stelle *(BE)* filling/petrol station; garage; *(AE)* gas station
Tanker tanker
Tante aunt
Tanz/tanzen dance
  Tänzer(in) ~r
Tasche *(Beutel, Reise~)* bag
  ~ *(in Kleidung)* pocket
  ~nbuch paperback
  ~ngeld pocket money
  ~nmesser pocket knife
  ~nrechner calculator
Tasse cup
Tastatur keyboard
Taste key
Tätigkeit activity
Tatsache fact
  tatsächlich indeed
taub deaf
  ~stumm ~ and dumb
tauchen dive
  T~ diving
  Taucher(in) diver

Taxi taxi
  ~fahrer(in) ~ driver
Team team
Techniker(in) technician
technisch technical
  ~e Fachschule ~ college
Technologie technology
Tee tea
  ~beutel ~ bag
  ~kanne ~pot
  ~löffel ~spoon
  ~pause ~ break
  ~tasse ~cup
  ~ trinken have ~ (have/had/had)
Teich pond
Teil part
  ein ~ von etw. sein be ~ of s.th.
  t~nehmen (an) take ~ (in) (take/took/taken)
  T~zeitbeschäftigung ~-time job
Telefax (tele)fax
Telefon/telefonieren (tele)phone
  am ~ on the ~
  ~buch telephone directory
  ~gesellschaft telephone company
  t~isch rufen ~ for
  ~karte phonecard
  ~leitung telephone line
  ~nummer ~ number
  ~vermittlung telephone operator
  ~zelle ~ box
Telegraf telegraph
Telegramm telegram
Teller plate
Temperatur temperature
Tennis tennis
  ~platz ~ court
  ~schläger ~ racket
  ~spieler(in) ~ player
Teppich carpet
Termin *(Verabredung)* appointment
Test test
teuer expensive
Teufel devil
Text text
Theater theatre
  ~karte ~ ticket
  ~programm ~ programme
  ~stück play
Theke bar; counter

Thema subject
Themse: die ~ the (River) Thames
tief deep
Tier animal
  ~pfleger zoo-keeper
  ~welt wildlife
Tiger tiger
Tinte ink
tippen *(maschine-schreiben)* type
Tisch table
  den ~ decken lay the ~
  ~tennis ~ tennis
  ~tuch ~ cloth
Tischler(in) carpenter
  Tischlern woodwork
Toast toast
  ~er ~er
Tod death
Toilette toilet
toll fantastic; great
Tomate/~n tomato/~es
Ton sound
  ~band tape
  ~~gerät tape recorder
  ~ingenieur(in) ~ engineer
Topf pot
  ~ *(mit Stiel)* pan
Tor gate
tot dead
töten kill
Tour tour
Tourist(in) tourist
tragen *(in der Hand ~)* carry
  (Kleidung ~) wear/wore/worn
Tragfläche wing
Trainer(in) coach
trainieren practise; train
Training practice
Traktor tractor
Träne tear
Transistor transistor
  ~radio ~ radio
Transport transport
  ~mittel means of ~
Trauben grapes
Traum/träumen dream
traurig sad; blue
treffen *(Ziel)* hit/hit/hit
  ~ *(jdm begegnen)* meet/met/met
  T~ meeting
Treffer hit
Treffpunkt meeting point
treiben/an~ drive/drove/driven

Treppe stairs
  die ~ hinunter down~
  die ~ hoch up~
treten (gegen) kick
  ~ (auf) step (on)
Trick trick
trinken drink/drank/drunk; have/had/had
trocken/trocknen dry
  Trockner dryer
Trommel drum
Trompete trumpet
Tropfen drop
trotzdem anyway
trügerisch false
tschüs bye; bye-bye; goodbye
  T~ für heute. Bye for now.
T-Shirt T-shirt
Tuch cloth
tun do/did/done
Tunnel tunnel
  der (Ärmel)kanal~ the Channel T~
Tür door
  ~klingel ~bell
Türkei Turkey
  Türke/Türkin Turk
  die Türken the Turks/the Turkish
  türkisch/T~ Türkish
Turm tower
Turnen gym(nastics)
  Turnhalle gym(nasium)
  Turnschuhe gym shoes
Typ *(Art)* type
  ~ *(Kerl)* guy
typisch (für) typical (of)

U

U-Bahn *(BE)* (the) Underground; *(AE)* subway
übel: Mir ist ~. I feel sick. (feel/felt/felt)
üben practise; train
über about; above; over
  ~ Nacht overnight
  (quer) ~ across
überall/~ hin everywhere; anywhere
  ~ im Land all over the country
überdenken: etw. ~ think s.th. over (think/thought/thought)

überfahren knock down
Überfall attack
überfüllt crowded
überhaupt: ~ nicht not at all
  ~ nichts nothing at all
  ~ keine(r/s) none at all
überholen pass
übermorgen the day after tomorrow
übernachten *(in einem Hotel)* stay (at a hotel)
überprüfen/Überprüfung check; test
überqueren cross
überraschen/Überraschung surprise
  ~d surprising
  überrascht surprised
Überstunden machen work overtime
überzählig spare
üblich usual; **~ly**
übrig *(überzählig)* spare
  ~(geblieben) left
  ~bleiben remain
  ~lassen leave/left/left
übrigens by the way
Übung exercise; practice; training
  ~ macht den Meister. Practice makes perfect.
Ufer bank
UFO UFO
Uhr *(Stand~/Turm~/Wand~)* clock
  Armband~ watch
  zehn ~ ten o' clock
um (a)round
  ~ 8 Uhr at 8 o'clock
  ~ zu (tun) to (do)
umdrehen/sich ~ turn round
umfallen fall over (fall/fell/fallen)
umgekehrt the other way round
umschauen: sich ~ look round
umsonst *(gratis)* free
umsteigen change
umstoßen knock/push over
Umtausch exchange
umwandeln in turn into
Umwelt environment
  ~verschmutzung pollution

umwerfen knock down
umziehen move
  sich ~ change
unbekanntes Flugobjekt (UFO) unidentified flying object (UFO)
unbeliebt unpopular
und and
  ~ so weiter (usw.) ~ so on (etc.)
uneben rough
unecht false
Unfall accident; crash
unfreundlich unfriendly
ungefähr about
ungefährlich safe
Ungeheuer monster
unglücklich unhappy
Uniform uniform
Union union
Universität university
unmittelbar right
unmodern out of fashion
unmöglich impossible
uns us; ourselves
unser(e) our
  unsere(r/s) ours
unten at the bottom (of); down
  ~ *(im Haus)* downstairs
unter under; below
  ~ *(zwischen)* among; non-stop
Unterbrechung: ohne ~ non-stop
Untergrund underground
  ~bahn *(BE)* (the) Underground; *(AE)* subway
unterhalb (von) below
Unterhaltung *(Gespräch)* conversation; talk
  ~ *(Vergnügen)* entertainment
  ~sbranche show business
  ~selektronik entertainment electronics
unterirdisch underground
Unterlippe lower lip
Unternehmen *(Firma)* business
unterrichten teach/taught/taught
  Unterrichtsstunde lesson
Unterschied difference
  u~lich different
unterstreichen underline

untersuchen check; test
Untertasse saucer
  fliegende ~ flying ~
unterwegs on one's way
  ~ *(nicht zu Hause)* out
unverheiratet single
unvorsichtig careless
Urenkel... great-grand...
  ~(kind) ~child
Urgroß... great-grand...
  ~eltern ~parents
  ~mutter ~mother
Urkunde certificate
Urlaub *(BE)* holidays; *(AE)* vacation
  in ~ sein/gehen be/go on holiday (go/went/gone)

V

Vater father
Vati dad
Verabredung appointment; date
verändern/Veränderung change
verängstigt frightened
veranlassen make/made/made
veranstalten organize; hold/held/held
Verband *(Vereinigung)* association
Verbandszeug first-aid kit
verbinden *(telefonisch)* connect
  Verbindung ~ion
Verbrechen crime
  Verbrecher(in) criminal; gangster
verbrennen burn/burnt/burnt
verbringen *(Zeit)* spend/spent/spent
verdammt damn; bloody
verdienen *(Geld)* earn; make (money) (make/made/made)
vereinigen/sich ~ unite
vereinigt united
  das V~e Königreich the U~ Kingdom (UK)
  die ~en Staaten the U~ States (US)
  die Vereinten Nationen the U~ Nations (UN)

Vereinigung union
verfehlen miss
verfolgen *(jagen)* chase
vergangene(r/s) past
Vergangenheit past
  ~sform past tense
vergessen forget/forgot/forgotten
vergleichen compare
Vergnügen *(Unterhaltung)* entertainment
  ~ *(Freude)* joy
vergraben bury
verhalten: sich ~ act; behave
verheiratet married
Verkauf sale
  v~en sell/sold/sold
  Verkäufer(in) (shop) assistant
Verkehr traffic
  ~sampel ~ lights
  (Fremden)~sbüro tourist information
  ~sstau ~ jam
verlassen leave/left/left
verletzen hurt/hurt/hurt; injure
  Verletzung injury
verlieben: sich ~ (in) fall in love (with) (fall/fell/fallen)
  verliebt sein (in) be in love (with)
verlieren lose/lost/lost
  Verlierer(in) loser
vermischen mix
vermissen miss
  vermißt missing
vermuten *(AE)* guess
veröffentlichen publish
verpassen miss
verpetzen: jdn ~ tell on s.o. (tell/told/told)
verrückt crazy; mad
verrühren mix
versagen *(Motor)* break down (break/broke/broken)
Versammlung meeting
verschieden different
verschmutzen pollute
  (Umwelt)verschmutzung pollution
verschneit snowy
verschwenden waste
verschwinden disappear
  verschwunden missing
versichern *(gegen Gebühr)* insure
  Versicherung insurance

versinken sink/sank/ sunk
versorgen look after; serve
versprechen/(ein) V~ promise
Verstand mind
verstecken/sich ~ hide/ hid/hidden
verstehen understand/ understood/ understood
sich mit jdm. ~ get on/along with s.o. (get/got/got)
Ich habe es nicht verstanden. I didn't get it.
Versuch/versuchen try
Vertreter(in) *(Beruf)* agent
verursachen cause
vervollständigen complete
verwandt (mit) related (to)
Verwandte(r) relative
verwirrend confusing
verwirrt confused
Verwirrung confusion
verwunden injure; wound
Verzeihung pardon
Verzeihen Sie bitte. I beg your ~.
verzollen declare
Video video
~kamera ~ camera
~kassette ~ cassette
~recorder ~ recorder
Vieh cattle
viel/viele a lot (of); lots (of); plenty (of); much (money); many (people)
V~en Dank. Thank you very much.
vielleicht maybe; perhaps
Viertel quarter
~finale ~ final
vierzehn Tage a fortnight; two weeks
Vogel bird
~käfig ~ cage
Volk people; nation
~smusik folk music
~stanz folk dance
voll full
~ *(überfüllt)* crowded
V~mond full moon

Volleyball volleyball
vollkommen perfect
vollständig complete
von (weg) from
~ ... bis ~ ... to
viele von uns many of us
vor *(zeitlich)* ago; before
~ *(örtlich)* in front of; outside
~ zwei Jahren two years ago
~ der Party before the party
~ langer Zeit long ago; a long time ago; once upon a time
zehn vor vier ten to four
vorbei over; past
~gehen/~kommen (an etw.) go past (s.th.); pass (s.th.) (go/went/gon)
vorbereiten prepare
sich ~ auf ~ for
Vorder.../~seite/ vorderer (Teil) front
~rad ~ wheel
~sitz ~ seat
Vorfahrt achten! Give way.
Vorgarten *(BE)* front garden; *(AE)* front yard
vorgehen *(sich ab- spielen)* go on (go/ went/gone)
vorgestern the day before yesterday
Vorhaben project
Vorhang curtain
vorher before
vorig careful
Vormittag morning
am ~/v~s in the ~
um 11 Uhr v~s at 11 am
vorn: nach ~ kommen come forward (come/ came/come)
Vorname Christian name; first name
Vorsicht care
v~ig careful
Vorsitzende(r) chairman/ chairperson
Vorspeise starter
vorstellen: sich etw. ~ imagine s.th.
Vorstellung *(Unter- haltungs~)* show

~ *((Idee)* idea
~sgespräch *(Beruf)* job interview
~skraft imagination
Vorteil advantage
vorüber over
~gehen pass
an etw./jdm. ~ pass s.th./s.o. by
vorwärts forward
vorziehen prefer

W

wach sein be awake
Wache/Wachposten guard
Wachablösung Changing of the G~
wachsen grow/grew/ grown
Waffen arms
Wahl *(Aus~)* choice
wählen *(aus~)* choose/ chose/chosen
~ *(Telefonnummer)* dial
~ *(Partei)* elect
wahr true
während (der Woche) during (the week)
~ (ich weg war) while (I was away)
Wahrheit truth
wahrscheinlich probably
~ tun be likely to do
Wald forest; wood
Wales Wales
Waliser(in) Welshman/ Welshwoman
die Waliser the Welsh
walisisch/W~ Welsh
Walze roller
Wand wall
wandern hike; walk
~ gehen go hiking (go/went/gone)
wann when
Warenhaus department store
warm warm; hot
Wärme heat
warten (auf) wait (for)
Warteraum/-zimmer ~ing room
warum why
was what
Was für eine gute Idee! What a good idea!

Waschbecken wash basin
waschen wash
die Wäsche ~ do the washing (do/did/ done)
Wäschetrockner dryer
Waschmaschine washing machine
Waschpulver washing powder
Wasser water
~hahn (~) tap
~rohr ~ pipe
~schlauch hose
~tropfen drop of ~
~verschmutzung ~ pollution
wechseln/Wechselgeld change
Wechselkurs exchange rate
wecken wake (up) (wake/woke/woken)
Wecker alarm clock
Radio~ clock radio
Weg way
~weiser signpost
weg away; off
wegen because of
berühmt ~ famous for
weggehen leave/left/ left
wegnehmen/wegschaf- fen take off (take/ took/taken); remove
weh tun hurt/hurt/hurt
wehen blow/blew/ blown
weiblich/Weibchen female
weich soft
Weide field
auf einer ~ in a ~
Weihnachten Christmas
Fröhliche ~! Merry Christmas.
Weihnachts... Christmas
~baum ~ tree
~karte ~ card
~lied ~ carol
~mann Father ~
erster ~tag ~ Day
weil because
Weile while
eine ~ *(eine Zeit- lang)* for a ~
Wein wine
~trauben grapes
weinen cry
Weise *(Art und ~)* way
auf diese ~ like this

weiß white
weit (weg) far (away)
  ~ *(breit)* wide
  meilen~ for miles and miles
  ~verbreitet popular
weiter further
  ~führende Schule secondary school
  ~geben pass on
  ~gehen go on (go/went/gone)
  ~machen go on; continue
  etw. ~hin tun go on/keep on doing s.th. (go/went/gone; keep/kept/kept)
  und so ~ and so on
welche(r/s) what; which
  welche *(einige)* any; some
Welle wave
Wellensittich budgie
Welt world
  der 2. ~krieg the Second World War
  ~meister ~ champion
  ~~schaft ~~ships
  ~raum space
  ~~flug space flight
  ~sprache ~ language
  w~weit ~wide
wem/wen who
wenig little; not much
  ~e few
  ~er less; fewer
  am ~sten least
  die ~sten fewest
  ~stens at least
  ein ~ a little; a bit
wenn *(falls)* if
  (dann) ~ when
wer who
Werbespot commercial
werden become/became/become; get/got/got; grow/grew/grown; will/would
werfen throw/threw/thrown
Werkstatt workshop
  Auto~ garage
Werkzeug tool
  ~kasten kit
Wert value
wert worth
wertvoll valuable
wessen whose
Westen/nach ~ west
  West.../westlich west; western

Western western
Wetter weather
  ~vorhersage ~ forecast
wichtig important
widersprechen: jdm. ~ argue with s.o.
wie *(Vergleich)* as; like
  ~ (z. B.) such as
  so (gut) wie as (good) as
  jemand wie ich someone like me
  ~? *(in Fragen)* how?
  Wie bitte? Pardon?
  Wie geht's? How are you?
  Wie ist er? What is he like?
  Wie ist es/wär's mit ...? How/What about ...?
  ~ oft how often
  ~viel how much?
  ~ viele how many?
  ~ es sich gehört proper; ~ly
  Wie schade! What a pity!
wieder again
  immer ~ ~ and ~
  Auf W~sehen. Goodbye.
wiederholen repeat
wiegen weigh
wieviel how much
wild wild
willkommen (in ...) welcome (to ...)
Wind wind
  windig windy
  ~schutzscheibe ~screen
winken wave
Winter winter
wir we
  ~ *(betont)* us
wirklich real; really; indeed;
Wirt(in) *(Haus~)* landlord/landlady
Wirtschaft *(Lokal)* pub
wischen/ab~ wipe
wissen know/knew/known
  W~ knowledge
  Fach~ know-how
Wissenschaft science
Witz/~e machen joke
  ~zeichnung cartoon
wo where
Woche week
  ~nende ~end

am ~~ at the ~~
  ~ntag ~day
woher where ... from
wohin where
wohl: sich ~ fühlen be comfortable
wohnen live; stay
Wohnung *(Etagen~)* flat
Wohnwagen caravan
  Parkplatz für ~ ~ park
Wohnzimmer living room
Wolke cloud
  ~nkratzer skyscraper
  wolkig cloudy
Wolle wool
wollen want
Wort word
  Wörterbuch dictionary
  wörtliche Rede direct speech
Wunde injury; wound
Wunder wonder
  w~bar ~ful
  w~schön lovely
Wunsch/wünschen wish
würde gerne would like
Wurst/Würstchen sausage
  Wurstbrötchen ~ roll
Wüste desert

Y

Yard yard

Z

Zahl number
zählen count
zahlen pay/paid/paid
Zahn/Zähne tooth/teeth
  ~arzt/~ärztin dentist
  ~bürste toothbrush
  ~pasta toothpaste
  ~schmerzen haben have (a) toothache (have/had/had)
  sich die Zähne putzen brush one's teeth
Zange pliers
  eine ~ a pair of ~
Zaun fence
Zebra zebra
  ~streifen ~ crossing

Zehe toe
Zeichen sign
Zeichentrickfilm cartoon
zeichnen draw/drew/drawn
  Zeichnung drawing
zeigen show/showed/shown; point
Zeile line
Zeit time
  ~abschnitt/~spanne period of time
  eine ~lang for a while
Zeitschrift magazine
Zeitung (news)paper
  ~sjunge paperboy
Zelt tent
  ~lager camp
  ~platz camping site; campsite
zelten camp
  ~ gehen go camping (go/went/gone)
  Z~ camping
Zensur *(Note)* mark
Zentimeter centimetre
zentral central
  Z~heizung ~ heating
Zentrum centre
zerbrechen break/broke/broken
zerfallen fall to pieces (fall/fell/fallen)
zerreißen tear/tore/torn
Zeugnis *(Schul~)* (school) report
ziehen/zu~ pull; draw/drew/drawn
Ziellinie finish line
ziemlich quite; rather
Zigarette cigarette
Zigarre cigar
Zimmer room
Zimmermann carpenter
Zitrone lemon
zittern shake/shook/shaken
Zoll *(~stelle)* customs
  ~ *(~gebühr)* duty
  ~ *(Längenmaß)* inch
  z~frei duty-free
  ~~er Laden duty-free shop
Zoo zoo
  ~wärter(in) ~-keeper
zornig angry
zu *(Zweck/Absicht/Richtung)* to
  etw. zu essen s.th. to eat
  um zu to

auf ... zu towards; up to
zum Bahnhof to the station
zu Hause at home
zu Weihnachten at Christmas
zum Mittagessen for lunch
zu/allzu *(übermäßig)* too
zuviel too much
zu viele too many
zubereiten prepare
züchten *(Pflanzen)* grow/grew/grown
Zucker sugar
zudecken cover
zuerst first/at ~

zufahren auf drive up to (drive/drove/driven)
Zufall chance
zufällig by ~; by accident
zufrieden pleased
Zug train
einen ~ erreichen catch a ~ (catch/caught/caucht)
den ~ verpassen miss the ~
im ~ on the ~
mit dem ~ fahren go by ~ (go/went/gone)
Zuhause home
zuhören: jdm. ~ listen to s.o.

Zukunft/zukünftig future
zulassen *(erlauben)* allow; let/let/let
zulaufen auf run up to (run/ran/run)
zunächst at first
Zunge tongue
zurück back
~kehren come/go ~ (go/went/gone; come/came/come); return
~lassen leave/left/left
zusammen together
zusätzlich extra
zuschließen lock (the door)

zustimmen agree
Zutritt entry
~ verboten no ~
zuviel too much
zuvor before
zuwenden: sich jdm. ~ turn to s.o.
zuziehen *(Vorhang)* draw (the curtain) (draw/drew/drawn)
Zweigstelle branch
zweimal twice; two times
zweite(r/s) second
Zwiebel onion
Zwiegespräch dialogue
zwischen among; between